Sexist Language

Sexist Language

A Modern Philosophical Analysis

Edited by

MARY VETTERLING-BRAGGIN

Lehigh University

1981
LITTLEFIELD, ADAMS AND CO.

Library of Congress Cataloging in Publication Data
Main entry under title:

Sexist language.

(Littlefield Adams quality paperback
series ; 353)
Bibliography: p.
1. Sexism in language. 2. Feminism.
3. Racism in language. 4. Truth. I. Vetterling-
Braggin, Mary.
[P120.S48S48 1981b] 401'.9   80-26248
ISBN 0-8226-0353-5 (pbk.)

Dedicated to the memory of Jane English

Errata

Page 2 of Contents, lines 25 and 26: *B. Impact of Sexist and Racist Statements on Theories of Truth* should follow line 28 and also be at top of page 290 instead of page 279.

Page 228, last two lines should appear as **NOTE** 1. referring to quotation on page 227 lines 17-20.

Contents

Preface

The current Women's Liberation Movement has made demands for a variety of social reforms: access to abortion-on-demand, equal pay for equal work, equal opportunity in employment, liberalization of laws relating to marriage and property, and so on. One demand, that for changes in the way women are talked and written about, has remained elusive and perplexing to many. It is the job of the philosopher to sort out and analyze ethical claims of the sort currently being advanced by feminists as well as the arguments that are adduced in support of such claims. To date, few philosophers have taken a deep or extended look at the claim that ordinary language is "sexist" and that use of such language ought to be altered or eliminated. This anthology is intended as an attempt to provide a beginning philosophical analysis of this claim insofar as it applied to certain words, sentences and statements in the (American) English language. But it is by no means intended as the final word on the subject. Its purpose is to elucidate current philosophical positions both in favor of and against the claim as well as the merits and demerits of each. It merely provides the groundwork for a more complex theoretical analysis of the feminist program with respect to language.

Very special thanks are due to Patrick Grim of the State University of New York at Stony Brook. Patrick's patient critical analysis of early drafts of the introductions to each part in this volume prompted many changes. I am also grateful to Elizabeth Beardsley, John Wieboldt, and Allan Braggin, all of whom provided continued and steady encouragement throughout the duration of the project.

General Introduction

The claim that ordinary language is sexist is by no means new. In 1895 Elizabeth Cady Stanton dramatized what she saw as the unjust way in which women are written and spoken about by rewriting the Bible to eliminate its sexist language. But what is new is the success that the current Women's Liberation Movement has had in getting people to think about this claim and the extent to which it is the source of debate even in ordinary conversation. Modern business practices have been altered to some degree to specify use of the word "Ms." as a proper form of address and modern writers are becoming increasingly sensitive to use of words such as "he" and "man." But the claim that ordinary language is sexist is neither self-evident nor very simple to prove; in order to be convinced of its truth, we must first come to some understanding of what "sexist" language is and how we can go about distinguishing it from "non-sexist" language. Various plausible definitions are offered and considered in PART I of this volume.

Because it is also not immediately evident why the use of sexist language is morally objectionable in the way that certain non-linguistic actions are obviously objectionable, PART II represents an examination of the moral significance of the feminist claim. There, it is asked *why* the use of sexist language ought to be avoided. Is it the language itself which is objectionable; or, is it rather what is *implied* by using sexist language that is objectionable? Several different plausible answers to these questions are presented along with a critical examination of each.

In PART III we turn to the debate over some examples of sexist language that seem to pop up frequently in the literature on the subject: a) so-called "gender-neutral" terms such as "he" and "man," b) terms describing or referring to sexual intercourse and c) titles (such as "Miss" and "Mrs."). It is asked in what sense(s) of the term these examples are cases of "sexist" language and why their uses should or should not be eliminated.

Lastly, PART IV represents an analysis of some analogies that have been claimed to hold between the use of sexist and the use of racist language. Specifically, it includes a debate over the claim that the user of sexist language has a tendency to behave toward women in morally unacceptable ways just as the user of racist language has a tendency to behave toward minority group members in morally unacceptable ways. Also included is a discussion of the possible impact of both racist and sexist statements on theories of truth. The volume concludes with a list of further references which includes relevant primary and secondary materials. Hopefully, this list will be of some value to those who might be prompted to further research on this subject.

Sexist Language

Part I

On Defining "X Is Sexist"

Introduction

The claim that we usually are able to distinguish "sexist" from "non-sexist" sentences is not unreasonable. For example, for the set of sentences

    1) "Women make terrible drivers."
    2) "She is a foxy chick."
    3) "Some women drive poorly."
    4) "She is an attractive woman."

it is likely that most of us would select 1) and 2) as "sexist" and 3) and 4) as "non-sexist." We would probably also consider as "sexist" the statements made by virtue of using (i.e. writing, typing, saying, etc.) sentences 1) and 2), but those made by virtue of using sentences 3) and 4) as "non-sexist."

Moreover, we seem to have a rough idea of what words in the English language are and are not "sexist." From the set of words

    1') "broads"
    2') "chicks"
    3') "women"
    4') "females"

it is likely that most us would select 1') and 2') as "sexist," 3') and 4') as "non-sexist." We would probably also agree that most[1] statements made by virtue of using sentences in which words 1') and 2') appear are "sexist," but that those made by virtue of using sentences in which words 3') and 4') appear need not be.

But words, sentences, and statements are not the only things to which these terms can be applied. Sometimes the *use* of words or sentences is called "sexist." In addition, the *assertion* of statements, people, beliefs (conceptions, attitudes, etc.) and behavior are but a few of the many items sometimes labelled "sexist." In order to come to some understanding of what the term means, we might begin by trying to determine what all the ►things that are called "sexist" have in common, but things called "non-sexist" do not have at all.

PATRICK GRIM calls "consequentialists" those who hold that all the things we call "sexist" do have one specific property in common that things we call "non-sexist" do not have and that is their *effect*. Grim cites the following as a consequentialist definition in that it defines "X is sexist" in terms of the effect that X has on women:

> a)   X is sexist if and only if X contributes to, encourages, causes, or results in the oppression of women.

A problem with this particular consequentialist definition is that in emphasizing effects on women only, it ignores the fact that it makes sense, in certain circumstances, to call something "sexist" by virtue of its being oppressive to men (e.g. use of the word "prick"). SARA SHUTE recognizes this difficulty and overcomes it in an alternative consequentialist definition of "sexist language exists in society S" (the effect in her definition is that such language "limits the activities of people of one sex but not the other").

Yet, as Grim goes on to point out, consequentialist definitions of "X is sexist," in general, have difficulty accounting for sexist language. We seem to understand what it means to call certain words or sentences "sexist" and yet words or sentences, if not used, cannot plausibly be construed as oppressing, denigrating, or limiting the activities of anyone.

This inability to locate that one effect that all things sexist have in common that things non-sexist do not has caused some to abandon a consequentialist approach in favor of a "distinctionist" approach. A distinctionist would point out that often things are called "sexist," not because they oppress or denigrate either of the sexes, but because they somehow point up a *distinction* between the sexes which is considered to be false, irrelevant, impertinent, or otherwise improper. The following is a distinctionist account:

  b)   X is sexist if and only if X creates, constitutes, promotes, or exploits any irrelevant or impertinent marking of the distinctions between the sexes.[2]

But although this definition, like the consequentialist definition, explains how beliefs, people, behaviors, sentence or word uses, and the assertion of statements can be considered "sexist," sexist words, sentences, and statements themselves pose a problem once again (since words or sentences, if not used, and statements, if not asserted, cannot plausibly be construed as advancing a marking of any distinction whatsoever).[3]

However, there does seem to be an element of truth in both of the above accounts, for sometimes a given thing is called "sexist" because it has an ill effect on women or men, and sometimes because it somehow points up an improper distinction between men and women. If this is so, then the consequentialist and the distinctionist are misguided only in their attempt to find necessary and sufficient conditions for the correct application of "sexist" to *all* of these things. In fact, there seem to be several different senses of the term; it simply has different meanings in different contexts. If this latter viewpoint is correct, we should really be trying to separate one sense of the word from another. The following are six different possible senses of the term:

  c) 1) A word or sentence is $sexist_1$ if and only if its use creates, constitutes, promotes, or exploits an unfair or irrelevant distinction between the sexes.

  2) A word or sentence use, a belief held, a statement made, a person, or a non-linguistic behavior is $sexist_2$ if and only if it creates, constitutes, promotes, or exploits an unfair or irrelevant distinction between the sexes.

3) A statement is sexist$_3$ if and only if its assertion creates, constitutes, promotes, or exploits an unfair or irrelevant distinction between the sexes.

4) A word or sentence is sexist$_4$ if and only if its use contributes to, promotes, causes, or results in the oppression of either sex.

5) A word or sentence use, a belief held, statement made, a person or a non-linguistic behavior is sexist$_5$ if and only if it contributes to, promotes, causes, or results in the oppression of either sex.

6) A statement is sexist$_6$ if and only if its assertion contributes to, promotes, causes, or results in the oppression of either sex.

ROBIN LAKOFF (PART II) presupposes a variant of "sexist$_4$" at certain points in her work when she refers to some words as being "derogatory to women as a group."[4] In other instances, she relies on a variant of "sexist$_1$" such as when she takes the words "Mr." and "Mrs." to illustrate a "lack of parallelism" between the sexes.[5] The first two paragraphs of this introduction to PART I presupposed the fourth sense of the term in its discussion of sexist words and sentences, the sixth sense of the term in its discussion of sexist statements. MARILYN FRYE uses a variant of the second sense of the term to define "sexist," PATRICK GRIM the fourth sense in objecting to the consequentialist definition he cites, and SARA SHUTE a variant of the fifth sense of the term in her arguments against the use of sexist language. In Part IV of this volume, we shall be concerned with the third and sixth senses of the term.

If this view that there is more than one sense of the term "sexist" is correct, the list of possible definitions is long. (It could be increased by finding other things called "sexist" in none of the senses defined above or by finding the same things "sexist" in some sense other than those defined above.) It is therefore imperative that the reader first review each piece in this volume with a view toward determining which sense or senses of the term is being presupposed (if not explicitly stated) by each author. The reason that this advance-work is so important is that it may well turn out that for any particular example of sexist language being offered (a set of such examples will be provided in PART III of this volume), that example may be "sexist" with respect to one sense of the term, "non-sexist" with respect to another, and indeterminable with respect to yet a third (as would occur if the sense of the term being considered were vague, imprecise or itself indeterminable). And it may well turn out that an apparent debate over whether any given instance of language used is or is not "sexist" is merely a disagreement over what sense of the term is being presupposed.

Lastly, there is a view which refuses to acknowledge any cognitive significance to *any* sense of the term "sexist." Michael Levin, for example, argues that the term can never be used in a meaningful way and that its use is similar, in intent and effect, to the use of words such as "grr!" or "ugh!"[6] It might be suggested, however, that he defeats his own purposes by specifying two possible meanings for the term and that his article shows only that neither meaning is tenable.

NOTES

1. Not all statements made by virtue of using sentences in which the words "broads" and "chicks" appear are "sexist." Statements in which these words are merely mentioned, as opposed to used, clearly are not. To see this, contrast the following two sentences:
    a) "The word 'broad' has six letters."
    b) "Those broads sure know how to have a good time."

2. Neither Sara Shute's definition nor definition b) is a purely consequentialist or a purely distinctionist one, as the reader has already undoubtedly noticed. Definition b) could be construed as at least partly consequentialist if contributing to the marking of an improper distinction between the sexes is viewed as having a negative effect on women or men. Shute's definition could be viewed as at least partly distinctionist insofar as it refers to a distinction between the limits of the effects certain language might have on one sex and the limits of the effects it might have on the other sex.

3. A third definitional approach (called "propositionalism") pops up in the literature from time to time, and it is described by Patrick Grim in his "Sexist Speech: Two Basic Questions" (in this volume). I have deliberately avoided mention of the approach in this Introduction to Part I because of my own belief that propositionalism can ultimately be analyzed as a form of either consequentialism or distinctionism. The propositionalist answers the question "What is it about sexist things said that makes them 'sexist'?" by reference to the beliefs, attitudes or propositions revealed in the sayings. This still leaves us with the question as to what property or properties these beliefs, attitudes or propositions have that those revealed in "non-sexist" sayings do not have. The answer to this latter question is virtually always expressed in terms of the *effect* such beliefs, attitudes and propositions have on women (men) or in terms of some unacceptable *distinction* between women and men marked by such beliefs, attitudes and propositions.

4. Robin Lakoff, *Language and Woman's Place* (New York: Harper and Row, 1975), p. 19, (p. 63 in this volume).

5. *Ibid.*, p. 36.

6. Michael Levin, "Doubts about 'Sexism,'" unpublished (in rough-draft stage only), Department of Philosophy, CCNY-CUNY, Brooklyn, New York.

Marilyn Frye

Male Chauvinism —
A Conceptual Analysis

Some years ago the new feminist rhetoric brought into common use the term 'male chauvinist.' The term found ready acceptance among feminists, and it seems to wear its meaning on its sleeve. But many males to whom it has been applied have found it rather puzzling. This puzzlement cannot properly be dismissed as a mere expression of defensiveness. In the first place, the term is frequently used as though it were interchangeable with the term 'sexist,' with the consequence that it can be difficult to see clearly that there may be different kinds of sin here. In the se-cond place, a bit of analysis of the phenomenon called male chauvinism shows that it is not likely to work in male psychology quite as a chauvinism should work, though it may bear con-siderable resemblance to a chauvinism when viewed from the position of the female. As if this weren't enough to cloud the picture, male chauvinism involves self-deception, and thus it is bound to escape notice on the first round of self-examination. So for this reason also, it is difficult for a male chauvinist, even

I am heavily indebted to Carolyn Shafer, with whom I thoroughly and profitably discussed all parts of this essay at all stages of its development; her contribution is substantial. I also profited from discussion with an audience of philosophers and others at Michigan State University, and an audience at a meeting of the Eastern Division of the Society of Women in Philosophy, in April 1974, at Wellesley College.
This paper is reprinted from *Philosophy and Sex*, Robert Baker and Frederick Elliston, eds. (Buffalo, N.Y.: Prometheus Books, 1975) by permission of the publisher and by permission of the author.

one eager to repent, clearly to discern the nature of his offense and the extent of his guilt.

One of my tasks here is to disentangle the notions of a male chauvinist and a sexist. The other is to provide the outlines of an analysis of male chauvinism itself. I shall to some extent be describing feminist usage and theory as I understand it, and to some extent be developing and improving upon it. There is no sharp line here between description and improvisation.

I. SEXISM

The term 'sexist' in its core and perhaps most fundamental meaning is a term which characterizes anything whatever which creates, constitutes, promotes or exploits any irrelevant or impertinent marking of the distinctions between the sexes. I borrow the term 'mark' here from a use in linguistics. Different distinctions may be "marked" in different languages. E.g., the distinction between continuous and instantaneous present action is marked in some languages and not in others, that is, some do and some do not have different syntactic or semantic forms corresponding to this distinction. Behavior patterns very frequently mark the distinction between the sexes. For instance, behavior required in polite introductions differs according to the sexes of the participants. This means, curiously enough, that one must know a person's genital configuration before one has made that person's acquaintance, in order to know *how* to make her/his acquaintance. In general, "correct" or "appropriate" behavior, both non-linguistic and linguistic, so frequently varies with (i.e., marks) the sexes of the persons involved that it is of the utmost importance that a person's sex be immediately obvious upon the briefest encounter, even in conditions relatively unfavorable to observation. Hence our general need for abundant redundancy in sex-marking.

The term 'sexist' can be, and sometimes is, used in such a way that it is neutral with respect to what if any advantage or favor is associated with the marking of the distinction between the sexes, and whether such advantage is enjoyed by the female or the male. But it is not standardly used in this neutral sense. As it is standardly used, the unqualified term denotes only those impertinent markings of the sexes which are in some way or sense associated with advantage to the male. To refer to such markings when they are associated with advantage to the female, one standardly must qualify the noun, using some such phrase as 'reverse sexism.' (There is a kind of irony here with which one is by now depressingly familiar. The word 'sexist' is itself male-centered — one may perhaps say, sexist. Nonetheless, for present purposes, I shall use and refer to the term 'sexist' in its male-centered sense.)

Although the term 'sexist' is commonly applied to specific acts or behavior, or to certain institutional processes, laws, customs and so forth when they irrelevantly mark the distinction between the sexes, these uses seem to me to be relatively unproblematic, and I shall not directly discuss them. I shall be focussing instead on the characterization of persons as sexists — the notion of *a sexist*.

II. THREE KINDS OF SEXISTS AND AN IMPOSTER

One would standardly characterize a person as a sexist in virtue of his sexist beliefs, opinions, convictions and principles.[1] A person might also be called a sexist in virtue of his acts and practices, but in general only if they are seen as associated with sexist belief. There may be people whose sexist behavior is nothing but an unthinking adoption of the habits of those around them, for instance, a door-opening habit whose genesis is like that of peculiarities of dishwashing or driving techniques picked up from parents. If a person's sexist behavior consisted solely of such habits, perhaps he would be found innocent of sexist belief. In that case I think that though his behavior might be labelled sexist (and he might reasonably be expected to change it), one should probably refrain from labelling *him* sexist. Actually, it is a bit difficult to imagine someone having many such habits and not developing sexist beliefs to link them to each other and to various aspects of social life. Perhaps much of our sexist training takes this route, from unthinking habit to conviction.

Speaking quite generally, sexists are those who hold certain sorts of general beliefs about sexual differences and their consequences. They hold beliefs which would, for instance, support the view that physical differences between the sexes must always make for significant social and economic differences between them in any human society, such that males and females will in general occupy roles at least roughly isomorphic to those they now occupy in most extant human societies. In many cases, of course, these general beliefs might more accurately be represented by the simple proposition: "Males are innately superior to females."

It is central to most feminist views that these general beliefs (assuming they are beliefs and not mere sentiments) are to be viewed as theories subject to the test of evidence and in principle falsifiable. And one kind of sexist is one who shares this attitude with respect to the epistemological status of such beliefs and differs from the feminist primarily in taking one version or another of them to be true, while the feminist holds that all such theories are false.[2] I call this person the *doctrinaire sexist*. When the feminist and the doctrinaire sexist are both fairly sophisticated, their debates tend to focus on preferred modes of empirical testing and the weights of various kinds of evidence.

There is another kind of sexist who would cheerfully assent to the same sorts of sexist propositions as those accepted by the doctrinaire sexist, but who does not view them as mere theories. Such people, whom I call *primitive sexists*, are committed to these propositions as *a priori* truths, or ultimate metaphysical principles. A value-laden male/female dualism is embedded in their conceptual schemes more or less as a value-laden mind/body dualism is embedded in the conceptual schemes of many people of our culture. Looking at things from the point of view of the primitive sexist, these beliefs or principles cannot simply be refuted by empirical evidence, for they are among the principles of interpretation involved in *taking in* evidence. Even so, there is a point in challenging and haranguing the primitive sexist, for the turmoil of attack and defense may generate a reorganization of his conceptual scheme, changing the role of his sexist beliefs. One may be able to convert the primitive sexist to doctrinaire sexism, which is vulnerable to evidence and argument. (I am inclined to think that much of what feminists are inclined to think of as unconscious sexism may really be primitive sexism.)

Borrowing a Quinean analogy, we might say the sexist beliefs of the doctrinaire sexist are relatively near the periphery of his conceptual net; those of the primitive sexist have a central position. Sexist beliefs may indeed be anywhere between the center and the periphery of a conceptual net, and accordingly sexists come in all shades from empirical to metaphysical.

The stances of the doctrinaire and primitive sexists mark ends of a spectrum. Another spectrum of cases differs from the doctrinaire position in the degree to which a person's sexist beliefs are internally coherent and distinct from sundry other beliefs. Certainly many people would assent (unless the new social pressure inhibited them) to quite a variety of statements the doctrinaire sexist would make, and yet could not in conscience be said to be adherents of a theory. There are those in whom such beliefs are scattered helter-skelter among religious persuasion, racist notions, beliefs and uncertainties about their own excellences and flaws, and so on. These sexist beliefs, though perhaps empirical enough, are not sufficiently organized or distinct from other networks of beliefs to constitute anything as dignified as a theory. Such sexists as these I call *operational sexists*. They live pretty much as though they were doctrinaire sexists, but they aren't so academic about it. Like the primitive sexist, the operational sexist may be more receptive to persuasion if first educated to the doctrinaire position.

There are other sorts of sexists who would have to be mentioned if we were striving for a complete catalog of the species according to the status of their sexist beliefs, but enough has been said to indicate the gist of the list. One other creature, however, should not go unmentioned, and that is the *Opportunist*. The Opportunist is an impostor — he either has no particular beliefs about sexual differences and their consequences, or even in one degree or another accepts feminist claims about them, but he pretends to sexist convictions in order to gain the privileges and advantages associated with their acceptance by others. Regularly carrying on as though it is one's natural destiny to have some woman tend to one's laundry has, in the context of our present lives, a tendency to bring about the regular appearance of clean and mended clothes without effort on one's own part. Such opportunities abound in our society and are not missed by very many persons of normal intelligence and normal distaste for distasteful tasks. (Many of us should recall here that in our youth we took advantage of such opportunities with respect to the rich variety of services our mothers were expected to perform, and which we could well have performed for ourselves.) The Opportunist furthermore can share not only the advantages but also the excuses of the genuine sexists. The privilege attendant upon the opportunistic pretense of sexism can often be protected by availing oneself of the excuses and sympathy available to the genuine sexist — sexism is, after all, deeply ingrained in our society and in our individual lives, and who can blame the poor soul if he can't rid himself of it overnight? One may well wonder how many of the people we identify as sexists are really cynical impostors; and while one's speculation on this question may place one on an optimist-pessimist spectrum, it is unfortunately not obvious which end of the spectrum is which.[3]

To accuse a person of being a sexist is to accuse him of having certain false beliefs, and in some cases, of having tendencies to certain reprehensible behavior presumed to be related one way or another to such beliefs. Those justly accused of being sexists may or may not be blameworthy in this matter; personal responsibility for holding false beliefs varies greatly with persons and circumstances.

III. MALE CHAUVINISM

The accusation of male chauvinism is a deeper matter than the accusation of sexism. 'Male chauvinist' is one of the strongest terms in feminist rhetoric; 'male chauvinist pig,' which to some ears sounds pleonastic, belongs to a vocabulary of stern personal criticism. In the more extreme instances, persons called male chauvinists are not seen as ignorant or stupid, nor as hapless victims of socialization, but as wicked, one might almost say, perverted. They are accused of something whose relation to belief and action is like that of a defect of character, or a moral defect — a defect which might partially account for an otherwise reasonable and reasonably virtuous person holding beliefs which are quite obviously false, and behaving in ways which are obviously reprehensible. I believe the defect in question is a particularly nasty product of closely related moral failure and conceptual perversity.

Prior to its new association with the term 'male,' the concept of chauvinism was connected primarily, perhaps exclusively, with excessive and blind patriotism and closely similar phenomena. Patriotism seems, at a cursory glance, to be some kind of identification with one's country. One is personally affronted if one's country is criticized, and one takes personal pride in the country's real or imagined strengths and virtues. A national chauvinism is an exaggerated version of this, in which the righteousness and intolerance are extreme, presumably because the identification is in some aspect extreme. Other chauvinisms will presumably be similar identifications with other sorts of groups, such as religious sects. In any of these cases the chauvinist will be convinced of the goodness, strength and virtue — in general the superiority — of the nation, the sect, or so on, and will have some sort of psychological mechanisms linking this virtue with his own goodness, strength and virtue, his own superiority.

Given roughly this view of chauvinisms, it might seem that if we could analyze and understand the mechanisms linking the supposed virtue and superiority of the nation or sect to the supposed personal virtue and superiority of the chauvinist, we could then transfer that account to the case of the male chauvinist and see how he is accused of ticking. But there is a serious obstacle to pursuing this course.

An analogy between national and male chauvinisms will not hold up because the objects of the identifications are not the same. Whatever the mechanisms of national or religious chauvinism might turn out to be, they are mechanisms associating a person with an entity which is pseudo-personal. Nations and sects act, and are responsible for their actions, and so on, and are therefore pseudo-persons. Identification with such an entity is identification with a pseudo-person, and its mechanisms therefore will presumably be similar in some fairly important and enlightening ways to those of identifications with persons. Now, if we take the label "male chauvinism" at face value, male chauvinism should be an identification with the group consisting of all male human beings from which the chauvinist derives heightened self-esteem. But the group of all male human beings is not a pseudo-person; it hasn't an internal structure which would give it an appropriate sort of unity, it does not act as a unit, it does not relate pseudo-personally to any other pseudo-persons; it is not virtuous or vicious. There cannot be a self-elevating identification with the group of all males the mechanisms of which would be like those of a national or sectarian chauvinism. The "group" with which the person supposedly identifies is the wrong sort of entity; in fact, one might say it is not an entity at all.

These reflections point to the conclusion that the phenomenon called male chauvinism is not in fact a chauvinism — a result which really should not be surprising. There clearly is some kind of mental set in which a male's knowledge that he is male[4] is closely connected with his self-esteem and with the perception and treatment of females as "other," or "alien." But the picture of this as a chauvinism is quite obviously odd. So diverse, varied and amorphous a group as that consisting of all male members of the species *homo sapiens* is a highly implausible peg on which to hang a self-esteem. I do think, however, that this phenomenon, like a chauvinism, critically involves an identification through which one gains support of one's self-esteem. Drawing on a prevalent current in feminist thought, I suggest it is at bottom a version of a self-elevating identification with Humanity or Mankind — a twisted version in which Mankind is confused with malekind. Superficially it looks something like a chauvinism, and a female's experience confronting it is all too much like that of an Algerian in France, but actually the feminist is accusing the so-called male chauvinist not of improperly identifying with some *group*, but rather of acting as though what really is *only* a group of human beings were all there is to the human race. Since this is not a chauvinism and calling it such can only be misleading, I shall hereafter refer to it instead as *phallism*.

IV. PHALLISM

Feminists have always been sensitive to the tendency to conflate and confuse the concepts of Man and male. We tend (we are explicitly taught) to think of distinctively human characteristics as distinctively masculine, and to credit distinctively human achievements like "culture," "technology" and "science" to men, *i.e.*, to males. This is one element of phallism: a picture of humanity as consisting of males. Blended with this, there is a (distinctively human?) tendency to romanticize and aggrandize the human species and to derive from one's rosy picture of it a sense of one's individual specialness and superiority.

Identifying with the human race, with the species, seems to involve a certain consciousness of the traits or properties one has, *qua* member of the species. In this, we generally focus on those specific differences which we can easily construe as marking our elevation above the rest of the animal kingdom; the powers of speech and reason, and moral sentiment are prime among them. Being the highest animals, the crowning achievement of evolution, we feel it morally acceptable to treat members of other species with contempt, condescension and patronage. We supervise their safety, we decide what is best for them, we cultivate and train them to serve our needs and please us, we arrange that they shall be fed and sheltered as we please, and shall breed and have offspring at our convenience (and often our concern for their welfare is sincere, and our affection genuine). Every single human being, simply *qua* human being, and regardless of personal virtues, abilities or accomplishments, has these rights and in some cases duties with respect to members of any other species. All human beings can be absolutely confident of their unquestionable superiority over every creature of other species, no matter how clever, willful, intelligent or independently capable of survival.

We are all familiar enough with this self-serving arrogance. It might suitably be called *humanism*. It is just this sort of arrogance and assumption of superiority that is characteristic of the phallist. It is an assumption of superiority, with accompanying rights and duties, which is not seen as needing to be justified by personal virtue or individual merit, and is seen as justifying a contemptuous or patronizing attitude towards certain others. What the phallist does, generally, is behave towards women with humanist contempt and patronage. The confusion of 'man' with lower case 'm' and 'Man' with upper case 'm' is revealed when the attitudes with which a man meets a lower animal are engaged in the male man's encounter with the female man.

It will be noted by the alert Liberal that women are not the only human creatures which are not, or not generally, treated with the respect apparently due to members of so elevated a species as ours. This is, of course, quite true. An arrogation of rights and duties fully analogous to humanism is carried out also in relation to infants, the aged, the insane, the criminal, the retarded, and other sorts of outcasts. It turns out that only certain of the creatures which are human (as opposed to equine, canine, *etc.*) are taken to be blessed with the superiority natural to the species; others are defective or underdeveloped and are not to be counted among the superior "us." The point here is just that phallists place females of the species in just this latter category. The words 'defective' and 'underdeveloped' and other similar terms actually are used, with deadly seriousness, in descriptions of female psychology and anatomy which are broadcast by some of those assumed to have professional competence in such things.

With this degree of acquaintance with the phallist, I think one can see quite clearly why women complain of not being treated as persons by those who have been called male chauvinists. Those human creatures which we approach and treat with not the slightest trace of humanistic contempt are those we recognize unqualifiedly as fully actualized, fully normal, morally evaluable *persons*. The phallist approaches females with a superiority and condescension which we all take to be more or less appropriate to encounters with members of other species and defective or underdeveloped members of our own. In other words, phallists do not treat women as persons.

(I speak here of "the slightest trace of humanist contempt" and "fully actualized, fully normal, morally evaluable persons." These heavy qualifications are appropriate because much of our behavior suggests that there are degrees of personhood. But for now, I wish to avoid this matter of degrees. I propose to simplify things by concentrating on unqualified fully actualized personhood. When in the rest of this essay I speak of persons or the treatment or recognition of someone as a person, it is "full" personhood I have in mind. Anything less than that, in any dimension, is covered by phrases like 'not a person' or 'not as a person.' I shall also confine my attention to females and males who are not extremely young, nor generally recognized as criminal or insane.)

V. THE PHALLIST FANTASY - I

The phallist does not treat women as persons. The obvious question is: Does he withhold this treatment in full awareness that women are persons; are we dealing with simple malice? I have no doubt there are cases of this transparent wickedness, but it may be more common for a person to shrink from such blatant immorality, guarding his conscience with a protective membrane of self-deception. The phallist can arrange things so that he does not experience females as persons in the first place, and thus will not have to justify to himself his failure to treat them as persons. In this and the succeeding section, I shall sketch out the phallist's characteristic strategies.

What makes a human creature a person is its possession of a certain range of abilities and traits whose presence is manifest in certain behavior under certain circumstances. Sacrificing elegance to brevity, I shall refer to these traits and abilities as person-abilities, and to the behavior in which they are manifest as person-behavior. As with abilities in general and their manifestation in behavior, certain circumstances are, and others are not, suitable for the manifestation of person-abilities in person-behavior.

Now, given this general picture, one can easily see that the possibilities for self-deceptive avoidances of attributing personhood are plentiful. (1) One can observe a creature which is in fact person-behaving, and deceive oneself straight out about the facts before one; one can come away simply denying that the behavior took place. (2) One can observe certain behavior and self-deceptively take it as a manifestation of a lower degree or smaller range of abilities than it in fact manifests. (3) One may self-deceptively judge circumstances which are adverse to the manifestation of the abilities to have been optimal, and then conclude from the fact that the abilities are not manifest that they are not present. I have no doubt that persons anxious to avoid perceiving females as persons use all of these devices, singly and in combination. But another more vicious device is at hand. It is not a matter of simple misinterpretation of presented data, but a matter of rigging the data and then self-deceptively taking them at face value.

Person-abilities are manifest only in certain suitable circumstances, so one can ensure that an individual will seem not to have these abilities by arranging for the false appearance that the individual has been in suitable circumstances for their manifestation. The individual will not in fact have been in suitable circumstances and this guarantees that the abilities will not be manifest; but it will seem that the individual was in suitable circumstances, and the deceived observer will sensibly perceive the individual to lack the abilities in question. Then, to wrap it up, one can deceive oneself about having manipulated the data, take the position of the naive observer, and oneself conclude that the individual lacks these abilities. Parents are often in a position to do this sort of thing. They "discover" that their daughters are incapable of learning certain things by presenting the girls with unsuitable learning situations which are self-deceptively arranged to appear suitable. A simple but illuminating example is frequently acted out by fathers attempting to teach their daughters to throw a baseball. They go through various superficial maneuvers and declare failure (her failure) without having engaged anything like the perseverence and ingenuity which would have been engaged in the training of sons.

But even this does not exhaust the tricks available to the phallist. A critical central range of the traits and abilities which go into a creature's being a person are traits and abilities which can be manifest only in circumstances of interpersonal interac-

tion wherein another person maintains a certain level of com-
municativeness and cooperativeness. One cannot, for instance,
manifest certain kinds of intelligence in interactions with a person who enters with a prior conviction of one's stupidity, lack of
insight, absence of wit; one cannot manifest sensitivity or loyalty
in interactions with someone who is distrustful and will not
share relevant information. It is this sort of thing which opens
up the possibility for the most elegant of the self-deceptive gam-
bits of the phallist, one which very nicely combines simplicity
and effectiveness. He can in one fell swoop avoid seeing the
critical central range of a woman's person-abilities simply by being uncooperative and uncommunicative, and can do it without
knowing he has done it by self-deceptively believing he has been
cooperative and communicative. The ease with which one can be
uncooperative and uncommunicative while self-deceptively
believing the opposite is apparent from the most casual acquaintance with common interpersonal problems. The manipulation
of the circumstances is easy, the deception is easy, and the effects are broad and conclusive.

The power and rigidity of the phallist's refusal to experience
women as persons is exposed in a curious perceptual flip he performs when he is forced or tricked into experiencing as a person
someone who is in fact female. Those of her female
characteristics which in any other woman would irresistibly
draw his attention go virtually unnoticed, and she becomes "one
of the boys." Confronted with the dissonant appearance of a
female person in a situation where he is unable to deny she is a
person, he denies that she is female.

The frustration of trying to function as a person in interaction
with someone who is self-deceptively exercising this kind of control over others and over his own perceptions is one of the
primary sources of feminist rage.

VI. THE PHALLIST FANTASY - II

It has been assumed in the preceding section that it is obvious
that women are persons. Otherwise, failure to perceive women
as persons would not have to involve self-deception. Some
women, however, clearly think there is some point in asserting
that they are persons, and some women's experience is such that
they are inclined to say they are denied personhood.

To some, there seems to be a certain silliness about the assertion that women are persons which derives from the fact that almost everybody, female and male alike, seems to *agree* that women are people. But in many instances this constitutes no more than acceptance of the fact that females are biologically human creatures with certain linguistic capacities and emotional needs, and those who accept this are committing themselves to no more than that women should be treated humanely, as we are enjoined to treat the retarded and the elderly. But the personhood of which we are speaking here is "full" personhood. We are speaking of unqualified participation in the radical superiority of the species, without justification by individual virtue or achievement — unqualified membership of that group of beings which may approach all other creatures with humanist arrogance. Members of this group are to be treated not humanely, but with respect. It is plain that not everybody, not even almost everybody, agrees that women belong to this group. The assertion that they do is hardly the assertion of something so generally deemed obvious as to be unworthy of assertion.

The other claim, that women are denied personhood, also seems a bit strange to some people. But it by no means emerges parthenogenetically from feminine fantasy. The concept of a person seems to some to be somewhat like the concepts which are sometimes called "institutional," like the concepts of a lawyer or a knight. To some it seems that 'person' denotes a social or institutional role, and that one may be allowed or forbidden to adopt that role. It seems that we (persons) have some sort of power to admit creatures to personhood. I find this view not very plausible, but it surely recommends itself to some, and must be attractive to the phallist, who would fancy the power to create persons. His refusal to perceive women as persons could then be taken as an exercise of this power. Some phallists give every sign of accepting something like this view, and some women seem to be taken in by it too. Hence, some women are worked into the position of asking to be granted personhood. It is a peculiar position for a person to be in, but such are the almost inevitable effects of phallist magic on those not forewarned. Of course one cannot make what is a person not a person by wishing it so. And yet some vague impression lingers that phallists do just that . . . and it is not without encouragement that it lingers.

Even apart from the cases of institutional concepts, there is in the matter of the employment of concepts, as in the employment of words, a certain collective subjectivity. Every concept has some standard use or uses in some community — the "conceptual community" whose usage fixes its correct application. Admitting that various hedges and qualifications should be made here, one may say that generally, if everyone in the community where the concept O is in general use declares x's to be O's, then x's are O's. For concepts employed only by specialists, or, say, only within certain neighborhoods, the relevant conceptual communities consist of those specialists or the residents of those neighborhoods. In general, the conceptual community whose use of a concept fixes its correct application consists simply of all the people who use it. To determine it's correct application, one identifies the people who use it and then describes or characterizes their use of it.

The concept of a person is a special case here. To discover the range of application of the concept of a person, one must identify the conceptual community in which that concept is used. It consists, of course, of all the persons who use the concept of a person. To identify that conceptual community, one must decide which human creatures are persons, for one will not want to take into account the usages of simply any and every human creature which shows the slightest sign of using concepts. The upshot is that the phallist who self-deceptively adjusts the range of application of the concept of a person is also manipulating appearances with respect to the constitution of the conceptual community. Males who live their lives under the impression that only males are persons (and in the belief that this impression is shared by other males), will see *themselves* (the persons) as completely constituting the conceptual community, and thence take *their* agreement in the (overt) application of the concept of a person as fixing its correct application, much as we all take our agreement in the application of the concept of a tree as fixing its correct application. We do not have the power to make what is a tree not a tree, but the collective subjectivity of conceptual correctness can be mistaken to mean that we do. Nor could the phallists, if they did constitute the conceptual community, thereby have the power to make what is a person not a person. But it is here, I think, that one finds the deepest source of the impression that women are *denied* personhood.

The self-deceptive denial that women are (full) persons adds up to an attempt to usurp the community control over concepts in general, by denying females membership in the conceptual community, or rather, failing to see that they are members of the conceptual community. The effect is not only the exclusion of females from the rights and duties of full persons, but a conceptual banishment which ensures that their complaints about this exclusion simply do not fit in the resulting conceptual scheme. Hence the phallist's almost incredible capacity for failure to understand what on earth feminists are talking about. His self-deception is locked into his conceptual framework not simply as his "analytic" or *a priori* principles are, but in the underlying determinants of its entire structure and content. The self-deception fixes his conception of the constitution of the conceptual community whose existence makes conceptualization possible and whose collective perceptions determine in outline its progress.

The rejection of females by phallists is both morally and conceptually profound. The refusal to perceive females as persons is conceptually profound because it excludes females from that community whose conceptions of things one allows to influence one's own concepts — it serves as a police-lock on a closed mind. Furthermore, the refusal to treat women with the respect due to persons is in itself a violation of a moral principle which seems to many to be *the* founding principle of all morality. This violation of moral principle is sustained by an active manipulation of circumstances which is systematic and habitual and self-deceptively unacknowledged. The exclusion of women from the conceptual community simultaneously excludes them from the moral community. So the self-deception here is designed not just to dodge particular applications of moral principles, but to narrow the moral community itself, and is therefore particularly insidious. It is the sort of thing which leavens the moral schizophrenia of the gentle, honest, god-fearing racist monster, the self-anointed *uebermensch*, and other moral deviates. The phallist is confined with the worst of moral company in a self-designed conceptual closet — and he has taken great pains to try to ensure that his escape will not be abetted by any woman.

———————————————————————————————

Postscript: It may seem that I have assumed here that all sexists and phallists are male. I do assume that in the paradigm cases phallists are male, but the suggestion that all sexists and all phallists are male arises innocently from the standard English usage of personal pronouns. 'He', 'him', and 'his' are of course to be understood in their generic sense.

NOTES

1. I will refer to beliefs, opinions, convictions and principles all indifferently as "beliefs." Not that it does not make any difference; a fuller analysis of sexism would take these distinctions into account.

2. It should be noted that such theories are sexist only if they are false; for if true, they would not count as marking the sexes irrelevantly or impertinently. Consequently my own use of the terms 'sexist' and 'sexism' in connection with such theories constitutes a certain commitment in this regard.

3. Women are warmly encouraged to view belief in the ubiquity of Opportunists as paranoia. In this connection, I refer the reader to a speech by William Lloyd Garrison, included under the title "Intelligent Wickedness" in *Feminism: The Essential Historical Writings*, edited by Miriam Schneir (New York: Vintage Books, 1972). He points out that men "manifest their guilt to a demonstration, in the manner in which they receive this movement (feminism) . . . they who are only ignorant, will never rage, and rave, and threaten, and foam, when the light comes . . . " One cannot but believe that there are also some who, well aware of the point Garrison makes, prudently refrain from foaming in public.

4. I am not attending to pathological cases in this essay, so I here ignore cases of females who fancy they are males.

Sara Shute

Sexist Language and Sexism

Having granted both the existence and the evil of sexism, often people debate about whether or not certain activities constitute cases of sexism.[1] For example, some people claim that the use of many terms in our language are "sexist," e.g., the use of the term 'girl' to refer to females over, say, 21 years of age. They advocate changing such terms to "nonsexist" terms. Opponents of changing terms which are claimed to be sexist sometimes make the following sort of argument: "Changing the language, even if it is 'sexist,' will not help to eliminate sexism. Sexism can be eliminated only by changing people's attitudes and requiring such things as equal pay for equal work. Changing 'sexist' language to 'nonsexist' language requires considerable effort, and since the effort is bound to be wasted, it would be irrational to make it." In short, it is an argument that changing "sexist" language to "nonsexist" language is irrelevant to solving the problem of sexism.

Against this, I argue in this paper that the elmination of sexist language is a necessary condition for eliminating sexism in any society. I show why this is true, and why proponents of the sort of argument above are mistaken.

I

A formal argument can be constructed for those who want to support the claim above that changing so-called sexist language to "nonsexist"[2] language does not help to eliminate sexism:

(1) Replacing "sexist" terms in a language with "nonsexist" terms can produce only the following results in what people say: (a) they use "nonsexist" terms to say the same as, or more than, or less than what they said using "sexist" terms, and (b) they use "nonsexist" terms to say with the same degree of, or more, or less clarity what they said using "sexist" terms.

(2) People do not help to eliminate sexism when: (a) they use "nonsexist" terms to say the same as, or more than, or less than what they said using "sexist" terms, and (b) they use "nonsexist" terms to say with the same degree of, or more, or less clarity what they said using "sexist" terms. Therefore, people do not help to eliminate sexism by replacing "sexist" terms in a language with "nonsexist" terms.

In (1), one can take 'replacing "sexist" terms in a language with "nonsexist" terms' to mean 'changing "sexist" language to "nonsexist" language' since the claim that "language" is sexist amounts to the claim that the use of certain terms (including names and expressions) in the language is sexist. Part (a) of premise (1) should be interpreted to mean that replacing "sexist" terms by "nonsexist" terms results in the intensions and/or extensions being either the same, broader, or narrower.

I discuss below attempts to support premise (2), but at this point I want to answer an objection to premise (1) which might be raised by those who want to support the conclusion. This objection is that using "nonsexist" terms does not result in people saying any *more* or any *less* than what they said using "sexist" terms, or in saying with any more clarity what they said using "sexist" terms. It is claimed rather that using "nonsexist" terms results only in people saying the same as what they said before, and with the same or less clarity, and that these results of course do not help to eliminate sexism. That is, it is a denial that "sexist" terms are sexist; that is why their replacement cannot help to eliminate sexism.

One might argue in support of this that when people say, e.g., that they want to hire the best man for the job, that the term 'man' includes women in its extension, and thus there is no need to replace it with 'person.' And one might argue that the terms 'chairman' or 'chairmen' can include women in their extensions, so that when people use a sentence such as, "The chairman of the math department was recently appointed Dean of the College," it can mean that the new dean is a woman; using 'chairperson' instead of 'chairman' says the same thing with the same degree of, or even less clarity.

It is true that if the intensions and extensions of "nonsexist" terms are the same as the so-called sexist terms they are to replace, and are just as clear as or less clear than "sexist" terms, then replacing them will not help to eliminate sexism. However, there is evidence to show that regardless of the intentions of speakers of our language, or of the pronouncements made by "experts" of the language, for the audience, more often than not, it is assumed that the referents of terms such as 'man,' 'chairman,' or 'he,' i.e., "sexist" terms, are male.[3] That is, there is evidence to show that the extensions of some "nonsexist" terms are broader than the "sexist" terms they are to replace. Or using a "sexist" term such as 'lady doctor,' e.g., in the sentence, "I went to dinner last night with a group of lady doctors" does result in saying more than one would say with 'doctor,' in that the intension of 'doctor' is narrower than that of 'lady doctor.' Thus replacing such "sexist" terms as 'man,' 'chairman,' or 'he' with "nonsexist" terms such as 'person,' 'chairperson,' or 'he or she' can result in people saying more than what they said using "sexist" terms; and replacing such "sexist" terms as 'lady doctor' with the "nonsexist" 'doctor' can result in people saying less than what they said using 'lady doctor.' Thus I find premise (1) acceptable. Now, precisely how using "sexist" terms contributes to sexism, i.e., why "sexist" terms are sexist, I discuss in section II of this paper.

Given that premise (1) is acceptable, there are two different ways to interpret and support premise (2), both of which fail. The first is the rather simple-minded claim that people cannot help to eliminate sexism merely by "talk," by replacing "terms" with other "terms," but only by *actions*. Such a claim embodies a failure to distinguish between words qua words and words qua used by speakers of the language. Words qua words are powerless to effect any change in the world, but the use of words is a human activity with nonlinguistic effects in the world.[4] Seen from this latter aspect, the use of words (terms) can have the same effect as activities (and their nonlinguistic effects) such as paying employees on the basis of sex rather than ability. Again, precisely how the use of sexist terms effects changes in the world, i.e., contributes to sexism, I show in section II of this paper.

The second way of interpreting and supporting premise (2) involves two steps. The first step is to agree[5] that if the intensions and/or extensions of "nonsexist" terms are the same as the "sexist" terms they are to replace, and are just as clear as or less clear than the "sexist" terms, then replacing them will not help to eliminate sexism. The second step is to claim that the result of people using "nonsexist" terms to say more than or less than they said using "sexist" terms would not be beneficial to anyone, and thus would not help to eliminate *sexism*. The elimination of sexism, either wholly or partly, is supposed to be beneficial to people, and if the result of a change is not beneficial, then whatever it has helped to do, it has not helped to eliminate *sexism*.

Proponents of this claim might argue, e.g., that although using 'Ms.' instead of 'Miss' or 'Mrs.' does result in people saying less than they did before (since reference to a female's marital status has been eliminated), this would not be a beneficial result. On the contrary, it might be argued, it is beneficial for both men and women that they know a woman's marital status. Or they might argue that although using 'flight attendant' instead of 'stewardess' (e.g., in the sentence, "Stewardesses are paid very little") does result in people saying more than before (in that the referent of 'flight attendant' can be male or female), this would not be a beneficial result. Some people may prefer to have female flight attendants, so identifying them as 'stewardesses' is beneficial to such people.

I am not interested here in arguing that it is beneficial to use "nonsexist" terms rather than "sexist" terms, especially since there are convincing arguments for this claim in the literature.[6] However, against the second way of supporting premise (2), I show precisely how the use of "sexist" terms contributes to sexism. Recall that this is needed also to complete my argument against the first way of interpreting and supporting premise (2). Thus unless there are other ways to support it, premise (2) is false and the argument in which it occurs is unsound. In addition, in showing precisely how the use of "sexist" terms contributes to sexism, I show that replacing sexist terms with nonsexist terms, i.e., the elimination of sexist language, not only can help to eliminate sexism, but is necessary for its elimination.

II

To show how the use of "sexist" language contributes to sexism, it is crucial to be clear about what sexism is. I offer the following definition of 'sexism' in any society S:

Sexism exists in S = df.

(i) Most people in S agree that there are two basic sexual categories, and the overwhelming majority of people in S are taken to belong either to one or to the other, and

(ii) There are in S people whose actions, practices, and use of laws, rules, and customs limit certain activities of people of one sex but do not limit those same activities of people of the other sex.

Now (i) is a part of the definition since for sexism to exist people must recognize the existence of sexes. Since there is disagreement about what biological, psychological, social, etc., characteristics one must possess to be said to belong to one sex or the other, I take it that at a minimum, one must possess certain biological reproductive characteristics to be said to be either male or female. This explains why in (i) not every person in S, only the over-whelming majority, belongs either to one sex or to the other.

The more important part of the definition is (ii). I believe that it, together with (i), is consistent with current uses of the term, and that it is superior to other definitions which have been given. A society past or present in which sexism did not exist would be one in which, regardless of its political or economic system, one's activities were not limited because of one's sex. This definition, then, would include all cases in any society where the sex of a person makes a difference in the activities of the person, relative to the activities of persons of the other sex.

One advantage of this definition is that it limits cases of sexism to cases where certain people are affected in concrete ways relative to the ways other people are affected.[7] A trival example of the kind of case which might be excluded by this definition is that in our society men's and women's trousers are constructed differently to accomodate differences in physiques between males and females, but this does not seem to limit any activities of one sex and yet not limit those same activities of the other. It seems to make only the most trival behavioral difference whether men's and women's trousers are constructed different- ly. If this is true, then no one should express any (moral) concern about it. The concern about sexism is not about differences qua differences. It is generally a concern about the way people of one sex are (negatively) affected in what they do, relative to what people of the other sex do. The definition rules out, as cases of sexism, differences which make no difference in limitations on what certain people do, relative to what certain other people do.

Further, (ii) is broad enough to encompass the enforcement of certain laws and rules, and narrow enough to exclude the mere existence of certain other laws and rules. For example, a law which excludes women but not men from owning property but which is ignored and is never forced would not count as an in- stance of sexism. So too a rule of some corporation or institu- tion which states, say, that women but not men shall dress only in skirts and blouses or dresses. If that rule is ignored and is never enforced then it is not an instance of sexism. Cases of sex- ism are cases where people are affected in concrete ways, and people are not affected by the mere existence of certain laws and rules.[8]

This definition is superior to others which have been given in that it does not claim that all these limitations are always disad- vantageous only to females, or advantageous only to males. For example, Mary Anne Warren says that 'sexism' in its primary sense means "unfair discrimination on the basis of sex," and in its secondary sense (i.e., indirect or covert, and paristic on primary sexism), "comprising all those actions, attitudes and policies which, while not using sex itself as a reason for discrimination, do involve sex-correlated factors or criteris and do result in an unfair impact upon (certain) women."[9] And Alison Jaggar says that a nonsexist society is one in which "those of one sex, in virtue of their sex, should not be in a socially advantageous position vis-á-vis those of the other sex."[10]

My definition leaves open the question of to whose advantage it is that different instances of sexism exist. Against many feminists, some and perhaps most people in societies past and present believe(d) that it is advantageous for some women that their activities are limited in ways that men's are not, e.g., that there are laws which are used to prohibit women but not men from combat duty in the armed services. And customs which limit a certain activity of people of one sex but not that same activity of people of the other sex can be disadvantageous to the latter, e.g., the custom in our society that males take out the trash in a household where there are people of both sexes. This definition allows people to agree that most societies are sexist, but allows for advantages or disadvantages in those societies to accrue to people of either sex.

If this definition of 'sexism' is acceptable, then one can understand sexist language in terms of it. For reasons given below, I offer the following definition of 'sexist language' in any society S:

Sexist language exists in S = df.

(i) There are names, terms, or expressions which are taken by speakers of the language to be appropriate to refer to or to characterize people who possess (at least) certain biological reproductive characteristics but which are inappropriate to refer to or to characterize those who possess (at least) certain other biological reproductive characteristics, and

(ii) There are names, terms, or expressions which are used limit certain activities of people who possess (at least) certain biological reproductive characteristics, but not to limit those same activities of those who possess (at least) certain other biological reproductive characteristics.

Sexist language is that language which is used to identify and characterize, and to limit certain activities of those who possess certain characteristics, and relative to those same activities of those who possess certain others. Part (i) emphasizes the use of language in sexual identification and characterization,[11] while (ii) emphasizes that language can be used further to limit an activity of those identified or characterized in one way, but not that activity of those identified or characterized in another way. It is important to understand in (ii) that it is not terms taken in isolation which are sexist, but the fact that they are used to limit certain activities of one sex but not those same activities of the other. In (i) the mere fact that we use names, terms, or expressions to identify or characterize people according to (at least) certain biological reproductive characteristics is not necessarily an instance of sexism. It is when, as is stated in (ii), such use limits an activity of people of one sex but not that same activity of the other that the language is sexist.

In a debate about "sexist" language I heard it suggested that a female doctor should be called 'doctrix,' since the 'or' in 'doctor' is a masculine ending. However, in our society 'doctor' is not used by speakers nor understood by audiences to refer exclusively to males. Thus when, e.g., I ask a friend if he or she knows a good doctor I could go to, I would not expect my friend to assume that I mean a good male doctor. But suppose this is assumed. In that case the activities of female doctors would be limited in a way that those of male doctors are not, since female doctors would have fewer patients referred to them. But the use of 'doctor' in our society is rightly excluded by my definition of 'sexist language' since its use does not limit certain activities of females and yet not limit those same activities of males.

Instances of the way language can be used to limit the activities of people of one sex relative to those of the other are numerous.[12] For example, the use of the pronoun 'he' can be used when the referent is known to be male, or when the referent is indefinite or unknown (unlike 'she'). 'He' is inappropriately used when the referent is known to be female. Thus the use of 'he' can be ambiguous—is the referent male, or is the referent either male or female? There is indirect evidence to show that regardless of the intentions of the speaker, for the audience, it is assumed that the referent is male.[13] This is unlike the use of 'he or she' where it is quite clear that the referent can be of either sex. If this is true, certain uses of male pronouns, even if intended to refer to people of either sex, serve to limit the activities of females in relation to the activities of males—in what is thought (or perhaps more appropriately, not thought) about them, in what is communicated (or not communicated) about them, and in what further actions are taken (or not taken) on the basis of that thought or communication.[14]

Or suppose that in a society roles in marriage are assigned on the basis of sex—a practice which is a case of sexism. This practice is communicated, taught, or justified by several means. For example, parents might require their daughters but not their sons to wash dishes. Physical rewards and punishments can be part of this role training, but part of it goes on by the use of language. Suppose that in a family in such a society a daughter asks her mother why she, not her brother, has to wash the dishes. Her mother replies, "Because it's not masculine for boys to wash dishes." From that statement the daughter learns (or is reinforced in her understanding) that boys are supposed to perform masculine activities, and that 'masculine activities' does not include washing dishes in its extension. A boy's activity of washing dishes is limited; a girl's is not. Thus certain uses of terms such as 'masculine' and 'boy,' as in the mother's statement, can effectively limit the activities of one sex but not limit those same activities of the other.

Sexist language, as I believe it should be defined, is thus a *part of* sexism in any society where sexism exists; it constitutes an instance of sexism. It is a human activity which limits the activities of one sex, but not those same activities of the other. Any society in which there is sexist language is a society which contains sexism, i.e., the existence of sexist language in a society is sufficient for one to say that there is sexism in that society.

Further, it is difficult to imagine a society where sexist language is not also necessary for sexism to exist. Only sexist societies which did not use language would be excluded. If a society uses language to justify or to give instructions about the activities of people in that society (which is virtually ineviatble), and that society contains sexism (as I define it), then its language is used as one tool among others to put limitations on the activities of the members of one sex but not on those same activities of the other.

The upshot of this is that elimination of sexist language is necessary for eliminating sexism in any society. It would be impossible to have a nonsexist society where there was sexist language, since sexist language serves to limit the activities of people of one sex but not those of the other, i.e., it is just another instance of sexism. (One might hypothesize that the extent of sexist language in a society is indicative of the local amount of sexism in that society.)

Recall that in section I of this article I outlined two ways to attempt to support the second premise of the argument that eliminating sexist language does not help to eliminate sexism. The second premise, once again, was:

(2) People do not help to eliminate sexism when: (a) they use "nonsexist" terms to say the same as, or more than, or less than what they said using "sexist" terms, and (b) they use "nonsexist" terms to say with the same degree of, or more, or less clarity what they said using "sexist" terms.

The first way to support this premise is the claim that people cannot help to eliminate sexism merely by "talk," by replacing "terms" with other "terms," but only by *actions*. The second is the claim that since replacing "sexist" terms by "nonsexist" terms is not beneficial to anyone, that therefore it does not help to eliminate *sexism*.

Against both of these claims I argue above that the use of sexist language, i.e., the use of sexist terms, is a part of sexism in any society where sexism exists, and that the elimination of sexist language is necessary for the elimination of sexism in any society. Thus if my account is correct, and if there are no other ways to support premise (2), or to support the conclusion of that argument, then people necessarily help to eliminate sexism by replacing sexist terms with nonsexist ones, and cannot totally eliminate sexism until they do.

NOTES

1. My thanks to Jan Wilbanks and Lee Francis for their valuable suggestions and criticisms of earlier drafts of this paper.
2. When the terms 'sexist' and 'nonsexist' are in double quotes in this paper they mean, respectively, 'so-called sexist' and 'so-called nonsexist.'
3. See Casey Miller and Kate Swift, *Words and Women* (Garden City, N.Y.: Anchor Press/Doubleday, 1976), pp. 19-38.
4. What J.L. Austin has called "perlocutionary acts" in *How To Do Things With Words* (New York: Oxford University Press, 1965), pp. 94-131.
5. See the discussion in Part I of this paper.
6. See, for example, Patrick Grim, "Sexism and Semantics," in *Feminism and Philosophy*, Mary Vetterling-Braggin, Frederick Elliston, and Jane English, eds. (Totowa, New Jersey: Littlefield, Adams & Co., 1977), pp. 109-116; and Elizabeth Lane Beardsley, "Referential Genderization," *Philosophical Forum* 5 (1973-74): 285-293.
7. Compare my definition with the definition of 'sexist' given by Marilyn Frye in "Male Chauvinism: A Conceptual Analysis," in *Philosophy and Sex*, ed. Robert Baker and Frederick Elliston Buffalo, N.Y.: Prometheus Books, 1975), p. 66 (p. 8 in this volume): "anything whatever that creates, constitutes, promotes, or exploits any irrelevant or impertinent marking of the distinctions between the sexes." Frye's definition would include, as sexist, activities which mine would exclude.
8. One might argue that the "mere" existence of certain laws and rules in a society makes certain future actions more probable than if they did not exist. But such a society is only potentially sexist, not actually so, and any society is always potentially sexist.

9. In "Secondary Sexism and Quota Hiring," *Philosophy and Public Affairs* 6 (Spring 1977); reprinted in *Philosophy and Women*, ed. Sharon Bishop and Marjorie Weinzweig (Belmont Cal.: Wadsworth Publishing Company, 1979), pp. 237-238.

10. In "On Sexual Equality," *Ethics* 84 (1974): 275.

11. What Elizabeth Lane Beardsley has called, respectively, "referential genderization" and "characterizing genderization" in her article "Referential Genderization," *op. cit.*

12. See, for example, Robert Baker, "'Pricks' and 'Chicks': A Plea for Persons,'" in *Philosophy and Sex, op. cit.*, pp. 45-64; the many examples throughout Miller and Swift's *Words and Women, op. cit.*, and Janice Moulton, "The Myth of the Neutral 'Man,'" in *Feminism and Philosophy, op. cit.*, pp. 124-137, (p. 100-115 in this volume).

13. Miller and Swift, *op. cit.*, pp. 19-38.

14. Masculine pronouns *can* legitimately be used to, and taken to refer to, people of either sex. But the empirical claim that they are often used and/or taken to refer to males only, if true, trivializes this objection. Proponents of nonsexist language claim that the most efficient way to change such usage is to adopt terms which are unquestionably used to, and taken to refer to, both males and females, such as 'he or she.'

Patrick Grim

Sexist Speech:
Two Basic Questions

There are two basic questions which must be answered in the course of any careful philosophical examination of the sexist things people say. The first is what 'sexist' means as applied to things said. The second is to what it applies; when something sexist is said, precisely what is it that is sexist? These are fundamental questions in at least the following sense: any further investigation of sexist speech must rely on certain claims that certain things said are sexist, and these two questions call for a clearer understanding of what such claims amount to. Precisely what is said or what when something said is said to be sexist?

Although I have tried to post them simply, I do not think these are simple questions. A philosophical understanding of sexist speech would be easier if either sexist speech were an isolated suburb of ordinary speech, capable of study in isolation, or if philosophy of language in general had progressed to the point that its conclusions and techniques could be applied second-hand to sexist speech in particular. But neither of these is the case. Sexist speech is not so much a particular type of ordinary speech as it is ordinary speech, with all its complexities, gone sexist. Thus fundamental questions in the philosophy of sexist language are no simpler or easier to handle than related questions, often unsettled or unanswered, in philosophy of language more generally.

In the preface to *Language and Woman's Place*, Robin Lakoff defends a linguistic approach to sexism on the grounds of the precision and perspicacity it affords us. In doing so, however, she seems to assume a quick and easy answer to each of the two questions above:

> Language is more amenable to precise reproduction on paper and unambiguous analysis than are other forms of human behavior; if we tell someone he has done something sexist, we often don't know how to describe exactly what he's done so that we can argue meaningfully about the truth of that assertion: the evidence vanishes before it can be studied. But if we say to someone, "You said . . . , which is insulting to women," provided he agrees that he has made the statement, it is available and open to close analysis.[1]

Here Lakoff glibly treats linguistic sexism as a matter of what is insulting to women, and what it is that is sexist in speech is apparently assumed to be utterances easily reproduced on paper. Neither of these answers, I think, does justice to the complexities of sexist speech or to complications involved in trying to answer fundamental questions concerning it. Part of what I hope to do in what follows is to point out difficulties that others have overlooked.

Though my concern is to work towards more adequate anwers to these two basic questions, much of what I will have to say involves merely outlining alternative approaches and different possible answers, without finally deciding between them. There are two major approaches to defining 'sexist' as it applies to sexist language which I will not decide between simply because I cannot; there seem equally compelling reasons for adopting each, though it does not appear that we can in the end accept both. Corresponding to these two definitional approaches are two approaches to answering the second question — what it is in sexist speech that is sexist — and two different philosophical approaches to sexist language in general. Here I will not try to decide between the two because they are at least largely complementary rather than competing approaches, and because a full understanding of sexist language requires both.

I. DEFINING 'SEXIST'

Consider first a handful of related difficulties which appear in trying to define the term 'sexist,' either in general or as it applies to things people say.

"What do you mean, 'sexist'?" In general, the term 'sexist' is used and understood — as most terms are used and understood — without recourse to formal definition. When the use of the term is challenged in some way, however, it is tempting to suggest a definition. But definition is often more difficult than it seems, and problems in defining the simplest of ordinary terms are notorious. As tempting as it may be to offer a definition when pressed, and as helpful as such a definition would be were we to have one, defining 'sexist' is no easier a task than defining a number of other terms in ordinary use.

Quite often definitions offered in response to a challenge turn on a consideration of consequences. As a first stab at what 'sexist' means we might start with the following as a rough 'consequentialist' definition:

Def. 1: X is *sexist* if and only if it contributes to, encourages, causes, or results in the oppression of women.[2]

There are a number of fairly glaring problems with this definition as it stands. The list of casual or quasi-casual terms appealed to — 'contributes to, encourages, causes, or results in' — seems of the type to positively invite devious counter-examples. The incorporated term 'oppression' itself calls for further clarification. Moreover, it appears that it is not merely oppression of women that is at stake but a particular form of oppression; oppression of women *qua* women, specifically, and because of their sex. Whatever the horrors of oppression facing women as a part of some large group (an economic class, nationality, or 'race,' for example), such oppression is not particularly sexist in that it is not directed against women in particular.

Let us put aside specific problems with definition (1) as it stands, however, and consider more generally the consequentialist approach to definition of which it is an example. A consequentialist definition of some type, more or less like (1), is often proposed in response to a challenge for clarification. Despite the particular problems facing (1), such an approach has much to be said in its favor.

It appears that some form of consequentialist definition is required in explaining at least some applications of the term 'sexist.' Sexist societies, sexist social institutions, and sexist actions of various types *do* variously encourage, contribute to, cause, and result in the oppression of women, whatever further clarification we offer for 'oppression.' It seems, moreover, that it is this oppression we have in mind in labelling such things 'sexist.' Furthermore, a consequentialist account offers a clear indication of why sexist societies, institutions, and the like are ethically objectionable; their sexism is a matter of consequences, and those consequences are clearly ethically objectionable.

The sexism of at least some attitudes, beliefs, and things people say also appears to fit a consequentialist approach. An attitude expressed may well contribute to oppression, as may a belief stated or acted upon, or something said and taken seriously.

There are a number of other things, however, which we readily and rightly consider sexist but which do not fit a consequentialist account, or at least do not fit it so neatly. An unexpressed or unrevealed attitude, it seems, might be as sexist as one which is expressed in action or speech. A sexist belief which is never stated and which never influences action is a sexist belief nonetheless, however secret. Perhaps we can take this line of thought further as well. A sexist belief which no one happens to hold is still sexist, and something sexist which might be said but which in fact goes unsaid is none the less sexist for that.

If we admit unspoken and unrevealed beliefs and attitudes as sexist, and are willing to countenance sexist claims which are (fortunately) never made or sexist beliefs which no one holds, it appears that a consequentialist definition of 'sexist' will prove inadequate to our purposes. Unexpressed attitudes will not contribute to oppression because they are unexpressed, and unrevealed attitudes will not result in oppression because they are unrevealed. Beliefs which no one holds and claims which are never made, on the other hand, do not even appear to be the *kinds* of things that can have causal consequences. Thus any account which will include some of these as sexist will have to involve more than a simple appeal to actual consequences.

We might try to deal with unspoken sexist beliefs, and with sexist things which might be said but which are in fact never said, by modifying a consequentialist account in one way or another. One such modification is considered below. But such cases might also be taken as suggesting the need for an importantly different approach.

In "Male Chauvinism: A Conceptual Analysis," Marilyn Frye proposes that an individual might "be called a sexist in virtue of his acts or practices, but in general only if they are seen as associated with sexist beliefs."[3] This suggests an alternative general approach to defining 'sexist.' Beliefs, attitudes, and things which might be said are perhaps *central* to what we mean by 'sexist,' rather than peripheral cases to be dealt with by adding appropriate riders to a consequentialist account.

What might be termed a 'propositional' approach to defining 'sexist' can be envisaged as a series of nested definitions. A 'core' definition would apply only to attitudes, beliefs, and things sayable or said, and would classify such things as sexist purely in terms of their content; what they are, beliefs, attitudes, or claims to the effect *that*. As a first rough guess, sexist claims, beliefs, and attitudes might be distinguished as those to the effect that women are in some way inferior because of, or in virtue of, their sex. The application of 'sexist' more widely to actions, social institutions, and the like might in turn be outlined in terms of appropriate ties to beliefs, attitudes, and things said which are sexist in content. The actual holding of a belief or attitude may be sexist in virtue of the belief held, and actions may be sexist in virtue of the attitudes they reveal or the beliefs they exhibit.

This is of course as rough an outline of a 'propositional' approach to defining 'sexist' as definition (1) was a rough indication of a consequentialist approach. I am sure there are difficulties with the 'core' definition proposed; although sexist beliefs and attitudes often involve some imagined inferiority of women, it is far from clear that they always do. Moreover, the appropriate ties to sexist beliefs called for in classifying actions, social institutions, and a variety of other things would be incredibly difficult to outline in detail.

A propositional approach of some type, however, has much to be said for it. In judging whether a particular action is sexist or not we often feel a need to know the motivation behind it or what attitudes it reveals, and may be less inclined to label it 'sexist' if it is not in some way tied to sexist beliefs or attitudes. It is also a point in favor of a propositional approach that we often seem able to distinguish sexist from non-sexist beliefs or attitudes on the basis of a consideration of their content alone, without tracing consequences to the extent that a rival consequentialist account would suggest. A propositional approach may also cast light on certain disagreements over whether certain things are sexist or not; a Freudian feminist may be more willing than others to label slips of the tongue sexist because he or she is more willing to take them as revealing beliefs and attitudes, and one's views on the sexism of particular economic measures may depend on what conspiracies one sees behind them. A propositional approach serves to some extent to illuminate the ethics of sexism as well. It is because it is so centrally tied to corrupt attitudes and distorted beliefs that sexism is such a personal failing, consequences aside.

In at least rough form, then, we have outlined two quite different approaches to defining 'sexist.' What I have termed a 'consequentialist' approach takes actual oppression as central, treating beliefs and attitudes as sexist to the extent that they contribute, however obliquely, to such oppression. A 'propositional' approach has also been suggested, however, which takes as central the *content* of sexist beliefs or things said (whether actually said or believed or not), dealing with sexist actions and institutions in terms of appropriate connections with sexist claims and beliefs.

That these are in some sense rival definitional approaches is, I think, clear. It is also clear that the sexism of particular institutions or practices may be differently understood in ways akin to each. Consider, for example, the ritual of asking of a newborn, 'Is it a boy or a girl?,' grunting meaningfully if it's male and tittering gleefully if it's female. Of two people who agree that such a custom is sexist, one may explain that it is sexist in that it reveals certain attitudes, while the other may condemn it as sexist on the grounds that it perpetuates oppression. That any such ritual both reveals attitudes and perpetuates practices is an indication of the difficulty involved in deciding between a consequentialist and propositional approach. Each may apply, and with comparable plausibility, to the same things.

Clear counter-examples to one definitional approach, with no corresponding counter-examples to the other, would be a clear indication of which approach is to be preferred. But this may not be as easy as the rough outlines of consequentialist and propositional approaches offered above suggest. Attitudes and beliefs which no one holds, and things which might be said but are not in fact said, were urged above as troublesome cases for a consequentialist account as simple as that proposed in definition (1). Such an account might be modified, however, so as to deal with these. Although unspoken sexist beliefs and sexist claims which (fortunately) are not made do not in fact contribute to oppression, they are of a *type* of thing which does, and if expressed or spoken in certain circumstances *would* contribute to oppression. Thus we might stretch a consequentialist definition far enough to include them by defining as 'sexist' things which do, or *would*, have certain consequences in the right circumstances. We could get much the same result by defining 'sexist' as applicable to types of things, members of which do contribute to oppression. Either modification, of course, would face further difficulties; we would have to specify relevant 'types' or more carefully characterize the 'right' circumstances. Any consequentialist definition designed to include unspoken beliefs and the like would have to be significantly more sophisticated than the rough sketch offered in definition (1), but there seems no reason to think that no consequentialist definition could be adequate to the task.[4]

There are similarly troublesome cases for a propositional account which call for similar modifications. At least some sexist actions, it appears, are *thoughtlessly* sexist. Such actions may be tied not so much to sexist beliefs and attitudes as to a lack of appropriate (non-sexist) beliefs and attitudes; sins of conceptual omission, as it were. Thoughtless sexism may at times reflect an unfortunate lack of conviction of any kind, rather than some buried sexist conviction. Cases of this kind can be dealt with on a simple propositional account such as that outlined above if they involve some 'deeper' sexist attitude or belief; that actions of a certain type and their effect on women are not worthy of serious consideration, for example. But it is not clear that we will be able to ferret out such an attitude in all cases we want to include as cases of thoughtless sexism. If not, some modification of a propositional account will be required in order to accomodate as 'sexist' actions which are not as nicely tied to sexist attitudes and beliefs as the simple propositional account considered above would suggest.

Here we might employ the same modificational gambit used in dealing with consequentialist difficulties. Although there may be (thoughtlessly) sexist actions which are not straightforwardly tied to sexist attitudes and beliefs, they are of a type which *is* characteristically tied to such attitudes and beliefs. Moreover they are actions which if performed on the basis of proper consideration and reflection *would* reveal sexist beliefs and attitudes. Thus we might stretch a propositional approach far enough to deal with thoughtless sexism by defining as 'sexist' things which do or would reveal sexist beliefs or attitudes in the right circumstances, or things of a type characteristically tied to such attitudes and beliefs. Here as before, of course, we would be left with the task of more clearly indicating the 'right' circumstances or the appropriate 'type.' What is of importance here, however, is that a propositional approach could be modified to the same extent as its rival, and moreover in much the same way, so as to deal with initially troublesome cases.[5]

It is not clear to me at present which approach to defining 'sexist' — consequentialist or propositional — is to be preferred. Despite their obvious differences, both have points of initial plausibility in their favor. Although simple forms of each seem plagued with counter-examples, comparably more sophisticated forms of each would seem capable of handling such examples. With appropriate tinkering on each side, moreover, it appears that at least some forms of consequentialist and propositional accounts will include and exclude the same things as 'sexist.' Neither, as far as I can see, has any blatantly absurd and hence disqualifying consequences.

It might be proposed that both approaches are to be accepted as valid and that the term 'sexist' has in fact two senses, one consequentialist and the other propositional. It seems to me, however, that the notion that 'sexist' is genuinely ambiguous is a position we should be forced to rather than an opportunity we should jump at. It would be an odd form of ambiguity, moreover, in that a sophisticated form of either 'sense' of 'sexist' alone would be adequate to distinguish sexist from non-sexist things in both senses. Both 'senses' would appear to apply to the same things, though for different reasons, and something sexist in one sense would thereby be sexist in the other as well. A resolution of the difficulty by proposing a single definition disjunctively consequentialist and propositional would seem similarly *ad hoc*, and it would still seem something of an embarassment that the disjuncts were extentionally equivalent.

We might also, at least in passing, suggest a more historical view. Terms often come into common usage without clearly specified definitions much as social practices are adopted without formal rules. The use and application of a term is, after all, a social practice, and thus it is not too surprising that it can evolve like one. The social history of an evolving practice or the use of a term, moreover, may to a greater or lesser extent be a history of social conflict or controversy. What a term is to mean is often more like something as yet to be decided than like something to be discovered, just as what form a social practice is to take may be a matter for social decision. Thus what a particular term means may not always be as simple a question as it appears; at a particular point in the history of a particular usage its meaning may remain a matter of social tension or disagreement, as yet to be resolved.[6]

As uncomfortable as this historical approach may be for those of us who would like to know quite precisely what our terms mean, it does suggest an interpretation of the conflict between definitional approaches sketched above. On a historical view, these might be viewed not as rival accounts of what 'sexist' does mean but as in some sense rival options for what 'sexist' is *to* mean. The extent to which such approaches conflict is an indication of tensions between different social interests as yet unresolved in the social history of the term.

At present I am content to let the two definitional approaches outlined above stand as rival options of some kind, without attempting further to decide precisely what kind of rivals they are or how their conflict is to be resolved. But these are not, I think, merely rival approaches to defining the term 'sexist.' More broadly, they suggest importantly different approaches to sexist speech in general.

II. SEXIST THINGS SAID

Corresponding at least roughly to the two approaches to defining 'sexist' outlined above are two general approaches to understanding linguistic sexism in general. But in working towards a fuller understanding of sexism in speech these appear to be largely complementary rather than competing approaches, unlike their definitional parallels. In working towards an answer (or set of answers) to the second basic question posed above, I will roughly sketch each approach and outline what each has to offer as well as indicating points at which they may conflict.

When something sexist is said, precisely what is it that is sexist?

Like many philosophical questions, this has a ready and trivial reply: when something sexist is said, it is what is said that is sexist. But like most ready replies to philosophical questions, such an answer remains peculiarly unsatisfying. 'What is said' can be used not only to refer to different things in different contexts, but to importantly different types of things. Thus the tasks of more straightforwardly trying to answer this second question requires, at the outset, a careful unravelling of relevant ambiguities.

We can indicate at least some of the ambiguities of 'what is said' by considering cases in which we are or are not willing to say that the *same* thing was said. In 1909, let us suppose, A.B. Smith publishes an article in which appears the line, "Einstein's theory has been conclusively disproven." In 1980 C.D. Jones publishes an article in which the same line appears. Here it seems we can quite legitimately claim that Jones has said the same thing — word for word, in fact — that Smith said years before. Even if we know that Smith was referring to the special theory and Jones to the general theory, and even if we know that Smith's claim was false whereas Jone's claim was true, there is a sense in which what they said was clearly the same. 'What is said' is commonly used in at least one sense such that syntactical features are of large importance; it is what is said word for word that counts, and that of course depends on the words.[7]

Often, however, we have something quite different in mind in speaking of 'what is said.' There is at least some sense in which Smith and Jones in the example above did *not* say the same thing; Smith was speaking of one theory and of disproof in 1909, whereas Jones was speaking of a different theory and of disproof at a significantly later time. In the sense in which Smith and Jones did not say the same things, though their texts may match word for word, two people may also say the same thing though their words are quite different. "My cousin is ill' and 'Susan's friend is under the weather' may amount to the same thing said if spoken by the right people at the right time, and one may say the same thing in two different languages though all the words are different. Let us label this second use of 'what is said' a 'propositional' sense, hoping that such a label and the lack of a more satisfactory definition will not cause unncessary trouble later.[8]

Such a distinction applies to the act of speaking as well as to what is said, and corresponding to the distinction noted above is a distinction between senses of 'saying something.' Propositional saying (if we may so call it) involves the making of a particular (propositional) claim. The same act of propositional saying may occur on different occasions though utterances differ word for word, and different acts of propositional saying may occur in which utterances are identical. 'Saying something' in this sense is an act identified and individuated in terms of content, and unspecifiable apart from it. 'Saying something' may also be used, however, in a manner more analogous to the first sense of 'what is said' outlined above; in some sense it is sufficient for saying the same thing that the same words are uttered. In this second sense 'saying something' amounts to little more than the act of utterance alone, or utterance of a particular set of words, rather than to the act of propositional assertion.

Speech and the use of language are paradigmatically a matter of both content and action. Saying things is, quite trivially, doing things, despite the fact that we often accord speech a distinct position (whether privileged or secondary) from other action. Unlike other cases of action, however, speech is characteristically tied to some content conveyed or expressed.[9] This double-edged character of speech — as an action and yet somehow unlike other actions — is evident, I think, in the distinctions outlined above. In one sense of the terms both 'what is said' and the act of 'saying something' are intimately linked with content, are identifiable and specifiable only in terms of content, and are to that extent distinct from other forms of action. But in another sense 'saying something' is an action like any other, to be specified (and perhaps evaluated) in ways similar to other actions.

Since language in general and sexist language in particular are in this way a matter of both content and action, there are often two different but equally viable approaches to understanding sexist speech. One approach will characteristically emphasize content, and attempt to outline and evaluate sexist speech as much as possible in terms of content conveyed or implied. But it is also possible to approach speech somewhat more simply as a form of action among others, to be understood and evaluated in at least roughly comparable ways. Similarities between these two general approaches to sexist speech and the two definitional approaches sketched in the preceding section are, I think, obvious. An approach to sexist language in which action is emphasized at least suggests a consequentialist approach to *defining* 'sexist.' A propositional approach to sexist language in general, like a propositional approach to definition, emphasizes the importance of content. But whereas the definitional approaches proposed seem to rivals, both analogous approaches to understanding sexist speech seem important and needed.

With the distinctions outlined in mind, and with at least some general contrast between possible philosophical approaches to sexist language, we can perhaps more fruitfully consider the question originally posed. When something sexist is said, precisely what is it that is sexist? Is it what is said or the act of saying it (or both) to which sexism is to be traced, and in which sense of each?

In at least some cases it seems inescapable that what is said in a propositional sense is sexist. Consider, for example, the claim that women are essentially lazy and stupid. Surely that is a sexist claim, and would be none the less sexist for being expressed in another language or in other words. In such cases it is not an unfortunate choice of words or a way of saying something which is sexist but the central claim or assertion made. Such a claim is sexist to its propositional core.

The fact that what is (propositionally) said in certain cases is sexist need not, of course, indicate that the act of saying what is said is not sexist as well. On the contrary, the fact that what is propositionally said is sexist is at least partial grounds for rejecting the propositional saying of such a thing as sexist too, and it may be that saying what is said is sexist in a non-propositional sense as well. Thus the conclusion that what is propositionally said is sexist in a particular case may contribute to rather than exclude judgments concerning what is said in a non-propositional sense and the different speech-acts involved.

There are other cases, however, in which it is harder to trace linguistic sexism to what is said in a propositional sense. Not everything said involves a (propositional) claim at all, and yet it is not hard to find sexist examples of nearly every category of utterance. Curses and oaths are perhaps obvious examples. Seething with disappointment, a rejected lover slams a door and yells "bitch." Muttering in frustrated confusion, a man at the bar grumbles "Goddamn broads." In neither case can it be what is explicitly claimed (in a propositional sense) which is sexist, since in neither case is anything straightforwardly claimed. In cases such as these there is in a sense no propositional content to *be* sexist, though the saying of what is said in a non-propositional sense is sexist just the same. Here an approach in terms of action alone, without an emphasis on content, appears more promising.

It seems safe to conclude that there are different cases of things said, and correspondingly of sexist acts of saying things, which call for each of the two general approaches outlined. In some cases a full understanding of sexist speech appears to demand an approach in terms of propositional content, whereas in other cases it seems more fruitful to deal with sexist speech simply as one among other forms of sexist action. These may moreover be complementary approaches even in cases where both apply — where, for example, what is said and saying what is said in both propositional and non-propositional senses are sexist. Some rivalry of the sort indicated in discussing definition may remain, however, in deciding whether it is the sexism of content or of act that is *primary* in some sense. There are also cases, less simple than those appealed to above, in which a decision as to which approach to take is significantly more difficult.

'Broads now have the right to vote.' Anyone saying such a thing would clearly have said something sexist, but in what sense what is said is sexist, and why, may here be somewhat more difficult to put a finger on. 'Women now have the right to vote,' on the other hand, is clearly non-sexist,[10] and so it may help to ask whether what is said in a propositional sense is the same in these two cases. If 'Broads now have the right to vote' involves a different propositional claim than 'Women now have the right to vote,' it may be that what is propositionally said in the first case is sexist. But if the same claim is at issue, the distinctive sexism of the first case must be due to some other feature; how what is said is expressed, perhaps, rather than strictly what is claimed to be the case.

It might be argued that these are different (propositional) claims either on the grounds that 'women' and 'broads' refer to different groups or that the two terms are not synonymous. The first, however, seems an unlikely alternative. 'Broads' is not, at least generally, used to refer to a particular sub-class of women (the lazy and stupid ones, for example); it is used rather to refer disparagingly to women as a whole. Thus it does not appear that differences between the two examples can be traced to different referents, and if there are two distinct propositional claims at issue it is not in virtue of what they are about that they are distinct.[11]

Even were it the case that the two examples differed in the referents of their subject terms, it would be difficult to trace the sexism of the first case to such a source. It is hard to see how a claim *could* be propositionally sexist solely in virtue of the individual or group it is about, regardless of what is claimed of (or about) the referent.

It might also be held that the two cases involve different propositional claims in that 'broads' means something different than 'women.' This, I think, is a somewhat trickier consideration. Certainly we don't want to claim that the terms 'broads' and 'women' are acceptably interchangeable, and if a thesis of synonymy comes at such a price it is to be rejected. Were 'broads' and 'women' strictly synonymous in such a sense, moreover, there would seem little basis left for distinguishing one example as sexist, and hence ethically objectionable, and the other not.

In rejecting synonymy there are, I think, two options. One is to claim that 'broads' and 'women' differ in meaning, and that the examples above thus involve two distinct propositional claims. Something is said of women in the first case which is not in the second, and it is presumably the additional claim made in the first that is the source of propositional sexism. At least at first glance something like this conclusion seems unavoidable. As long as we are properly to distinguish the terms 'broads' and 'women,' and as long as the only grounds for doing so are differences of either referent or meaning, it appears we must conclude that the examples above involve different propositional claims.

It is not clear, however, that this is the most plausible alternative. In rejecting synonymy we might also reject the emphasis on meaning it involves, proposing that the distinctive sexism of 'broads' is to be attributed to something other than what the term strictly *means*. To use the term 'broads' is to refer scathingly or disparagingly to women, but it need not be explicitly to claim anything disparaging about women. It would indeed be difficult to define 'broads,' and this may not be because its meaning is vague or elusive but because its distinctive use is not to be understood as strictly a matter of meaning.

This second alternative may go a long way toward explaining both nagging similarities and obvious differences between 'Broads now have the right to vote' and 'Women now have the right to vote.' 'Broads,' like 'niggers' and a score of other terms in common use, is a form of scathing reference or a referential slur. It is because 'broads' is a form of reference, co-extentional with 'women,' that the two terms seem so close and the examples above so alike. It is because it is a *disparaging* form of reference that it seems linked to explicitly disparaging assertions. But 'broads' is not merely a form of reference, on an equal footing with 'women,' nor is the disparagement it carries strictly a matter of the meaning of the term or explicit claims made in using it. Disparaging reference is unlike other reference in being disparaging, but at the same time unlike (propositional) disparagement in being referential.

Whether or not this particular example is to be dealt with along these lines, there clearly will be cases which call for such an approach. The sexism of saying things and of things said may lie in the use of particular referential terms, adjectives and adverbs with similar overtones (consider in this light 'bitchy,' 'catty,' and 'effeminate'), selective mention of one or another group, or the use of particular pronouns.[12] Not all cases of this sort will plausibly be dealt with as involving explicitly sexist propositions. But how are we to work towards a systematic understanding of sexist speech in cases in which a search for explicitly sexist propositional content fails?

It is in such areas of ignorance that a contrast between the two general approaches outlined becomes most obvious, simply because they here become rival options for further work. In abandoning an account of some aspects of sexist speech in terms of explicit propositional content we might concentrate instead on sexist speech-arts as one among other types of sexist action, only incidentially involving words rather than obscene gestures or physical assault. A referential slur such as 'broads,' for example, may be seen as a form of verbal assault, and perhaps we need not examine content in order to understand its sexism any more than we need examine some imagined 'content' of a weapon in order to understand physical assault.

On the other hand, however, we might continue a search for propositional content and its contribution to sexist speech while recognizing that not all sexist things said will involve such content explicitly. What is not asserted may nonetheless be implied, and what is not explicitly claimed may nonetheless be suggested or insinuated by saying something a certain way, choosing a particular emphasis, phrasing, or form of words, by saying one thing rather than another or nothing at all. Thus an account of aspects of sexist speech may be offered even where it is admitted that it is not what is said in a propositional sense that is sexist. Sexism might nonetheless be traced to a sexist proposition, though it is a proposition lurking in the linguistic wings or carried by informal implication of one sort or another. 'Women are properly referred to as "broads",' we might maintain, is a sexist proposition carried as an implication of 'Broads now have the right to vote,' though not explicitly stated.

As a matter of temperament, at least, which of these general approaches one favors in particular cases may be linked to which of the definitional approaches sketched above one finds most plausible. Those who see content as in some sense central to sexism will consider an approach purely in terms of action a last resort only to be taken when all else fails. Those who view linguistic sexism as only incidentally linguistic will be less patient with what may at times appear an *ad hoc* invention of implicit content. Nonetheless both approaches, I think, are of significant value and both are worthy of careful pursuit. There will be cases in which one approach proves more fruitful than another, and cases in which work in line with one approach will augment work in line with the other. We have at present neither a systematic understanding of speech-acts, including sexist speech-acts, nor a satisfactory outline of conversational implicature. The pursuit of both is required for a fuller understanding of sexist language, as it is for a more complete understanding of language in general.

III. CONCLUSION

Sexist things said are all too familiar to us all. But precisely what 'sexist' means as applied to things said, and to precisely what it applies in particular cases, may be quite difficult to specify. I have tried above to indicate some of the difficulties facing any attempt to answer even these fundamental questions concerning sexist language, and in the process to outline at least roughly two approaches to defining 'sexist' and to understanding sexist language in general.

Somewhat paradoxically, it appears that approaches which conflict in attempting unequivocally to define 'sexist' are nonetheless largely complementary in attempting to understand sexist language. I am not sure what moral to draw from this. Perhaps it simply indicates a common temptation to adopt as definitional matters which are merely relevant to understanding a phenomenon, and some third definitional approach different from those suggested will prove more satisfactory then either. If on the other hand we adopt a historical view of definitional conflict suggested in passing — that 'sexist' is as yet in search of a definition consonant with a number of different social concerns

— we might conclude that even quite basic theoretical questions concerning sexist language embody a variety of those social concerns.[13]

NOTES

1. Robin Lakoff, *Language and Woman's Place* (New York: Harper and Row, 1975), p. 1.
2. 'Sexist' is generally understood in terms of discrimination against women in particular, rather than simply discrimination on the basis of sex. This definition and those which follow it reflect this emphasis, though it is fairly easy to see how a more 'neutral' definition of the term might be constructed.
3. Marilyn Frye, "Male Chauvinism: A Conceptual Analysis", in *Philosophy and Sex*, Frederick Elliston, eds. (Buffalo, New York: Prometheus Books, 1975), p. 67 (p. 8 in this volume).
4. Perhaps being thought of in a certain way (whether we know it or not, and whether that thought is revealed or not) is something we have a right against and is a form of victimization or oppression. In that case a 'consequentialist' account might deal with unrevealed beliefs and attitudes without resort to conditional considerations, though claims never made and beliefs never held would still pose the same difficulties.

    It should also be noted that a consequentialist account might be made to accord better with cases of attitudes by allowing a claim made to be sexist in revealing a particular attitude, though the attitude is to be considered sexist purely in terms of its consequences.
5. Though the modification of both a consequentialist and propositional account in terms of conditionals allows them each to deal with certain troublesome cases, such modification may in each case come at a significant cost. As long as it is *actual* consequences that are at issue, the ethical force of a consequentialist approach is obvious, and as long as *actual* attitudes and beliefs held are at issue the ethical importance of a propositional approach is equally clear. But if it may be merely hypothetical consequences or attitudes which may be at issue the ethical implications of sexism become importantly less direct.
6. This historical approach is very much akin to some of Alasdair MacIntyre's work. See especially *Against the Self-Images of the Age* (New York: Schocken Books, 1971).
7. One of the most careful discussions of senses of 'what is said' to date appears in Alan R. White's little book *Truth* (Garden City, New York: Anchor Books, 1970).

8. Despite the intuitive force of the distinction at issue, a satisfactory definition would be hard to come by. In outlining a 'propositional' sense of 'what is said' it might be tempting to insist that it is not the words said that matter but the claim or statement made. But unfortunately the terms 'claim' and 'statement' (as well as a large number of other common terms which might be suggested in definition) have ambiguities corresponding to those of 'what is said' and are thus of little use in trying to distinguish the senses at issue. In a sense Smith and Jones made the same claim (word for word) and the same statement, just as in a sense they said the same thing. We might attempt to isolate the 'propositional' sense of 'what is said' by way of a technical term 'proposition,' but that would of course merely forestall rather than alleviate definitional difficulties.

9. It is unfortunately popular at present to undermine a distinction between speech and other action, either by ignoring the communicative aspects of speech or by treating all action as communicative. A crude approach to all forms of sexist language as 'forms of violence' is perhaps a symptom of the former. 'Body language' and an attempt to 'understand' what someone is 'trying to tell us' in beating their children or turning to rape is a symptom of the latter.

10. At least characteristically or in most circumstances. But with a little ingenuity we can rig hypothetical circumstances so that almost any claim is sexist in context.

11. Whether certain sexist claims are true is also at issue here, though I have skipped past questions regarding truth because they are more directly considered elsewhere. See "Sexism and Semantics" in *Feminism and Philosophy*, Mary Vetterling-Braggin, Frederick A. Elliston, and Jane English, eds. (Totowa, New Jersey: Littlefield, Adams and Co., 1977). A number of questions in the theory of reference may also be involved, along with the possibility of sexist claims *necessarily* true or false. A full consideration of these, however, would require another paper.

12. Whatever their theoretical failings, linguists are marvelous as sources of examples. Robin Lakoff's *Language and Woman's Place* is to be recommended if for no other reason for the wealth of raw data it includes.

13. I am grateful to Kriste Taylor, Sherry Floyd, and David Pomerantz for helpful discussion of some of the main points of the paper, and to Deborah Merritt for comments on an earlier draft.

Part II

On The Moral Significance of Using Sexist Language

Introduction

Having come to at least a rudimentary understanding of in what senses of the term words, sentences and statements in the English language could be called "sexist," it would be natural for us now to ask what it is that feminists find wrong with such language. Are they saying that sexist language is itself morally objectionable? Or is it the use of such language? Or is it rather what the use of such language implies, either about our conception of things or things themselves that is claimed to be morally objectionable?

This thesis that sexist language is itself morally objectionable has an initial implausibility and none of the authors whose work is represented in this volume would, if pressed, subscribe to it.[1] The reason for this is clear: even if words or sentences are "sexist₄," they cannot plausibly be construed as contributing to, promoting, causing or resulting in the oppression of anyone if they are not used. And even if they are "sexist₁," they cannot plausibly be construed as creating, constituting, promoting, or exploiting any distinction between the sexes if they are not actually used. Yet a word or sentence is not "sexist" at all in any of the other major senses of the term that we found in the introduction to PART I. (A similar argument can be advanced for sexist statements.) The feminist demand for linguistic reform, if we are to be careful in our attempt to understand it, cannot be interpreted as a demand for the purging of certain words, sentences or statements from the English language. It is rather to be interpreted as a demand for halting the *use* of such words, sentences, or statements, either because the use is itself objectionable, or because what the use implies (either about our conceptions of women and men or about women's and men's roles in society) is morally objectionable.

ROBIN LAKOFF seems to be advancing the view that the reason the use of sexist language is wrong is that it implies that women have socially inferior roles in society. She begins her work by telling us that "the way we feel about things in the real world governs the way we express ourselves about these things."[2] If we feel positively towards any given thing in the world, we are more likely to describe that thing by using words with positive connotations than we are by using words with negative connotations. For example, if I admire a person who is capable of independent thinking, I am more likely to describe that person as "strong-minded" than I am to describe that person as "pig-headed." This relationship between the words we use and the way we feel is not always one-to-one (we are all, after all, capable of hiding our feelings behind a linguistic mask) but on the whole, our feelings are usually reflected in the language we use. Because this is so, adds Lakoff, "we can use our linguistic behavior as a diagnostic of our hidden feelings about these things,"[3] and she concludes that an examination of the use of language about women can provide evidence "for one type of inequity that has been claimed to exist in our society: that between the roles of men and women."[4]

This argument can be expressed in the following general form:

a) 1) The language we use about women will show us how we conceive of women.

2) We use sexist language about women.

3) Women have inferior social roles.

The conclusion of this argument does not follow from these premises. For even if the language we use about women does show us something about our conceptions of women, it may well show us nothing at all about the inferiority of women's social roles.[5]

Perhaps Lakoff really meant to describe the significance of the use of sexist language in the following way:

b) 1) The use of sexist language about women implies that women have inferior social roles.
2) We use sexist language about women.

3) Women have inferior social roles.

The conclusion of this argument does follow from the premises and Lakoff gives considerable indication that she believes b 1) to be true as well. She says, for example, that each of the disparities she shows us in language about women and men "reflects in its patterns of usage the difference between the role of women in our society and that of men."[6] And b 1) is consistent with an ancillary claim made in her work, namely that an improvement in women's social roles will be accompanied by the elimination of the use of sexist language. She says, "social change creates language change, not the reverse,"[7] "social change must precede lexical change,"[8] and "one cannot, purely by changing language use, change social status."[9]

VIRGINIA VALIAN disagrees with b 1). For her, the use of sexist language implies nothing about women's social roles, for it is entirely possible that we will continue to use sexist language even when the lot of women is improved to a state of equality with that of men. History has shown us, she says, that the social roles of Jews has improved without a corresponding elimination of the use of racist language about Jews. Perhaps the same thing will happen in the case of women. But as Valian herself points out, the validity of this analogy rests on what is meant by "social roles"; if Lakoff means something other than things like "economic self-determination" by the term, the analogy may be subject to debate, for history has not shown us that Jews suffer no discrimination whatsoever in modern-day society.

JACQUELINE FORTUNATA disagrees with premise b 2). She takes a close look at .the examples Lakoff cites as being "sexist" in the sense of "being derogatory to women as a whole" and decides that none of them are actually sexist in that sense of the term. This is not, however, to deny that they could be examples of "sexist" language in some other sense of that term.

Notice that Lakoff can also plausibly be interpreted as advancing the following argument:

c) 1) The use of sexist language about women implies that women are conceived of as inferior beings.

2) We use sexist language about women.

3) Women are conceived of as inferior beings.

However, this argument will not go far enough for her stated purpose which is to show that women have inferior social roles. The reason for her desire to connect up data about language use with social injustice is easily guessed at. For if the use of sexist language about women only implies that we have an unfair conception of women, we might well ask, "So what? Even if our conceptions are unfair, why are unfair conceptions so terrible? We can, after all, imagine a world in which everyone thought about women in a discriminatory or unfair way and yet no one behaved unfairly toward women. What women are really worried about are actual inequities in treatment, not how someone might or might not conceive of them."

There is more than one possible response to this objection to argument c), however. The thesis that thinking about women as inferiors causes us to behave in unfair or discriminatory ways toward women would rescue c) from the objection and it has a good deal of initial plausibility. For we expect the person who conceives of women as inferiors to behave toward women in an unfair or discriminatory way. An analogous expectation is often made of the person who thinks of minority group members as inferiors; we do not expect such a person to advance blacks in his or her firm, to invite blacks into his or her home or, for that matter, to have any black friends. Questions about the validity of this analogy between racist and sexist conceptions are raised in PART IV of this book.

Another possible response would be to argue that there is a link between the use of sexist language and conceptions of women which would justify the view that the use of sexist language ought to be eliminated solely because of what it has to show us about these conceptions. On this view, the conceptions themselves *are* "terrible" in the sense of being morally objectionable. ROBERT BAKER (PART III B), for example, defends this response in advancing a variant of argument c). Clearly, he says, having derogatory conceptions of women is morally objectionable in its own right; sexist language should not be used precisely because it implies the presence of such conceptions. Notice that Baker does not deny the existence of a relationship between social change, conceptual change and changes in linguistic usage. (He agrees with Lakoff that social change causes conceptual change which in turn causes changes in linguistic usage.) However, he also believes that one need not link up social inequality with the use of sexist language in order to demonstrate that the use of sexist language is morally objectionable. It might be argued in response to Baker's view that it is possible for a person to use sexist language about women without having a corresponding derogatory conception of women. Or, it might be argued that none of the examples of sexist language use Baker cites actually are "sexist" in the sense of the term he presupposes. (See PART III B for a full discussion of these responses.)

Others object to the use of sexist language on grounds other than those advanced by either Baker or Lakoff. Both VIRGINIA VALIAN and SARA SHUTE (PART I) argue that using sexist language is in and of itself a morally objectionable act. In Valian's view, we should want to eliminate such usages just as we would want to eliminate the symptoms of a disease just as much as the disease itself. For her, even if social inequality (the disease) were removed, linguistic oppression (a symptom) would remain. She says, "linguistic oppression is not a symptom that will disappear when more fundamental social inequalities are removed."[10] This symptom, she adds, is objectionable in and of itself: "While we are curing the disease — no overnight affair — we can use a little relief from the symptoms."[11] A problem could arise with this disease/symptom analogy, however, were we to question whether something could really be a symptom of a disease if it would remain after the disease itself were cured. Moreover, if using sexist language is itself a form of oppression, it is not clear that it is not itself a part of the disease of social inequality rather than a symptom of it.

SARA SHUTE (PART I) offers other grounds for holding that the use of sexist language is in and of itself morally objectionable. In her view, the use of sexist language is a behavior which is itself "sexist" in the sense of "limiting the activities of people of one sex, but not the other" and it is wrong to so limit the activities of one group but not another. She gives two examples to demonstrate her point. In the first, a speaker utters the sentences "Do you know a good doctor I can go to?" If the hearer assumes that "doctor" refers only to male physicians, he or she will not respond to the question by giving the name of a female doctor. The activities of female doctors are then "limited" in the sense that they would be having one less patient being referred to them. But this example fails to show that the use of sexist language alone is morally objectionable, although it might be claimed to show that the use of sexist language *in conjunction with* certain assumptions on the part of the hearer can have morally objectionable results, as Shute recognizes.

The second example offers a stronger defense of the view that using sexist language is itself morally objectionable. It supports the view that if we systematically use sexist language, then we will condition women to the belief that they are not capable of doing things they they actually are capable of doing, thereby preventing them from engaging in these activities. Of course, a detractor might argue that it remains to be shown that the use of sexist language does have this effect on women; even if women are conditioned to the belief that they are not capable of doing things they actually are capable of doing, this conditioning may be the result of some behavior(s) other than the use of sexist language. But if it is agreed that the use of sexist language is at least a part of what causes such conditioning and if it is also agreed that such conditioning of women exists, then we would also have to agree with Shute that the systematic use of sexist language is itself morally objectionable (not necessarily because it alone has an adverse effect on women, but at least because it, in conjunction with other non-linguistic behaviors, might have such an effect).

Lastly, there is a view which denies plausibility to any of the above accounts. In this view, the term "sexist" has no cognitive significance whatsoever and therefore no sense can be made out of a plea to ban the use of sexist language. But problems with the only current written philosophical defense of this view were pointed out in the introduction to PART I of this volume.

NOTES

1. In another volume, Barbara Lawrence suggests that a word's etymology can make it denigrating to women, which seems, at least on the surface, to be a variation of this viewpoint. (See her "Four Letter Words *Can* Hurt You" in Robert Baker and Frederick Elliston, eds. *Philosophy and Sex* [Buffalo, N.Y.: Promethus, 1975], pp. 31-33.) But even supposing that all words in current usage do carry their etymologies with them and that a word's origin can thus give us a clue to its current meaning, it is the *use* of a word with a certain meaning, not the word itself, which is objectionable. See STEPHANIE ROSS (PART III B) for a full discussion of Lawrence's position.

2. Robin Lakoff, *Language and Woman's Place* (New York: Harper and Row, 1975), p. 3 (p. 60 in this volume).

3. *Ibid.,* pp. 3-4, (p. 60-61 in this volume).

4. *Ibid.,* p. 4, (p. 61 in this volume).

5. This argument could be shored up by adding the thesis that "social roles" are at least in part a matter of beliefs, conceptions, attitudes, etc. But Lakoff does not herself argue for this thesis, so we cannot assume that she subscribes to it.

6. Lakoff, *op. cit.,* p. 49, (p. 66-67 in this volume).

7. *Ibid.,* p. 47, (p. 66 in this volume).

8. *Ibid.,* p. 42, (p. 65-66 in this volume).

9. *Ibid.,* p. 41, (p. 65 in this volume).

10. Virginia Valian, "Linguistics and Feminism," in *Feminism and Philosophy*, Mary Vetterling-Braggin, Frederick Elliston and Jane English, eds. (Totowa, N.J.: Littlefield, Adams and Co., 1977), p. 155, (p. 69 in this volume).

11. *Ibid.,* p. 161, (p. 76 in this volume).

Robin Lakoff

Language and Woman's Place

(Excerpts)

I. INTRODUCTION

Language uses us as much as we use language. As much as our choice of forms of expression is guided by the thoughts we want to express, to the same extent the way we feel about the things in the real world governs the way we express ourselves about these things. Two words can be synonymous in their denotative sense, but one will be used in case a speaker feels favorably toward the object the word denotes, the other if he is unfavorably disposed. Similar situations are legion, involving unexpectedness, interest, and other emotional reactions on the part of the speaker to what he is talking about. Thus, while two speakers may be talking about the same thing or real-world situation, their descriptions may end up sounding utterly unrelated. The following well-known paradigm will be illustrative.

      (1)   (a)   I am strong-minded.
             (b)   You are obstinate.
             (c)   He is pigheaded.

If it is indeed true that our feelings about the world color our expression of our thoughts, then we can use our linguistic behavior as a diagnostic of our hidden feelings about things. For often — as anyone with even a nodding acquaintance with modern psychoanalytic writing knows too well — we can interpret our overt actions, or our perceptions, in accordance with our desires, distorting them as we see fit. But the linguistic data are there, in black and white, or on tape, unambiguous and unavoidable. Hence, while in the ideal world other kinds of evidence for sociological phenomena would be desirable along with, or in addition to, linguistic evidence, sometimes at least the latter is all we can get with certainty. This is especially likely in emotionally charged areas like that of sexism and other forms of discriminatory behavior. This book, then, is an attempt to provide diagnostic evidence from language use for one type of inequity that has been claimed to exist in our society: that between the roles of men and women. I will attempt to discover what language use can tell us about the nature and extent of any inequity; and finally to ask whether anything can be done, from the linguistic end of the problem: does one correct a social inequity by changing linguistic disparities? We will find, I think, that women experience linguistic discrimination in two ways: in the way they are taught to use language, and in the way general language use treats them. Both tend, as we shall see, to relegate women to certain subservient functions: that of sex object, or servant; and therefore certain lexical items mean one thing applied to men, another to women, a difference that cannot be predicted except with reference to the different roles the sexes play in society.

* * *

II. TALKING LIKE A LADY

"Women's language" shows up in all levels of the grammar of English. We find differences in the choice and frequency of lexical items; in the situations in which certain syntactic rules are performed; in intonational and other supersegmental patterns. As an example of lexical differences, imagine a man and a woman both looking at the same wall, painted a pinkish shade of purple. The woman may say (2);

     (2) The wall is mauve,

with no one consequently forming any special impression of her

as a result of the words alone; but if the man should say (2), one
might well conclude he was imitating a woman sarcastically or
was a homosexual or an interior decorator. Women, then, make
far more precise discriminations in naming colors then do men;
words like *beige, ecru, aquamarine, lavender,* and so on are
unremarkable in a woman's active vocabularly, but absent from
that of most men. I have seen a man helpless with suppressed
laughter at a discussion between two other people as to whether
a book jacket was to be described as "lavender" or "mauve."
Men find such discussion amusing because they consider such a
question trivial, irrelevant to the real world.

* * *

As an experiment, one might present native speakers of standard American English with pairs of sentences, identical syntactically and in terms of referential lexical items, and differing
merely in the choice of "meaningless" particle, and ask them
which was spoke by a man, which a woman. Consider:

      (3) (a) Oh dear, you've put the peanut butter in
              the refrigerator again.
          (b) Shit, you've put the peanut butter in the
              refrigerator again.

It is safe to predict that people would classify the first sentence
as part of "women's language," the second as "men's
language." It is true that many self-respecting women are
becoming able to use sentences like (3) (b) publicly without flin-
ching, but this is a relatively recent development, and while
perhaps the majority of Middle America might condone the use
of (b) for men, they would still disapprove of its use by women.

* * *

III. TALKING ABOUT WOMEN

We have thus far confined ourselves to one facet of the problem
of women and the English language: the way in which women
prejudice the case against themselves by their use of language.

But it is at least as true that others — as well as women themselves — make matters so by the way in which they refer to women. Often a word that may be used of both men and women (and perhaps of things as well), when applied to women, assumes a special meaning that, by implication rather than outright assertion, is derogatory to women as a group.

When a word acquires a bad connotation by association with something unpleasant or embarrassing, people may search for substitutes that do not have the uncomfortable effect — that is, euphemisms. Since attitudes toward the original referent are not altered by a change of name, the new name itself takes on the adverse connotations, and a new euphemism must be found. It is, no doubt, possible to pick out areas of particular psychological strain or discomfort — areas where problems exist in a culture — by pinpointing items around which a great many euphemisms are clustered. An obvious example concerns the various words for that household convenience into which human wastes are eliminated: toilet, bathroom, rest room, comfort station, lavatory, water closet, loo, and all the others.

In the case of women, it may be encouraging to find no richness of euphemism; but it is discouraging to note that at least one euphemism form "woman" does exist and is very much alive. The word, of course, is "lady," which seems to be replacing "woman" in a great many contexts. Where both exist, they have different connotations; where only one exists, there is usually a reason, to be found in the context in which the word is uttered.

*   *   *

This brings us to the consideration of another common substitute for *woman*, namely *girl*. One seldom hears a man past the age of adolescence referred to as a boy, save in expressions like "going out with the boys," which are meant to suggest an air of adolescent frivolity and irresponsibility. But women of all ages are "girls": one can have a man, not a boy, Friday, but a girl, never a woman or even a lady, Friday; women have girl friends, but men do not — in a nonsexual sense — have boyfriends. It may be that this use of *girl* is euphemistic in the sense in which *lady* is a euphemism: in stressing the idea of immaturity, it removes the sexual connotations lurking in *woman*. Instead of the ennoblement present in *lady*, *girl* is (presumably) flattering to women because of its stress on youth. But here again there are pitfalls: in recalling youth, frivolity, and immaturity, *girl* brings to mind irresponsibility: you don't send a girl to do a woman's errand (or even, for that matter, a boy's errand). It seems that again, by an appeal to feminine vanity (about which we shall have more to say later) the users of English have assigned women to a very unflattering place in their minds: a woman is a person who is both too immature and too far from real life to be entrusted with responsibilities and with decisions of any serious nature. Would you elect president a person incapable of putting on her own coat? (Of course, if we were to have a married woman president, we would not have any name for her husband parallel to *First Lady*, and why do you suppose that is?)

* * *

Also relevant here are the connotations (as opposed to the denotative meanings) of the words *spinster* and *bachelor*. Denotatively, these are, again, parallel to "cow" versus "bull": one is masculine, the other feminine, and both mean "one who is not married." But there the resemblance ends. *Bachelor* is at least a neutral term, often used as a compliment. *Spinster* normally seems to be used pejoratively, with connotations of prissiness, fussiness, and so on. Some of the differences between the two words are brought into focus in the following examples:

  (a)Mary hopes to meet an eligible bachelor.
  (b)*Fred hopes to meet an eligible spinster.

It is the concept of an *eligible spinster* that is anomalous. If someone is a spinster, by implication she is not eligible (to marry); she has had her chance, and been passed by. Hence, a girl of twenty cannot properly be called a spinster: she still has a chance to be married. (Of course, *spinster* may be used metaphorically in this situation, as described below.) But a man may be considered a bachelor as soon as he reaches marriagable age: to be a bachelor implies that one has the choice of marrying or not, and this is what makes the idea of a bachelor existence attractive, in the popular literature. He has been pursued and has successfully eluded his pursuers. But a spinster is one who has not been pursued, or at least not seriously. She is old unwanted goods. Hence it is not surprising to find that a euphemism has arisen for *spinster*, a word not much used today, *bachelor girl*, which attempts to capture for the woman the connotations *bachelor* has for a man. But this, too, is not much used except by writers trying to give their (slick magazine) prose a "with-it" sound. I have not heard the word used in unselfconscious speech. *Bachelor*, however, needs no euphemisms.

* * *

Although blacks are not yet fully accorded equal status with whites in this society, nevertheless *black*, a term coined to elicit racial pride and sense of unity, seems to have been widely adopted both by blacks and whites, both in formal use and in the media, and increasingly in colloquial conversation. Does this constitute a counterexample to my claim here? I think not, but rather an element of hope. My point is that linguistic and social change go hand in hand: one cannot, purely by changing language use, change social status. The word *black*, in its current sense, was not heard until the late 1960s or even 1970, to any significant extent. I think if its use had been proposed much earlier, it would have failed in acceptance. I think the reason people other than blacks can understand and sympathize with black racial pride is that they were made aware of the depths of their prejudice during the civil rights struggles of the early 1960s. It took nearly ten years from the beginning of this struggle for the use of *black* to achieve wide acceptance, and it is still often used a bit self-consciously, as though italicized. But since great headway was made first in the social sphere, linguistic progress could be made *on that basis*; and now this linguistic progress, it is hoped, will lead to new social progress in turn. The women's movement is but a few years old, and has, I should think, much deeper ingrained hostility to overcome than the civil rights movement ever did. (Among the intelligentsia, the black civil rights struggle was never a subject for ridicule, as women's liberation all too often is, among those very liberals who were the first on their blocks to join the NAACP.) The parallel to the black struggle should indicate that social change must precede lexical change: women must achieve some measure of greater social independence of men before *Ms.* can gain wider acceptance.

* * *

IV. CONCLUSION

If we can accept the facts already discussed as generally true, for most people, most of the time, then we can draw from them several conclusions, of interest to readers in any of various fields.

People working in the women's liberation movement, and other social reformers, can see that there *is* a discrepancy between English as used by men and by women; and that the social discrepancy in the positions of men and women in our society is reflected in linguistic disparities. The linguist, through linguistic analysis, can help to pinpoint where these disparities lie, and can suggest ways of telling when improvements have been made. But it should be recognized that social change creates language change, not the reverse; or at best, language change influences changes in attitudes slowly and indirectly, and these changes in attitudes will not be reflected in social change unless society is receptive already. Further, the linguist can suggest which linguistic disparities reflect real and serious social inequalities; which are changeable, which will resist change; and can thus help the workers in the real world to channel their energies most constructively and avoid ridicule.

* * *

. . . Each of the nonparallelisms that have been discussed here (as well, of course, as the many others I have mentioned elsewhere, and still others the reader can no doubt supply himself) would in such treatment be nonparallel for a different reason from each of the others. Yet the speaker of English who has not been raised in a vacuum *knows* that all of these disparities exist in English for the same reason: *each reflects in its pattern of usage the difference between the role of women in our society and that of men.* If there were tomorrow, say by an act of God, a total restructuring of society as we know it so that women were in fact equal to men, we would make certain predictions about the future behavior of the language. One prediction we might make is that *all* these words, together, would cease to be nonparallel. If the curious behavior of each of these forms were idiosyncratic, we would not expect them to behave this way en masse. If their peculiarity had nothing to do with the way society was organized, we would not expect their behavior to change as a result of social change. Now of course, one cannot prove points by invoking a cataclysmic change that has not occurred and, in all probability, will not. But I do think an appeal is possible to the reader's intuition: this seems a likely way for these forms to behave. In any event, I think this much is clear: that there is a generalization that can be made regarding the aberrant behavior of all these lexical items, but this generalization can be made only by reference, in the grammar of the language, to social mores. The linguist must involve himself, professionally, with sociology: first, because he is unable to isolate the data that the sociologist can use in determining the weaknesses and strengths of a culture (as we have done, to some extent, here); and then because if he does not examine the society of the speakers of the language along with the so-called purely linguistic data, he will be unable to make the relevant generalizations, will be unable to understand why the language works the way it does. He will, in short, be unable to do linguistics.

*   *   *

Virginia Valian

Linguistics and Feminism

At least three important issues arise from a reading of Robin
Lakoff's articles "Language and Woman's Place" and "Why
Women are Ladies."[1] One issue is methodological: it is concerned with how to evaluate data about language use in making
claims about the utility of men's and women's speech. The
second issue is linguistic: it concerns the definition of language
and the nature of the domain that linguists study. The third issue
is political: it concerns the relation between language and other
areas of oppression. It also concerns the proper advisory role of
linguistic "experts" who are exploring how language can be
used to oppress women.

This paper explores three questions related to these issues.
(1) With respect to the first issue, is women's speech
inferior to men's?
(2) Do men and women speak different languages?
(3) What is the relationship between linguistic and social
change? It concludes that:

First, some of the alleged differences between men's and
women's speech argue for the superiority of women's speech.

I dedicate this paper to J. J. Katz and T. G. Bever. I would also like to thank M.
Garrett of M.I.T., M. Parlee of Wellesley College (now of Barnard College), and
T. G. Bever of Columbia University for making available the subjects who
served in the experiment reported in the text.
This paper is reprinted from *Feminism and Philosophy*, Mary Vetterling-
Braggin, Frederick Elliston and Jane English, eds. (Totowa, N. J.: Littlefield,
Adams and Co., 1977) by permission of the publisher and author.

Lakoff notes that women make finer color distinctions, use more adjectives, and are more courteous. If this is indeed so, the first two characteristics would enable one to make more true statements than would be possible with a leaner vocabulary. The stereotyped male view that such refinements are trivial reflects sexist values rather than a scientific assessment.

Second, criteria such as those Lakoff offers are not sufficient to establish the claim that men and women speak different languages. It is necessary to draw a distinction between speech and language in order to avoid the reductio that people speak a different language from one minute to the next, and that everyone is a polyglot. The distinction between speech and language is politically important as well: women should not erroneously think that in order to overcome their oppression they must learn another "language."

Third, the paper concludes that linguistic oppression is not a symptom that will disappear when more fundamental social inequalities are removed.

I

Lakoff claims that, compared to men, women make finer color distinctions, use more adjectives, use tag questions more, and are more courteous. The claims have been questioned by Dubois and Crouch,[2] but the argument here depends not upon the truth of the claims but on what conclusions can be drawn from them, assuming that they are true. Lakoff concludes that such differences are evidence for "triviality in subject-matter and uncertainty about it." The conclusion does not follow. If a color is mauve or ecru or crimson, being able to say so is an advantage rather than a liability: there are more true statements that can be made with such a vocabulary than without it. There is nothing trivial about this ability.

Lakoff's treatment of non-color adjectives also leads to erroneous conclusions. Lakoff claims that women use more "women's" adjectives than do men, who use "neutral" adjectives. Examples of "women's" adjectives are words like "lovely," "adorable," and "divine." "Neutral" adjectives include words like "terrific" and "great." There are actually two separate issues here: one has to do with what adjectives can modify what nouns, independent of the speaker's sex; the other has to do with what adjectives speakers commonly use as a function of their sex.

Lakoff confuses the two issues. For example, she finds the sentence "What a lovely steel mill" to be unacceptable if uttered by a man, and acceptable if uttered by a woman. A steel mill, however, normally cannot properly be termed lovely, regardless of the speaker's sex, since a steel mill is normally not an aesthetic object, and to judge something as "lovely" is to judge it favorably as an aesthetic object. If a chair is described as "lovely," it is the chair's aesthetic, rather than functional, qualities that are being praised.[3]

If this analysis is correct, what could it mean for Lakoff to claim that the sentence "What a lovely steel mill" is unacceptable only if a man utters it? Are women ignorant of the meaning of "lovely?" Even if they are, that would seem to be a matter independent of the language. It would only reflect women's knowledge and use of the language. Or is the unacceptability to be interpreted not relative to the sentence, but relative to the speaker? That is, perhaps Lakoff is claiming that a semantically deviant sentence is socially unacceptable if a man utters it, but acceptable if a woman utters it. If this is so, the use of a double standard needs to be justified.

Lakoff's discussion indicates that she has something slightly different in mind. She suggests that even women can only use "women's" adjectives if "the concepts to which they are applied are not relevant to the real world of (male) influence and power."[4] That is, the use of such adjectives automatically connotes triviality, and women will use them only if they are willing to be trivial. Again, there seems to be a confusion between adjective appropriateness independent of the speaker and speakers' usage. The confusion is accompanied by a negative value-judgment of women's usage.

Let us consider adjectives in more detail. The adjectives Lakoff categorizes as "neutral" are multi-purpose and have a broad range of application, e.g., "terrific." The "women's adjectives" have a narrow range of application, e.g., "divine." There is a parallel here with words like "small," which can be used to describe any extent, whereas words like "short" are limited to things having vertical extension. Compared to men, do women also use more specific words like "short" just as they use more specific color adjectives? This hypothesis is not considered, although its verification would challenge an image of women as trivia-mongers and substitute an image in which women are more precise and have larger vocabularies than men.

Lakoff narrows the range of possible explanations for women's adjective use in another way. Returning again to the analogy of "short," there is a counterpart term, namely "tall." Similarly, there are counterparts to the "trivial" adjectives Lakoff lists for women, such as "magnificant," "dynamic," "brilliant," "powerful," "hideous," "forceful," etc. Do women also use words like "forceful" more than men? Lakoff fails to consider the possibility that her selection is biased, that there exists a counterpart category that is also more frequently used by women than men, because women have larger vocabularies than men. In almost all of her comparisons between men's and women's usage, Lakoff assumes that the women's usage is somehow inferior.[5] That assumption seems unwarranted.

II

Lakoff distinguishes between "women's language" and "men's language" and discusses the implications of the distinction for women's role. There are two principal criticisms of her view: first, that Lakoff fails to distinguish language and speech and only argues for sex differences in speech; second, that she erroneously complicates the task of women by implying that we will have to learn another "language." What is the criterion by which people are held to speak different languages? This is never discussed. It is assumed that because women may use different vocabulary items from men, and may use some linguistic constructions more than men, women and men speak different languages.

There are two separate, though related, problems here. One is how to determine what are the criteria for languagehood; the other is how to distinguish between speech and language. By confusing speech and language, Lakoff accepts the evidence that men and women have different speech habits as also being evidence that men and women speak two different languages.

Let us first explore what the criteria for languagehood are. If vocabulary and favored use of one construction over another are sufficient, then no two people speak the same language: no two people use just the same vocabulary and linguistic constructions. One is also led to the conclusion that the language I am speaking today is different from the one I spoke yesterday and the one I will speak tomorrow, since I will use different words and constructions on each of these occasions. Even if individual differences are somehow exempted from the criterion, there is still the problem of differences between groups. If men and women speak different "languages" by virtue of using different vocabulary items and different constructions, then many groups could be distinguished on the basis of the vocabulary items and constructions they use. In fact, there is no *a priori* reason to limit the number of such groups: there are skiers vs. non-skiers, parents vs. the childless, students vs. non-students, etc.

Lakoff claims that some women become "bilingual" in men's and women's language and that this may be a strain on them, reducing their performance. (Presumably it is also a strain on male intellectuals, clergy, and upper-class Britons who, according to Lakoff, have speech more similar to women than to other men.) By this argument, if I were a student mother who skis I would speak at least four "languages" and add another for each new classification I fall under. Therefore, by this argument, all of us are extraordinary polyglots, and under extraordinary strain, since each of us falls into an extremely large number of such categories. Are we also to conclude that each of these "languages" has the same status as genuine languages like French and Russian? If Lakoff is satisfied with the conclusion that everyone speaks a different language from everyone else (or the alternate conclusion that everyone speaks indefinitely many languages) then we must understand her to be using "language" in a metaphorical rather than technical sense. If she is not satisfied with the conclusion, she must provide and justify alternate criteria so that only men and women will end up speaking different "languages."

The *reductio ad absurdum* occurs because Lakoff confuses speech with language. An analogy with another field may clarify matters. Perhaps men and women add and multiply differently. That is not evidence for "women's mathematics" and "men's mathematics," but for different computational styles. The structure of mathematics is the same, no matter who uses it. Similarly, there is a difference between the English language and how people use that language, and nothing is served by obscuring that difference, except to make it seem as if linguists have "discovered" that women and men speak English I and English II and that linguists therefore have some special competence in discussing sex differences in this realm. Lakoff maintains the confusion when she says "my feeling is that language use by any other name is still linguistics." In saying this, Lakoff denies the linguistic distinction between competence and performance. Competence refers to the speaker's knowledge of the language, and is described by a rule system called a grammar; performance refers to the speaker's use of language, and is described by a model of processing.[6]

The confusion between speech and language is also maintained in Lakoff's discussion of women's inability to express themselves strongly. She argues that women do not have the linguistic means to express themselves strongly, rather than saying that they lack the social will to use the available forms. Assume that it is true that women find it difficult to express strong emotion, that they find it difficult to swear. Is this due to speaking a different language or to an upbringing that demands that women not be assertive, not argue, not fight? We can accept as fact that women have difficulty being assertive and angry, and that the difficulty is reflected in our manner of speaking (as well as in other ways.) There can be no quarrel with this; it is a truism from the women's movement. The quarrel is with dressing the understanding up in linguistic clothes and drawing conclusions such as that some women learn to be "bilingual" in both men's and women's languages and that this is a strain.[7] Such conclusions are based on premises that have never been proved in the first place (i.e., that there really are different languages.)

The failure to make a speech/language distinction is finally seen in Lakoff's discussion of what information a grammar should include. She argues that significant generalizations will not be captured in a grammar that ignores the social causes for differential word meanings. For example, she points out that "a professional" has two different meanings depending on whether it is applied to a man or a woman. When applied to a man it means that he is a doctor, lawyer, or has some other profession. When applied to a woman it means that she is a prostitute. There are also word pairs that have similarly non-parallel meanings, such as "bachelor" and "spinster." Unless the grammar contains information about social and political conditions, the generalization that all these cases reflect the oppression of women cannot be made by the grammar.

The claim may be true, but it does not constitute an argument for including such information in the grammar. Lakoff's reasoning is an argument for making appropriate generalizations; a separate argument is needed to support the claim that an appropriate place to make such generalizations is in the grammar of a language, rather than in ancillary fields such as sociolinguistics. She does not supply such an argument.

There is one further point in this connection: Lakoff never states what the generalization is. She offers no hypotheis that would account for the non-parallels that exist. The oppression of women is not a sufficient hypothesis, because there are cases of a parallel usage. In fact, the non-parallelisms are a small minority compared to the number of words that apply equally to men and women, including explicitly sexual or gender terms, such as "horny" and "man/woman" (where the two forms have equivalent connotations).

In summary, Lakoff incorrectly identifies the differences between men's and women's speech as differences between men's and women's language. The problem occurs because she fails to distinguish between speech and language. Two unfortunate consequences are her suggestions that women need to overcome their linguistic background by learning "men's language," and that the grammar should include social and political information.

III

In the final sections of "Language and Women's Place" Lakoff analyzes the relation between social change and linguistic change; she also considers which changes in linguistic usage, on the part of both men and women, are desirable. Her position is that linguistic change follows from social change, and that some changes in usage will be impossible to effect even under conditions of social equality. Let us examine in detail Lakoff's position on the relation between social and linguistic change. Lakoff writes:

> The presence of the words is a signal that something is wrong, rather than (as too often interpreted by well-meaning reformers) the problem itself.[8]

Linguistic imbalances are worthy of study because they bring into sharper focus real-world imbalances and inequities. They are clues that some external situation needs changing, rather than items that one *should* seek to change directly. A competent doctor tries to eliminate the germs that cause measels, rather than trying to bleach the red out with peroxide. I emphasize this point because it seems to be currently fashionable to try, first, to attack the disease by attempting to obliterate the external symptoms; and, secondly, to attack *every* instance of linguistic sexual inequity, rather than selecting those that reflect a real disparity in social treatment, not mere grammatical nonparallelism; we should be attempting to single out those linguistic uses that, by implication and innuendo, demean the members of one group or another, and should be seeking to make speakers of English aware of the psychological damage such forms do. The problem, of course, lies in deciding which forms are really damaging to the ego, and then in determining what to put in their stead.[9]

It should be recognized that social change creates language change, not the reverse; or at best, language change influences changes in attitudes slowly and indirectly, and these changes in attitudes will not be reflected in social change unless society is receptive already. Further, the linguist can suggest which linguistic disparities reflect real and serious social inequalities; which are changeable, which will resist change; and can thus help the workers in the real world to channel their energies most constructively and avoid ridicule.[10]

The only substantive claim in these discussions is an inconsistent one that linguistic change follows social change and not vice versa. The thesis seems to be that linguistic oppression is a symptom of the disease of social inequality, rather than the disease itself. Thus there is no point in trying to eliminate the symptoms alone; the disease itself must be attacked. But Lakoff is not consistent on this point. Shifting ground somewhat, she says that we should not try to eliminate all linguistic inequality at once; this implies that it does make sense to try to change some of the external symptoms. She also says that we should try to make people realize the psychological harm that oppressive usage inflicts, again as if to say that the symptom can have its own ill effects on top of the disease. In another place, she vacillates between saying that social change creates linguistic change and saying that linguistic change is slow and can only create social change if social change has already been in the wind. Lakoff nowhere defines social change or tells us what the disease is of which oppressive language is one of the symptoms.

There are three different arguments against the point she wants to make about linguistic change, and each accepts the disease analogy as valid. First, while we are curing the disease, no overnight affair, we can use a little relief from the symptoms. Second, not only is reduction of suffering a good in itself, it often gives the patient the strength necessary to fight the disease more effectively.

The third argument is more basic and more complex. It requires a definition of social inequality and the nature of the disease. Are the two identical? Social inequality could refer to salary, the distribution of women in different kinds of jobs, the number of women with paying jobs, or educational level; Lakoff is not specific. Is changing the socioeconomic status of women attacking the disease rather than the symptoms? By all socioeconomic criteria, Jews do very well. Yet there is prejudice against Jews, and no lack of epithets to refer to them. If the disease has been cured in the case of Jews, why do the linguistic symptoms remain? The point of the example is that social change does not guarantee linguistic change; we can imagine women being socioeconomically equal but still linguistically oppressed. It could be argued that the linguistic oppression was formerly much worse, or at least more widely practiced; but my point is that linguistic oppression can exist in a socioeconomic vacuum.

That argument, however, only proves that social change is not sufficient to guarantee linguistic change. But even if it is insufficient, it could still be necessary. If we look at the early years of the recent women's movement, there is evidence from the radical movement as a whole that linguistic change can occur before social change. Before there were any tangible changes in women's education or jobs, feminists changed the way they themselves spoke, and also changed the speech habits of non-feminist radical women and men.

One counter-argument Lakoff could make is that I have incorrectly defined social inequality: that I am incorrectly using it as synonymous with economic and educational equality. She might propose a more abstract definition, such as a lack of self-determination or power over one's own life. Having asserted such power, women become an important influence on the radical movement. The linguistic effect of feminists on the radical movement was then a consequence of their having more political power. The problem changes, however, if put in these terms. Now the chain of events is not properly described as first social change and then linguistic change, but rather as first self-determination and then choices about what changes are desirable. The disease is therefore not social inequality but lack of power over one's life; all forms of oppression—be they economic, psychological, social, or linguistic—are merely symptoms of it.

On my analysis, feminists have already developed the correct strategy with respect to oppressive linguistic usage: eliminate it wherever it exists. On Lakoff's analysis, the feminist strategy is incorrect. On the acceptance of "Ms." as a title for women, she says:

> One must distinguish between acceptance in official use and documents (where Ms. is already used to some extent) and acceptance in colloquial conversation, where I have never heard it.[11] . . . it would seem that trying to legislate a change in a lexical item is fruitless. The change to Ms. will not be generally adopted until women's status in society changes to assure her an identity based on her own accomplishments.[12]

On the desire of many women to do away with forms of "he" being used as the generic pronoun:

> I think one should force oneself to be realistic: certain aspects of language are available to the native speakers' conscious analysis, and others are too common, too thoroughly mixed throughout the language, for the speaker to be aware each time he uses them. It is realistic to hope to change only those linguistic uses of which speakers themselves can be made aware, as they use them. One chooses, in speaking or writing, more or less consciously and purposefully among nouns, adjectives, and verbs; one does not choose among pronouns in the same way. My feeling is that this area of pronominal neutralization is both less in need of changing, and less open to change, than many of the other disparities that have been discussed earlier.[13]

> Many speakers, feeling this is awkward and perhaps even discriminatory, attempt a neutralization with *their*, a usage frowned upon by most authorities as inconsistent or illogical.[14]

With respect to changing the use of "he" as the generic pronoun, Lakoff says that she does not think it is important, and that in any event it is not possible to stop using "he" as the generic. That is, even if women suddenly stopped being discriminated against, "he" would continue, because speakers do not have control over this aspect of their speech. No evidence is offered for the claim.

Lakoff acknowledges that many women object to the use of "he" as the generic, but asserts that an attempt to change the use is futile. But the women who object to "he" have presumably been able to control their speech. Perhaps Lakoff is arguing that these women may have been able to, but that other people cannot or will not. There does not, however, seem to be anything in the way except lack of motivation or lack of a suitable alternative. Lakoff's pessimism seems to be a personal statement rather than a scientific judgment. This is also apparent in her remarks on the use of "Ms." as a title. The danger is that her assertions could have a pernicious effect on feminists: a linguist, who apparently should know, is stating that a certain change is not possible. But the linguist does not know and presents neither argument nor evidence.

Lakoff's willingness to use an appeal to authority as an argument is apparent in the brief remark she makes about the suggestion they "they" be used instead of "he." "Most authorities" frown upon it as "inconsistent or illogical." Who are these "authorities?" What is their evidence? Inconsistent or illogical in what way? "They" in fact seems an admirable substitute, since it already freely occurs in speech. Bodine demonstrates that "they" was commonly used until the end of the 18th century, when social and political pressures were responsible for its demise.[15]

There has been little research on the frequency with which "they" is used as the generic. In an experiment Carla Fink and I ran to see what pronoun male and female college students would use to fill in the blank of a generic sentence like "Everybody should wipe _____ feet before entering," we found that subjects used the appropriate form of the generic pronoun "they" about 45 percent of the time. Further, many subjects who used the masculine third-person singular reported remembering being taught not to use the third person plural in grammar school. The evidence is scanty, but does suggest that "they" is a useful substitute for "he."

If women think "he" should be eliminated, the role of linguists should not be to tell us either that they do not think it is important or that they do not feel it is possible. Rather, they should help supply a substitute. For example, the creation of new pronouns will be less useful than the resurrection of "they," because in general it is easier to increase the frequency of a behavior that already exists than to create a new behavior.

In her discussion of the neologisms "herstory" and himicanes," I think Lakoff misses the point. (Since she does not quote any sources, however, I cannot be sure.) Women do not necessarily believe that these words are etymologically sexist. By using "herstory" they believe that they can point out that women are ignored in most historical accounts and that they themselves are involved in doing history from a feminist viewpoint. It is a play on words to make a point. With hurricanes, it is politically and sociologically interesting that until recently they were all named after women, and calling them "himicanes" could be a play on words in which only this fact is intended to be brought out. Surely even non-linguists are entitled to have a little fun with words. Lakoff's concern over these suggestions is shown by her statement that

> If this sort of stuff appears in print and in the popular media as often as it does, it becomes increasingly more difficult to persuade men that women are really rational beings.[16]

Even if the "himicane" suggestion were dead serious, who are these unworthy creatures who generalize that all women are irrational on the basis of the irrationality of a few? Their sexism should be attacked rather than catered to.

To sum up, Lakoff's views on the value of attacking oppressive linguistic usage have been criticized here on two grounds. First, her analysis of the relation between linguistic and social change is faulty. Second, her claim that some usage is unalterable is supported by neither logic nor evidence. The feminist strategy of trying to eliminate all oppressive usage is preferable.

To return to one of the issues posed at the beginning of this paper: how can linguists (as linguists) contribute to the feminist strategy? The answer is, by helping to implement it, rather than by using a presumed linguistic expertise to answer a political question. No linguist can properly tell us to learn to live with a certain amount of oppression, or to try not to think of it as oppression, because our decisions about what we will tolerate are not linguistic decisions but political ones.

NOTES

1. Robin Lakoff, "Language and Woman's Place," *Language in Society* 2 (1973): 45-80; reprinted in *Language and Woman's Place*, Robin Lakoff, ed. (New York: Harper and Row, 1975); and *idem*, "Why Women Are Ladies," in *Language and Woman's Place*.

2. B. L. Dubois and I. Crouch, "The Question of Tag Questions in Women's Speech: They Don't Really Use More of Them, Do They?" *Language in Society* 4 (1975): 289-94.

3. When "lovely" modifies nouns that are not physical objects, the analysis is more complicated. For example, in "What a lovely day for a picnic" the adjective "lovely" is not simply making an aesthetic evaluation, but a functional one as well. It can be seen, however, that the functional evaluation only carries because of the implicit aesthetic evaluation: if "What a lovely day to stay indoors" is uttered because it is raining outside, there is still something odd about the sentence. One can properly say "What a good day to stay indoors" in such a situation because "good" has no independent aesthetic meaning.

4. Lakoff, *Language and Woman's Place, op. cit.*, p. 13.

5. The one exception is in her discussion of women's tendency to speak indirectly, where she suggests that both direct and indirect styles of talking are of value. See *Language and Woman's Place*, p. 74.

6. See Noam Chomsky, *Aspects of the Theory of Syntax* (New York: Harper & Row, 1965) and my "The Relation between Competence and Performance: A Theoretical Review," *CUNY Forum in Linguistics* 1 (1976): 64-101.

7. Lakoff, *Language and Woman's Place, op. cit.*, pp. 6-7.

8. *Ibid.*, p. 21.

9. *Ibid.*, p. 43.

10. *Ibid.*, p. 47 (p. 66 in this volume).

11. *Ibid.*, p. 36.

12. *Ibid.*, p. 41.

13. *Ibid.*, p. 45.

14. *Ibid.*, p. 44.

15. A. Bodine, "Androcentrism in Prescriptive Grammar: Singular 'They,' Sex-Indefinite 'He,' and 'He or She,'" *Language in Society* 4 (1975): 129-46.

16. Lakoff, *Language and Woman's Place, op. cit.*, p. 46.

Jacqueline Fortunata

Lakoff on Language
and Women

Does our language discriminate against women? Robin Lakoff
has argued convincingly that, in certain ways, it does. The present paper will discuss some puzzling aspects of her seminal
work, "Language and Woman's Place," as it originally appeared in *Language in Society*.[1] Lakoff has raised many of these
same issues in her recent book, *Language and Woman's Place*,
but I believe my criticisms still have not been met.

Robin Lakoff examines speech by women and speech about
women and concludes that "the marginality and powerlessness
of women is reflected both in the ways women are expected to
speak, and the ways in which women are spoken of."[2] Her first
claim, that the language patterns women are expected to use are
distinct from those men are expected to use, I have no comment
on. This question is outside my realm of expertise. Her second
set of claims, that "speech about women implies an object,
whose sexual nature requires euphemism, and whose social roles
are derivative and dependent in relation to men,"[3] I will
criticize. These attitudes toward women, which Lakoff claims to
prove are embodied in language about women, are attitudes
which at least some women find demeaning. If Lakoff means
that in a single offensive piece of linguistic behavior, irrespective
of context and the personal feelings toward women of the
speaker, the speaker demeans or causes "psychological

damage"[4] to women, then her thesis is far from obvious. The situations that come to mind are those in which the speaker has no intent to demean (or praise) and the audience does not feel demeaned (or praised). Are the demeaning uses that she uncovers demeaning in these situations? Unless Lakoff's thesis extends to these situations, her claim reduces to the trivial thesis that women can successfully be demeaned. That Lakoff is attempting to prove the stronger thesis, namely that women as a whole are demeaned by certain linguistic uses, seems obvious from parts of her paper quoted later. After an attempt to prove her thesis, she calls for replacing these uses with some neutral, non-psychological damaging patterns.[5]

My criticism of Lakoff's thesis and plea for linguistic revision takes the following form. First, I argue that the concept of a linguistic usage demeaning to women as a whole is opaque. In an attempt to understand this concept and, thereby, her thesis, the reasons Lakoff gives for censoring particular linguistic uses are examined. I show that all but one of these reasons cannot be general reasons for censoring linguistic uses suspected of demeaning women, blacks, or any other group. In other words, I state counter-examples to the general applicability of Lakoff's reasons for saying that certain uses are demeaning to women as a whole. Also, I briefly discuss what it is to demean and, correspondingly, to be demeaned, in an attempt to illustrate some of the difficulties involved in making unaware people aware that they are demeaning (or being demeaned).

Does Lakoff attempt to prove that women in general are demeaned by certain ways of talking about them? In the first paragraph of the section entitled "Talking About Women," she states:

> Often a word that may be used of both men and women (and perhaps of things as well), when applied to women, assumes a special meaning that, *by implication rather than outright assertion, is derogatory to women as a group.*[6]
> [Italics mine].

One example of such a word is "professional."[7] Typically, when a man is termed a "professional," it means that he is a doctor or a lawyer, and so on. But when a woman is termed a "professional," it means that she is a prostitute. I interpret this argument in the following schematic way: if *prima facie* sexually neutral terms do not apply in the same way to women as they do to men, and the application to women is derogatory, women as a whole are being demeaned by the usage. In the case in question, "professional" is a *prima facie* sexually neutral term which does not apply to women as it does to men, and "professional," as it applies to women, is derogatory; therefore, women as a whole are being demeaned by the usage. This argument will be discussed later. I cite it now to justify my claim that Lakoff is arguing that certain linguistic uses demean women as a whole.

There is further evidence that this is her thesis. In the first paragraph of the subsequent and final section of her paper, entitled "Suggestions and Conclusions," Lakoff states:

> . . . we should be attempting to single out those linguistic uses that, by implication and innuendo, demean the members of one group or another, and should be seeking to make speakers of English aware of the psychological damage such forms do. The problem, of course, lies in deciding which forms are really damaging to the ego, and then in determining what to put in their stead.[8]

I interpret these remarks to mean that there are certain linguistic uses which are always demeaning, regardless of the speaker's intent to demean and the awareness on the part of the women allegedly demeaned that they have been demeaned. It is these language uses which must be uncovered by the linguist.

Lakoff is trying to prove that particular uses are demeaning to women in general, by their very presence in the language. This is distinctly different from the trivial claims that women in general may be demeaned, that particular women may be demeaned, and that there are ways of demeaning women in general, or in particular, that are almost exclusively ways of demeaning women. As long as language can be used to demean, people will demean other people, and it would seem futile and even undesirable to change the language in an attempt to temporarily stymie demeaners. At most, we may convince them that what they are doing is often immoral.

Can we clarify Lakoff's thesis by examining her arguments to prove that particular linguistic uses are demeaning to women in general? Her first argument, an attempt to prove that "lady" is one such usage, may be divided into three stages. First, "lady" does not have the same connotation as "woman." At least for some speakers of English, Lakoff points out, this is true. She cites cases in which "lady" functions differently from "woman." One example is the difference in connotation between "lady sculptor" and "woman sculptor."[9] Second, "lady" is a euphemism for "woman"; because of this status, its existence demeans women. She gives two main reasons why "lady" is a euphemism for "woman." "Lady" is used to euphemize certain occupations, as in "cleaning lady." Also, the presence in the language of many derogatory words for women indicates the felt need for a euphemism. Third, at the present time "lady" does not function in the same way as either "gentleman" or "lord." However, at some past time "lady" and "gentleman" and "lady" and "lord" had parallel uses. This divergence of use is indicative of the difference in roles women and men have in this society, according to Lakoff. This divergence is similar to what Lakoff calls "Bull-Cow-Shifts" and will be discussed with other divergences in use of this type.

First, does "lady" have a different connotation than "woman"? Certain uses suggest this. For example, Lakoff compares "woman doctor" to "lady doctor" and finds the latter to be demeaning.[10] If questioned, people will often agree that "lady doctor" is demeaning. The question asks about an expression devoid of context. I have encountered "lady doctor" twice in the past year, once in a journalistic autobiography and once in a conversation. In neither instance was the use demeaning, nor was there any intention to demean. Context must count for something. However, if Lakoff is asserting here the simple point that most language users feel that the use of "lady doctor" in most contexts is demeaning and, therefore, that "lady doctor" is a demeaning expression, I have no quarrel with her. I would argue that this is the most appropriate and widely used test for a demeaning expression: the feelings of the speaker and his or her audience.

Lakoff's second claim is that "lady" is a euphemism and, like all euphemisms, demeans the euphemized object. I argue that it is not clear that "lady" is a euphemism and that it is false that all euphemisms demean, because they trivialize the object euphemized. Ignoring the separate question, "Is 'lady' demeaning?" consider the question, "Is 'lady' a euphemism?"

How does Lakoff prove that "lady" is a euphemism for "woman"? First, she claims that "lady" is used to euphemize professions. For example, we have the expressions "cleaning lady" and "sales lady." However, is it the professions of cleaning and selling or the sex of the cleaner and seller that must be euphemized? It seems to me that it is the profession that is the source of our discomfort. We euphemize the professions of cleaning and selling when the cleaners and sellers are male, also. Consider the words "janitor," "sanitary engineer," "maintenance man," and "broker," "counselor," and "sales representative."

Secondly, Lakoff claims that we feel a need to euphemize "woman" because of the sexual connotations present in "woman." Lakoff supports this claim by citing contexts in which "woman" has a sexual connotation.[11] In some contexts, "woman" has a sexual connotation, just as in some contexts "man" has a sexual connotation; however, there are many contexts in which neither word has a sexual connotation. For example, "woman" and "man" have no sexual connotation in the context, "the man and woman who entered the room were strangers." She further supports the claim that there are sexual connotations present in "woman" by pointing out that derogatory terms for women are often overtly sexual.[12] Thus, she concludes that what bothers us about women is their sexual nature and, therefore, we must euphemize "women." Her second point ignores certain pertinent facts. Even though, according to Lakoff, no euphemisms are needed for "man," many derogatory terms for men are overtly sexual. I found no other argument to prove "lady" is a euphemism, except possibly the following obviously invalid one:

> The use of lady tends to trivialize the subject matter under discussion. Euphemisms tend to trivialize the subject matter under discussion. Therefore, lady is a euphemism.

I do not wish to attribute this argument to Lakoff and have no comment on it.

Suppose that "lady" is a euphemism. Are all euphemisms demeaning? Lakoff's proof is as follows: euphemisms are not employed in serious discussions and the use of a euphemism tends to trivialize the subject matter under discussion. Euphemisms, for these two reasons, demean the euphemized object. If "lady" is a euphemism, then we can conclude that it, too, demeans the euphemized object, namely women. It is true that euphemism of some types, such as "little boys room" (Lakoff's example)[13] are not employed in serious discussions. However, other euphemisms are employed in many serious discussions and cannot, therefore, be said to necessarily trivialize and demean the euphemized object. There are many examples of non-trivializing euphemisms in military language:

"anti-personnel weapon" for "bomb," "preemptive strike" for "attack," "defensive maneuver" for "retreat," and so on. These euphemisms attempt to remove the bad connotations of "bomb," "attack," and "retreat" but they do not have the effect of trivializing the war.

Lakoff has described a cluster of considerations about the related uses of "woman" and "lady." In reply to her point that the use of "lady," as in "lady doctor" is demeaning, I stated that this depends on the context. In making her point that "lady" is a euphemism for "woman," Lakoff gives two reasons: (1) We use it to ennoble professions such as cleaning and (2) we feel a need to euphemize "woman" because of the sexual connotations of the word. These sexual connotations are apparent in some contexts. Also, the derogatory words for "woman" point to the source of our discomfort: her sexual nature. I argued that we euphemize the profession, cleaning, and not the sex of the employed person in "cleaning lady." I also argued that there are contexts in which "man" has a sexual connotation and that there are many derogatory words for "man" that emphasize his sexual nature, yet this is anomalous given Lakoff's reasoning about the euphemistic nature of "woman." In reply to her final point that all euphemisms demean by trivializing the object euphemized (by being employed in nonserious discussions), I pointed out that euphemisms appear in some of the least trivial discussions of all, those about war.

Lakoff has described a cluster of considerations that may, in their totality, lead to hypothesis that the use of "lady" is demeaningly euphemistic. Perhaps it is unjustifiable to question each reason in turn, for singly they do not seem sufficient to confirm her hypothesis.

Her second example of a euphemism which demeans women is "girl."[14] According to Lakoff, "girl" removes the sexual connotations of "woman" in stressing the idea of immaturity. But it demeans women because "girl" brings to mind irresponsibility. For weeks I pointed out to every woman (I only heard women use the expression) that "girl" and "gal" were insulting for those two reasons and all I got were blank stares and polite silences. Girls are immature, but "girl-gals" are not girls. My experience illustrates, I think, a feature of the act of demeaning. People must, at least on some occasions, spontaneously recognize that they are being demeaned, and/or that they are demeaning. This elementary fact is generally overlooked and ignored by many who speak to the problem of verbal discrimination against women. The question is, what does "demeaning" mean in the contexts in which Lakoff claims women are being demeaned? Her underlying assumption seems to be that people don't know they are being demeaned and, therefore, they don't know what the meaning of "demean" is. The rest of my paper, in discussing Lakoff's arguments, illustrates the difficulty of reassessing what it means to demean. I will argue that words are demeaning only if they spontaneously elicit feelings of being demeaned on the part of those to whom the terms are applied.

Lakoff's next set of arguments are termed "Bull-Cow-Shifts." She states:

> Suppose we take a pair of words which, in terms of the possible relationships of an earlier society, were simple male-female equivalents, analogous to bull: cow. Suppose we find that . . . society has changed in such a way that the primary meanings now are irrelevant. Yet the words have not been discarded, but have acquired new meanings, metaphorically related to their original senses. But suppose these new metaphorical uses are no longer parallel to each other. By seeing where the parallelism breaks down, we can intuit something about the different roles played by men and women in this culture.[15]

She later supplements this argument in a way that indicates that she does not intend it to be a valid argument. Her conclusion, that "we can intuit something about the different roles played by men and women in this culture," is considered as a hypothesis for explaining why the "Bull-Cow-Shifts" have occurred.[16] A linguist writing a descriptive grammar must otherwise be content with *ad hoc* rules of language. If certain social facts about the place of women in society are assumed, the nonparallel linguistic uses are understandable. Presumably, these explanatory social assumptions about the roles of men and women can then be verified to see if in fact they do hold for a particular society.

The problem with "intuiting" the different roles played by men and women in this culture (whatever that could mean) is that we can do better than "intuit" them. We know the different roles played by men and women in this culture (and, also, for nearly every culture for which we have a history).

Lakoff's program seems to be this: (1) We determine that a linguistic usage is demeaning to a particular group of people;

(2) We suppose that certain social facts explain the linguistic usage; (3) We verify our hypothesis that certain facts explain the linguistic usage by checking society. Obviously, there will be archaic usages, making (3) superfluous. If Lakoff does not think (3) is necessary, I have no wish to attribute (3) to her. The problem with this view of a suspect usage is that it is self-confirming. The social facts cannot be tied down as the causes of any specific usage. The social facts explain everything and, therefore, nothing. The demeaning nature of an expression must first be discerned by independent testing. The test for demeaning nature in the case of a Bull-Cow-Shift seems to be the following: sex-linked pairs of terms which had parallel uses at some time in the past and no longer have parallel uses in the present may be demeaning to women as a whole. They are demeaning if they are derogatory. I will refer to this as the Bull-Cow-Shift Test.

Lakoff's earlier argument that "lady" demeans women may be seen as a variation on the Bull-Cow-Shift Test. In the past, there were the pairs "lady"/"gentlemen" and "lady"/"lord" and "lady" no longer functions in a way parallel to either "gentleman" or "lord." If "lady" is derogatory, we can conclude this usage is demeaning to women as a whole.

I dispute the rationality of the Bull-Cow-Shift Test. I do not think we can conclude that it uncovers demeaning linguistic expressions. Consider the following so-called Bull-Cow-Shift: "bachelor" and "spinster."[17] It seems to me that if there is some linguistic expression which serves to describe women, some other linguistic expression which serves to describe men, and the two uses essentially say the same thing about men and women respectively, it is not reasonable to say that the Bull-Cow-Shift in question demeans women as a whole.

"Bachelor" and "spinster," while each refers to an unmarried person, have different connotations. The use of "spinster" is cited by Lakoff as a usage which demeans women as a whole because it fails the Bull-Cow-Shift Test. I would agree with her conclusion about "spinster" if and only if all unmarried women were spinsters, all unmarried men were bachelors, and those were the sole ways the two groups could be described. In other words, I agree that a woman is demeaned by "spinster" and, if "spinster" were the only word for an unmarried woman, I would agree that all (unmarried) women would be demeaned. But the world of unmarried people includes bachelors, spinsters, singles, swinging singles, bachelor girls, maidens, monarchs, celibates, old maids, misogynists, career women, free spirits, libertarians, and Shakers.

Are there any other tests proposed by Lakoff for discerning linguistic uses which are demeaning? She discusses titles such as "Miss," "Mrs." "Mr." and other ways status is signaled in our society. I have no comment on these usages. She implies other tests in criticizing two well-known arguments for the general thesis that language demeans women. Lakoff criticizes the argument that calls for neutralization of third person singular pronouns and one version of the argument that calls for changing or abandoning words with parts composed of "man," "his," "brother," "son" (and so on) when these words apply to women as well as men. Her criticisms of these well-known arguments imply certain tests for determining if a linguistic usage is demeaning to women. I do not wish to attribute these tests to her, but consider them in their own right.

Lakoff does not advocate pronominal neutralization but she admits that since so many women do, they may have a valid point. She writes:

> I have read and heard dissenting views from too many anguished women to suppose that this use of "he" is really a frivolity.[18]

Here, Lakoff seems to consider the feelings of women as relevant to which uses are demeaning to women. This seems to me to be the most acceptable test for determining if a linguistic usage is demeaning. At the very least, a usage is demeaning only if people spontaneously see it as demeaning.

The next argument Lakoff considers is that for changing the word "history." The argument goes as follows. A part of the word "history" is the masculine "his" (you can read the word as "his story") but women also make history; therefore, the usage demeans women. Lakoff states that this argument is irrational and she bases this charge on the etymology of "history." Is this then a general test for linguistic sexism? A word's etymology cannot yield a sufficient condition of linguistic sexism unless "woman" is itself demeaning to women. "Woman" has its origin in "wif man" or "wife of man." Neither can it yield a necessary condition of linguistic sexism because "lady," "professional," and other sexist words cited by Lakoff are unrelated to any masculine root. Is the etymology of a word a necessary condition of linguistic sexism for all and only those words that have as a proper part some masculine root? This test would ensure that we would need an etymologist to point out words that are demeaning to women. What is again ignored is the genesis of feeling demeaned. The feeling one has when one feels demeaned typically has little to do with etymological considerations.

It is obvious that one could use "history" in a punning way to demean women. Perhaps Lakoff would reply that women could be demeaned, but the mere existence of the word "history" is not demeaning to women. However, is it clear that the mere existence of any linguistic usage is demeaning to women as a whole?

Is the etymology of a word always a sure sign that a linguistic expression, especially a derogatory one, is demeaning to some group? "Sinister," a derogatory expression, has its origin in the belief that the left hand is the devil's hand. Left-handed people are not as a group demeaned by the word "sinister." Why not? Lack of appropriate intentions to demean on the part of those who use "sinister" and the lack of feeling demeaned on the part of the left-handed is surely relevant.

I have been arguing that "lady" and other suspect uses are demeaning only if "lady" and other uses elicit feelings of being demeaned on the part of those termed "lady." Because demeaning and feeling demeaned are reciprocal socially-acquired linguistic acts, we can make an expression a demeaning one if we convince enough people to feel demeaned. It would seem that Lakoff's linguistic task must be secretive or self-defeating (if you are an optimist) or self-confirming (if you are a pessimist). She purports to describe, but the description influences self-conscious people to feel demeaned at the sound of "lady." What may have once been neutral becomes demeaning. Her theory makes itself true if it is published and taken seriously, but then the taboo was not successfully described by the missionaries, for it was they who taught it to the natives.

NOTES

1. Robin Lakoff, "Language and Women's Place," *Language and Society,* vol. 2 (1973): 45-80.
2. *Ibid.,* p. 45.
3. *Ibid.*
4. *Ibid.,* p. 73.
5. *Ibid.*
6. *Ibid.,* p. 57 (p. 63 in this volume).
7. *Ibid.,* p. 64.
8. *Ibid.,* p. 73.
9. *Ibid.,* p. 60.
10. *Ibid.,* p. 59.
11. *Ibid.,* p. 62.
12. *Ibid.,* pp. 58-59.
13. *Ibid.,* p. 62.
14. *Ibid.,* pp. 61-62 (footnote).
15. *Ibid.,* p. 53.
16. *Ibid.,* pp. 76-77.
17. *Ibid.,* pp. 66-67.
18. *Ibid.,* p. 75.

Part III

Examples

Introduction

Suppose we can all agree that the use of sexist language ought to be avoided either because this use is itself morally objectionable or because it implies a morally objectionable conception of women (men) or a morally objectionable difference in the social roles of women and men. If it can be demonstrated that there is sexist language (i.e. that there are words, sentences or statements which are "sexist" in some sense of that term), we would also all have to agree that the use of such language ought to be avoided.

Because it would be impossible to examine all words, sentences or statements which ever have been or ever will be claimed to be "sexist," in PART III we shall confine ourselves to three types of examples of sexist language which seem to pop up most frequently in the literature on the subject: a) so-called gender-neutral terms such as "he" and "man," b) terms describing sexual intercourse and c) titles such as "Mrs." and "Miss." The point of this exercise will be to try to come to some understanding of what sense(s) of the term "sexist" such words are claimed to be sexist and to determine whether or not the arguments for these claims are convincing.

A. THE DEBATE OVER "HE" AND "MAN"

Four different types of justifications have been advanced in support of the claim that "he" and "man" are sexist, one of which interprets "sexist" in one way, the other in a different way.

One type of justification denies that "he" and "man" are gender-neutral (i.e. that they can be used to refer to males and females alike). According to this view, anyone who attempts to use "he" and "man" to refer to males and females alike will fail to do so. Moreover, this failure points up a mistake on the part of the speaker (writer) of these words, not the hearer (reader); the speaker thinks that he or she is using "he" and "man" gender-neutrally, but is in fact referring to males only.

This view is advanced by JANICE MOULTON who takes "he" and "man" to be "sexist" in the sense that "they can only be used by a speaker (writer) to refer to males, not females." She offers as a paradigm example the speaker who asserts the following statements:

        1) All men are mortal.

        2) Socrates is a man.

        3) Socrates is mortal.

Replacement of "Socrates" with "Sophia" in the second and third statements, she says, makes the second statement "false" or "insulting" and she adds that 'Sophia is a man' cannot be taken (presumably either by a speaker or hearer) to mean that Sophia is a member of the human species.

There do seem to be a couple of problems with this line of reasoning, both of which are illuminating. Firstly, in order to show that it is impossible to use "he" and "man" gender-neutrally, it is not enough to show that there may be some cases in which the attempt is made and failed at; rather, it has to be shown that there is a failure in all such cases. Secondly, as JANE DURAN points out, the paradigm case offered does not conclusively demonstrate that there is even one such failure. For if the speaker did intend for "he" and "man" to be referring to males and females alike, he or she would also have to assent to the statement that Sophia is a man. That is to say, it can be argued that any speaker who denies that Sophia is a man really had no intention of using "man" gender-neutrally in asserting 'All men are mortal' in the first place.

CAROLYN KORSMEYER offers a second type of argument for the view that "he" and "man" are "sexist" in a different sense of that term. On her view, the two words can be used gender-neutrally by a speaker (writer). But they are "sexist" in the sense that "although they can be used to refer to both males and females, 'she' and 'woman' can be used only to refer to females." The use of "she," says Korsmeyer, always remains the exception to the rule, the deviating case, which directs a disproportionate amount of attention to the sex of the referent.

But even though this may well be the case, Korsmeyer's argument could be construed as good reason for banning the gender-specific uses of "she" and "woman" rather than the generic uses of "he" and "man."

A third view accepts Korsmeyer's claim that "he" and "man" can be used gender-neutrally but argues that the terms are "sexist" in that "their uses can be construed by a hearer (reader) to refer to males, but not females." ELEANOR KUYKENDALL points out that some feminist linguists in philosophy, for example, do construe then in this way. She says, "If persons of either sex can drive cars, for example, feminist linguists will perceive a cultural assumption in a sentence like 'Will the person with New York license plates please remove his car' which is inconsistent with the assumption that the driver could be female." Given that such construals on the part of hearers (readers) do seem to be commonplace, proponents of the third view argue that gender-neutral use of "he" and "man" ought to be avoided on the grounds that, wherever possible, one ought not give rise to misinterpretation. This moral objection to the gender-neutral use of "he" and "man" could, however, be forstalled by a variety of tactics, such as forthrightly stating that the intended referents are both males and females.[2]

A fourth view, advocated by ELIZABETH BEARDSLEY,[3] is that "he" is "sexist" in the sense that "it, but not 'she,' can be used to refer to a human being whose sex is unknown, on pain of saying something deemed linguistically incorrect or inappropriate." Use of the generic "he," she concludes, has negative moral implications bearing on the concepts of personhood and selfhood. Beardsley's position is subject to the charge that what is "deemed linguistically incorrect or inappropriate" is not entirely clear in that it is not spelled out who the persons are who are making the judgement or why their judgements are justified. But if adequate answers to these questions can be given, then it could be concluded that uses of the generic "he" should, indeed, be avoided and replaced with uses of the disjunctive phrase "he or she," as Beardsley suggests.[4]

B. TERMS DESCRIBING SEXUAL INTERCOURSE

ROBERT BAKER argues that many of the words we use to describe the activity of sexual intercourse are "sexist" in the sense that "their use marks the presence of a conception of women's and men's sexual roles which is denigrating to women, but not to men.'' He begins by assuming the Wittgensteinian thesis that the terms we utilize to identify something reflect our conception of it. If I refer to an adult Afro-American as a "boy" instead of as a "black," my use of "boy" is a form of metaphorical identification which indicates that I think of him as less than an adult. Likewise, says Baker, an examination of a group of verbs which are often used interchangeably with "had intercourse with" in "A had intercourse with B" shows that these verbs turn out to be metaphorical descriptions of sexual activity. For a large number of these verbs, he adds, the names for males are subjects of sentences with active constructions (where the active constructions do not indicate that the male is being harmed) whereas the names for females require passive constructions (where the passive constructions do indicate that the female is being harmed). Thus, the reason it is wrong to use words describing sexual activity which are "sexist" in the above sense is that the use marks the presence of a *conception* which is denigrating to women (but not to men).

In order to reject Baker's line of reasoning, one would have to show either a) that the words we use to describe or identify sexual activity do not reflect our *conception* of that activity (perhaps, for example, what is actually reflected is merely a perception of the difference in the physiology of men and women) or b) that although some conception of women is reflected by these word usages, it is not the conception Baker has in mind, or c) that the conception Baker thinks is reflected actually is, but it is not in any way denigrating to women.

Although she is not explicitly responding to the Baker piece, JANICE MOULTON offers a position which could be used to support thesis b) above. Moulton agrees with Baker that words used to describe sexual intercourse mark the presence of a morally objectionable conception of men's and women's sexual roles. But rather than arguing that this conception is one of a woman's being harmed by sexual intercourse, she thinks that the conception marked by use of these terms is one of a woman's sexual role as not being *as important* as that of a man. She says, "The grammar of the word 'fuck' does not imply that he and she are equally involved in the activity." On Moulton's view, the moral objection is to the *falsity* of the conception whose presence is implied by use of metaphorical descriptions of sexual activity since, as she points out, women's sexual roles are in fact just as important as men's.[5]

STEPHANIE ROSS offers a viewpoint which could be used to support thesis a) above. The use of metaphorical descriptions of sexual activity does not, on her view, necessarily reflect the presence of a conception of women as being harmed or of a false conception of the insignificance of women's sexual roles. Rather, what she thinks is being marked is the presence of a derogatory *attitude* toward women. On her view, it is possible for a speaker to consistently utter phrases such as "Sam screwed Jane" without having a corresponding conception of Sam's harming Jane or without having a false conception that Jane's role in the activity is insignificant. But in uttering sentences like this, the speaker does indicate that he or she does have a less-than-morally-acceptable derogatory attitude toward women.

No philosopher has advanced thesis c) above in print to date.

C. TITLES SUCH AS "MISS" AND "MRS."

Recently there has been much agitation within the Women's Liberation Movement for the replacement of the women's titles "Miss" and "Mrs." with "Ms." on the grounds that the former two words are "sexist," whereas the latter is not. The claim is not that "Miss" and "Mrs." are "sexist" in the sense that "they can only be used to refer to females or that "Mr." is "sexist" in the sense that "it can only be used to refer to males." Rather, the claim seems to be that "Miss" and "Mrs." are "sexist" in the sense that "they are used to mark an irrelevant distinction of marital status between women," whereas "Mr." cannot be used to mark an irrelevant distinction of marital status between men. The use of words which are "sexist" in this sense of the term is morally objectionable, say the defenders of "Ms.," because marking the irrelevant distinction of marital status can be detrimental to women in a large number of important contexts (such as when women are hunting for jobs or seeking entrance to universities). Note that if this argument is correct, the moral objection to using "Miss" and "Mrs." cannot be eliminated by substituting "Mrm." and "Srs." for "Mr." depending on marital status, as Russell Baker once suggested in a humor column. For using these new words would only compound the problem by marking the irrelevant distinction of marital status for men just as use of "Miss" and "Mrs." currently does for women.

Both ALAN SOBLE and LAURA PURDY hold that "Miss" and "Mrs." are sexist words and that their use is morally objectionable on the grounds cited above. MICHAEL LEVIN, however, disagrees. Although Levin admits that use of "Miss" and "Mrs." does mark a distinction of marital status among women, whereas use of "Mr." does not convey information about the marital status of men, he argues that the distinction marked for women is by no means "irrelevant." In fact, he says, it is of crucial importance for a man to know the marital status of women he comes into contact with; this information is conveyed to him by the use of "Miss" and "Mrs." which helps him in that it facilitates his heterosexual encounters.

Several problems with this point of view are discussed by Soble and Purdy. Although it might be granted that use of "Miss" and "Mrs." does convey to a male whether or not a woman is single, it has yet to be demonstrated that use of "Miss" and "Mrs." also conveys to a male whether or not a woman is eligible for heterosexual encounters. (Many married women are eligible for them, many single women are not.) Secondly, even if single women were more eligible than married women, it is by no means clear that the advantage of using "Miss" and "Mrs." for purposes of facilitating heterosexual encounters would outweigh the disadvantages for women posed by their continued use in contexts which may be of greater importance to them than those in which sexual communication might be initiated.

NOTES

1. There is at least one sense of each of the terms "he" and "man" which must be defined in terms of maleness only (as opposed to maleness and femaleness). This is, of course, the specific, not the so-called generic, sense. Since the feminist debate has, for the most part, revolved around claims about the so-called generic senses, I have confined muself to a discussion of this latter topic in this Introduction to PART III. Clearly, however, there is also a pressing need for a similiar examination of the use of the terms "he" and "man" in their specific senses. Refer to Carolyn Korsmeyer's piece (in this volume) for a beginning analysis of the use of terms in their specific senses.

2. Marilyn Frye, for example, uses this tactic. See the last line of her "Male Chauvinism-A Conceptual Analysis," in this volume, p. 21.

3. See her "Referential Genderization," Philosophical Forum, V, nos. 1-2 (1973-4):289-90. Beardsley's argument against the use of the so-called generic "he" is to be distinguished both from her position on the use of "man" (explicated in that same article) and from her position on the use of words with "— man" as a suffix (explicated in "Degenderization," in this volume).

4. Of course, another alternative would be to use the term "she" to refer to human beings where the sex of the referent is unkown. But, as Beardsley points out, this tactic is subject to the charge of "reverse imperialism." ("Referential Genderization," op. cit., p. 290).

5. It might be claimed that it is unclear in what sense a person's having a false conception of something is *morally* objectionable. On this view, such a person merely mistakenly holds a false belief, but is not necessarily therby engaging in a morally objectionable act. Moulton, could, however, respond to the objection by arguing that having *this particular* false conception is morally objectionable on the grounds that it is now a matter of common knowledge that it is false. To have the conception is thus deliberately (and not mistakenly) to hold a false belief.

Part III (A)

"He" And "Man"

Janice Moulton

The Myth of the Neutral "Man"

I

Here are two riddles:

(1) A man is walking down the street one day when he suddenly recognizes an old friend whom he has not seen in years walking in his direction with a little girl. They greet each other warmly and the friend says, "I married since I last saw you, to someone you never met, and this is my daughter, Ellen." The man says to Ellen, "You look just like your mother." How did he know that?

(2) A boy and his father were driving when suddenly a large truck careened around a corner and hit their car head-on. The car was crushed, and when their bodies were removed from the wreck the father was already dead. The son, badly injured but still alive, was rushed to the hospital, where hasty preparations were made for immediate surgery. As the boy was brought in for

This paper owes a special thanks to G. M. Robinson and Cherin Elias for their comments and encouragement. Many other people at the Society for Women in Philosophy, the American Philosophical Association meetings, and the University of Maryland philosophy department gave me valuable comments. I would particularly like to thank Mary Vetterling-Braggin, Virginia Valian, Larry Stern, Christine Pierce, Susan Rae Peterson, Stan Munstat, Susan Moore, W. G. Lycan, Ron Laymon, Adele Laslie, Gale Justin, Carl Ginet, Alan Donagan, Richard Brandt, and H. D. Block.

the operation, the surgeon saw him and said, I can't operate, that's my son.'' How is that possible?

If you have not heard these riddles before and they puzzle you, that's an important datum for this paper.

II

Recently it has been argued that the words "he," "man," etc. should not be used as gender-neutral terms because it is unfair to women; anyone who looks for the best *man* for the job or tells an applicant to send *his* credentials is less likely or less able to consider a female candidate fairly.

Two claims should be distinguished here. The first accepts that there is a gender-neutral meaning for terms like "he," "man," etc. Adherents of this view consider the gender-neutral uses of these terms an *effect* of, and an unpleasant reminder of, the lower status of women, and urge that the gender-neutral use be eliminated as a sign of good will and for symptomatic relief.

The second claim denies that terms such as "he" and "man" have gender-neutral uses. It argues that using these terms as if they were neutral terms *causes* unfairness. This is because not really being gender-neutral, the use of such terms leads one to apply the context to males, and makes it difficult to apply it to females.

The first claim is sometimes followed up with a shift to the second claim: once the first claim has been articulated, the second claim is thought to become true. Refusing to adopt this sign of good will indicates a lack of good will — that is, sexism. Continued use of "he" and "man" as neutral terms indicates that the attitude of the speaker is not gender-neutral. It will be recognized on some level of awareness that the speaker intends men to be preferred to women, and intends terms such as "he" or "man," although hitherto neutral, to apply primarily to men. Only people who have these intentions will continue to use these terms as if they were neutral. Such an argument defends and reinforces the first claim by appeal to the second claim.

The first claim, that there *are* neutral uses but they are symptoms of unfairness and should be eliminated, has greater initial plausibility than the second. Using "he" and "man" as neutral terms may well be the result of the greater prominence of men in our culture. But once this use has been established, it appears that it can be both intended and understood neutrally. There is no initial reason to suppose that these terms are less likely to be applied to women than men, *if* used neutrally.

I am going to defend the second claim, but I would like to do so without appealing to any connection with the first claim. I believe that the second claim can be defended on its own, without appeal to sexist attitudes of the speakers. I shall try to show that however innocently and neutrally they are intended, the words "he," "man," etc. may not function as genuine gender-neutral terms; that their use is unavoidably somewhat gender-specific; and that male gender-specific descriptions make it difficult to recognize that descriptions in that context could apply to a female.

III

Let us first consider the criticism of the use of "he," "man," etc. as gender-neutral terms which, while allowing that the uses may be neutral, nevertheless requests relief from these symptoms of other injustices. This criticism reminds us that there are other neutral terms: One can look for the best *person* for the job, tell *applicants* to send their credentials to one, etc. It continues: If we change our language, we will increase awareness of past unfair treatment of women and save women from being constantly reminded of the male priority and domination that the neutral uses of "he" and "man" indicate. Although some of the suggested changes will be awkward at first, they will be signs of a spirit of sympathy and cooperation with the criticism and therefore with efforts of women to attain equal human status.

Once this request has been made, the continued use of "he" and "man" as gender-neutral terms does not *make* a person less likely to consider a woman for the job. Nevertheless it may be an indication that the person is not especially sympathetic to the problems of being automatically assigned a lower status, and therefore that the person may be less likely to consider a woman for the job. On this view, the gender-neutral use of "he," etc. is a consequence, or a symbol, not a cause, of existing unjust attitudes.

This request seems to be asking very little, just that a few words be changed, but is actually asking more than that. The change in language might also publicize a political position, or challenge friends and colleágues. In our language where a lower socioeconomic class is detectable by dialect variants such as the use of "gutter," "nylons," and "light bill," instead of "street" or "road," "stockings," and "electric bill," and a graduate education turns a "resume" into a "vita," a "convention" into "meetings," and "manuscripts" into "stuff" (as in "send me your stuff"), the change of few words is likely to announce a life style, broadcast a political position, or misdirect attention to the wrong issue.

If, after their relation to male status has been pointed out, "he" and "man" continue to be used in place of other neutral terms, it does not necessarily follow that the user lacks good will toward females. Small variations in language may have great social significance. It may not be a lack of good will, but a desire to concentrate on more significant issues or a shyness about taking political stands in casual conversations, that leaves the request unfulfilled.

IV

Perhaps you've recognized by now that the above riddles are intended to illustrate that assuming that a description (a surgeon, the friend of a man) applies to a male makes it difficult to recognize that the description could also apply to a female.

The second riddle is frequently presented as an illustration of our sexist presuppositions. We automatically assume that the surgeon has to be a man. But the first riddle has a similar effect without the presence of a professional description to receive the blame. I do not believe that the surgeon riddle does show sexism. What it shows is that once the assumption is made that a description is of a man, it is very, very hard to change that assumption. In the first riddle the assumption is probably made merely because an old friend of a man is somewhat more likely to be a man than a woman. (The assumption about gender need not have any empirical basis. There appears to be a tendency to assume that "my cousin," if spoken by a woman, refers to a female, and if spoken by a man, refers to a male.) Yet however weak the basis for the assumption, the perplexity caused by the riddles shows that it is still very hard to change one's assumptions about gender.

Note that these riddles do not show that the use of "he" or "man" in their alleged neutral sense makes it difficult to realize that a description in that context could be of a female. The only thing the riddles show is that if one assumes that a description applies to a male, it is hard to realize that the description could apply to a female. But genuine gender-neutral terms should not foster such an assumption. Therefore I still have to show that the alleged gender-neutral uses of these terms are, in fact, somewhat gender-specific.

V

It is not legitimate to assume that any use of "he" makes people think of a male instead of a female. Language has an influence on thought, but there are many other influences, too. Consider another example: "being doctored" has worse connotations than "being nursed." Things that have been doctored are in a worse condition than if left alone, whereas things that have been nursed are frequently in a better condition as a result. However, such linguistic usage does not prevent people from seeking doctors rather than nurses for serious illnesses. It seems very likely that these verb forms are derived from the functions of doctors and nurses. Yet there is no reason to suppose that use of these expressions causes discrimination against doctors in favor of nurses.

So even though the use of "he" as a gender-neutral pronoun is related to the position of males as compared with that of females in this culture,[1] and even though women are in a position inferior to men, it still has to be shown that gender-neutral uses of "he," "man," etc. affect people's thinking by preventing them from applying the context in question to women.[2]

The claim that there is no really neutral use might not need defense if there were no other terms that had both a neutral and non-neutral use. But such is not the case. Many adjectives that refer to one of a pair of opposite qualities can be used neutrally to indicate the dimension whose extremes are the opposites. One can ask "How tall is she?" of a short person, and "How wide is that?" of a narrow object. "Tall" and "wide" are used not only as opposites of "short" and "narrow," but as neutral terms to describe the quality or dimension of which the opposites are extremes. One *can* ask "How short is she?" or "How narrow is that?" but doing so expresses the expectation that the answer will lie on one end of the range of possible answers. In contrast, any tendency to suppose that anyone of whom it is asked how tall they are is in fact a tall person, is certainly very slight. Such uses of "short," "narrow," as well as "young," "impure," "bad," and "small" are called *marked* while similar uses of the opposite terms, "tall" and "long," "wide," "old," "pure," "good," and "big" are termed *unmarked*.[3]

In this respect, unmarked and marked adjectives behave very much like the he-she, man-woman, his-her pairs. The use of "he" or "man" may be either gendered or neutral. However, if one uses "she" or "woman," one conveys the expectation that a person who fits the description will be female, not male.[4] If one is going to argue that "he" and "man" cannot function as gender-neutral terms, it cannot be merely because such terms also have gender-specific meanings.

VI

It might be argued that, given that there are other neutral terms ("they," "one," "human," "person"), perpetuation of a neutral use of one of a pair of opposites gives that quality a priority or superiority over the opposite quality. There is some evidence that the unmarked term of a pair of opposites has higher positive associations. The use of a marked term often has a pejorative tone.[5] It is not an accident that "good" and "pure" are unmarked, "bad" and "impure" marked. If by perpetuating the neutral uses of "he" and "man" one encouraged the continuation of the unfair priority of males, then there would be a sense in which such uses were not really neutral.

Granted that people usually do have higher positive associations for the term with the neutral use than with its opposite.[6] And people have higher positive associations for "he" than "she." But it is far from clear that the positive association is a *result* of the neutral use; it may well be the other way around. The neutral uses of "tall," "wide," "high," "long," "big," etc. tell us that, in general, the larger size is better, or standard, or ideal. I suspect the reason for this is that children, during the time of first language learning, are expected to increase in size and are often praised for doing so and worried over when they do not. Thus at the outset they learn the term for the extreme that is their goal, and then come to use it to stand for the whole dimension.[7] (This would explain why "old" is unmarked even though youth is so much admired and valued. The post-adolescent youth that is valued is many years older than the language-learning child.) When one uses an adjective that can stand for one end of a dimension neutrally to name the dimension, one presents that end of the dimension as expected or standard. For example, "How cold is it?" vs. "How hot is it?"; "How hard is it?" vs. "How soft is it?". If one end of a dimension is a standard independently of a particular context, the term for that end would acquire a neutral use. If this explanation of the origin of unmarked adjectives is correct, the similarity to unmarked adjectives is no reason to suppose that the more positive evaluation of "he" is the *result* of its neutral use. It indicates, instead, that men's being more highly regarded than women promotes the neutral uses of male terms.

In any case, the higher positive associations of adjectives with neutral uses do not affect evaluations in particular cases. Although "wide" has a higher positive association for people than "narrow," wider objects are not necessarily valued more than narrower objects. For example, pocket calculators are touted for their narrow dimensions (although in advertisements one is more likely to hear the term "slim" than "narrow"). And so there is no reason to suppose that using "he" and "man" as unmarked neutral terms affects evaluations of females in particular cases. If one is going to argue that such uses are not really neutral, one has to show something more about these terms — something other than that they have the properties of other unmarked terms.

VII

There are important differences between unmarked adjectives and words like "he" and "man." The neutral use of adjectives is quite unambiguous, restricted to contexts in which a quantity or amount of that dimension is the topic (i.e., three inches *high*, 99 & 44/100% *pure*). The neutral uses of "he" and "man" have no restricted contexts to clarify them. Moreover, uses of these terms are frequently in need of clarification. We might be inclined to say that "man" in "The Neanderthal man was a hunter" was being used neutrally to mean "human." But this sentence could be used to describe just males. One might say, "The Neanderthal man was a hunter. The Neanderthal woman raised crops." In this context "man" is clearly intended to mean "male human." In an example from an introductory philosophy text, an apparently neutral use of "he" turns out to be intentionally gender-specific. This ambiguity is resolved only by the last word:

Consider, firstly, two comparatively simple situations in which a cyberneticist might find himself. He has a servomechanism, or a computing machine, with no randomising element, and he also has a wife.[8]

Although "he" and "man" behave like unmarked adjectives in some respects, their double roles as both gender-specific and gender-neutral terms permit ambiguity in ways that the double roles of unmarked adjectives do not.

The ambiguity in the beginning of these examples allows an intended gender-specific "he" or "man" to be interpreted as a neutral term so that a context may be inadvertently applied to women. And ambiguity may also allow an intended neutral "he" to be interpreted as a gender-specific term so that the context is accidentally not applied to women. But if this is so, the culprit is ambiguity, which could be resolved without forsaking the neutral uses of male terms. Add that you are an equal-opportunity employer and there should be no gender-specific interpretation of "man" in "the best man for the job." One need not eliminate the neutral use of "he" and "man" in order to eliminate ambiguity. There will be other ways of resolving the ambiguity besides using other neutral terms that are not ambiguous.

VIII

Here's the problem: However the use of a term gets started, it would seem that if it was intended a certain way when used, and understood that way by others, then, on any available theory of meaning, that's what it means. If "man" or "he" are intended neutrally, as they often are, and if people know that, as they do, then it would seem that "man" and "he" do refer to the members of the human species, and that they are as neutral as "human" and "they."

In order to show that "man" and "he" and like terms are not really neutral, I propose to show that it is not enough that one *intend* a term to have a particular meaning for it to have that meaning; that intended neutral uses of "he," "man," etc. can fail to be neutral; and that such failures have implications for all other allegedly neutral uses.

Let's compare "he" and "man" with other terms whose gender neutrality is not in dispute, such as "one," "they," "human," and "person." One striking difference is the inability to use "he" and "man" to refer to a female human. It would be a rare person who could say without irony "She's the best *man* for the job" or say of a female, "He's the best." Yet the undisputed gender-neutral terms can indeed be used this way: "She's the best person;" "That one is the best" (of a female). If "he" and "man" are genuinely gender-neutral, then they ought to be applicable to any person regardless of gender.

One might argue that one does not say "he's the best" of a female for the same reason one does not merely say "I believe" when one knows. On Grice's account of the latter, it is not that believing *implies* not knowing, but that one does not usually convey less information than one can.[9] Therefore if one says one believes, people may assume one does not actually know. Similarly, one might argue, if it is clear in some context that the gender of a referent is known to the speaker, then the speaker is expected to specify that gender. It is not that uses of "he" and "man" *imply* that the referent is male, but simply that one does not convey less information than one can. If one uses "he" or "man," people may assume that either a male is being referred to or that the gender is not known.

This explanation, however, does not account for all the facts. It offers no explanation for why "She's the best man" is not permissible since gender *has* been specified. Moreover, it would predict that undisputed neutral terms could not be used if the gender were known. If the problem were only that speakers are expected to specify gender when known, the sentence "That's the best person" would be as inappropriate to say of either a male or a female as "That's the best man" is to say of a female.

On some theories of meaning, the meaning of a term is a function of its use. I have already pointed out that "he" and "man" do not have the same uses as undisputed gender-neutral terms. Recent theories of meaning have analyzed meaning as a function of the intentions of the speaker. Yet failures of gender-neutrality of "he" and "man" occur even though the speaker may intend a gender-neutral use. For example, Bertrand Russell in his classic paper "On Denoting" says:

> Suppose now we wish to interpret the proposition, "I met a man."
> If this is true, I met some definite man; but that is not what I
> affirm. What I affirm is, according to the theory I advocate: — "I
> met x and x is human' is not always false."[10]

If Russell were correct, then parents familiar with his theory would have no cause for anxiety if their young female child, on arriving home several hours late from kindergarten, said, "I met a man." Russell did not notice that "man" is not used neutrally in his context. This example shows that one cannot account entirely for the meaning of a term by the intentions of the speaker on a particular occasion. The meaning of a term involves, among other things, its expected interpretation, the way it functions with other terms, and its use in linguistic enterprises such as reasoning. This is important for the next point.

"He" and "man" cannot be used in some contexts where undisputedly gender-neutral terms can. But what about other contexts? Suppose it can be shown that a familiar and paradigmatic example of a gender-neutral use of "man" or "men" is not really neutral at all? Then I think it can be argued that there is no real gender-neutral meaning of these terms. Consider the first line of the familiar syllogism:

All men are mortal.

Most people would agree that the occurrence of "men" is intended to be neutral; this is a statement about the whole human species. But if it is a neutral use, then this syllogism, that paradigm of valid syllogisms, is invalid, for the second line usually reads,

Socrates is a man.

The occurrence of "man" in this sentence is *not* a neutral use. If it were a neutral use, then replacing "Socrates" with the name of a female human being or a child would not affect the syllogism. Yet the usual interpretation of

Sophia is a man

makes it false, or insulting. It is not taken to mean that Sophia is a member of the human species.

Let me add two explanations here. (1) The meaning of a term is not determined by the interpretation of one person alone. How others will understand it must be considered as well. Although some people might argue that in this context the syllogism "Sophia is a man" can be read as "Sophia is a human being," they will recognize that many other people will not take it this way (this is due in part to our inability to use "man" to refer to a female in other contexts). Although *some* people might be able to *read* "man" neutrally in this context, it does not follow that this is what it means. Further examples where "man" and "his" fail to be gender-neutral will be given to convince those who can make a gender-neutral reading in one case.

(2) It might be argued that I have changed the meaning of "man" in the syllogism by substituting "Sophia" for "Socrates." The original syllogism might have had a neutral occurrence of "man" which changed with the substitution. For example, if I substituted "The Outer Banks" for "savings and loan institutions" in "_____are banks," I would change the meaning of "banks." However, if "man" *has* a gender-neutral use, it should retain that use regardless of the gender of the referent. There is no reason to claim that it has a gender-neutral meaning unless it has a use that can be applicable to females as well as males. Gender-neutral terms such as "human" and "person" are not affected by the substitution of a female name in their context.

Thus the inference from "All men are mortal" and "Socrates is a man" to "Socrates is mortal" is invalid if the occurrence of "men" is intended to be gender-neutral in the first premise. Instead of a paradigm of valid inference we would have an equivocation, because the meaning of the terms has changed. It would be just like the argument:

All banks are closed on Sunday.
The Outer Banks are banks.
Therefore, the Outer Banks are closed on Sunday.

That the occurrence of "men" in the first premise is believed to be gender-neutral, and that the syllogism is believed to be neither enthymematic nor invalid, is evidence either that we are confused about neutral uses or that we are confused about validity even in the simplest cases. There is further evidence that it is the former. Consider another example:

Man is a mammal.

This use of "man" is neutral if any use is. But if this is conjoined with the dictionary definition of "mammalia":

the highest class of Vertebrata comprising man and all other animals that nourish their young with milk, that have the skin usu. more or less covered with hair, that have mammary glands . . . [11]

it should be legitimate to conclude:

Man has mammary glands.

But this conclusion is less acceptable than:

Humans have mammary glands.

because "man" does not function in the same gender-neutral way as "human" in this context. A statement that members of the human species have mammary glands is not peculiar, but a statement that males have mammary glands is. Although both men and women have mammary glands, only the mature glands of women are ordinarily likely to be topics of conversation. If "man" could be used gender-neutrally, its occurrence in a context that applied to both male and female humans, particularly to female humans, would be given a gender-neutral interpretation. Instead, its occurrence in such a context is plainly gender-specific.

Alleged neutral uses of "he" are not as frequently found in syllogisms. But *if* it sounds strange to ask an applicant about the interests of his husband or wife, to instruct a child on the cleaning of his vagina or penis, or to compliment a guest on his gown or tuxedo, then something is less than neutral about "he" and "his" as well. Note that there is no ambiguity about these uses. The contexts make it clear that "man" and "his" are supposed to be understood to be gender-neutral, if possible. Other obvious failures of gender neutrality are:

Man has two sexes.

Some men are female.

There are many more contexts in which attempts to use terms such as "he" and "man" gender-neutrally produce false, funny, or insulting statements, even though the gender-neutrality was clearly intended.

The failure of "he," "man," etc. to be gender-neutral can be demonstrated in examples where a reference to a particular person, or a grammatical context in which these terms cannot be used neutrally occurs. But what about other cases? Surely I cannot *prove* that there is never a case in which "man" means human, you will say.

Similarly I could not prove that there was never a case in which "wash-bucket" meant "justice" or "Watch out!" (Imagine a feud in a laundry room.) But that's not the sense of meaning that's at issue here. As I've said earlier, the meaning of a term involves its expected interpretation, the way it functions with other terms and its use in reasoning and other discourse. And what we've seen with "he" and "man," etc. is that some uses which may appear gender-neutral at first turn out to be gender-specific because of what is said in some other place.

To give an idea of the variety of ways that gender-neutrality can fail, or can be shown to have failed, let me offer another example first pointed out by Ruth Lucier:

> All men and all women are philosophers; or, let us say, if they
> are not conscious of having philosophical problems, they have, at
> any rate, philosophical prejudices. Most of these are theories which
> they unconsciously take for granted, or which they have absorbed
> from their intellectual environment or from tradition.
>
> Since few of these theories are consciously held, they are
> prejudices in the sense that they are held without critical examina-
> tion, even though they may be of great importance for the practical
> actions of people, and for their whole life.
>
> It is an apology for the existence of professional philosophy that
> men are needed who examine critically these widespread and
> influential theories.[12]

In these three paragraphs by Karl Popper, he begins by speaking of men and women, using the pronoun "they" and then in
the third paragraph switches to "men." Were it not for his talk
of men *and women*, we might be tempted to interpret his use of
"men" as intended gender-neutrally. But because there is a shift
from men and women to men, whether deliberate or not, I
believe that the reference to men is unquestionably gender-
specific.

The difficulty is that there is no way of guaranteeing a gender-
neutral use, because one cannot predict how that use will be connected with other discourse and behavior. One can imagine that
an entire book might be written with attempted neutral uses of
"he"and "man," while the title alone or some advertising copy
shows that these uses are gender specific (for example, the
SPLEEN OF THE DIABETIC MALE, or *MEN OF THE
FUTURE* — "essential reading for their wives and girlfriends"
— I. M. Mailer).

One might want to claim that the gender-specific contexts do
not make the other neutral uses gender-specific. Instead there
has been a change in meaning — as if one had switched from a
discussion of different color greens to salad greens, from sand
banks to commercial banks.

However, a shift in meaning, like a pun, is usually noticeable
and often a bit funny. This is not the case for the alleged shift
with "he," "man," etc. If there is a shift it takes place
smoothly, and usually goes unnoticed, particularly by the people
who are most likely to claim that there has been one. The
noticeable and funny examples occur only when a gender-
neutral use is attempted (as in "Man has two sexes") and not
when a gender-specific reference is made. Because the gender-
specific references are *not* noticeable shifts in meaning, I think it

is justified to conclude that they were not genuinely neutral uses in the first place.

One might argue that all uses of "he," "man," and like terms are simply gender-specific. But I think a weaker conclusion is easier to support: that attempts at gender-neutrality with these terms fail, not because they are simply gender-specific but because something else is going on. This conclusion is supported by empirical studies that show the use of "he" rather than "they" or "he or she," makes it more likely, but not inevitable, that people will think of males. I try to explain what else is going on in the next section.

IX

How can the failure of gender-neutrality be accounted for when people think they are using "he," "man," etc. in a gender-neutral sense? Rather than attribute the failure to peculiar properties of each context in an ad hoc fashion, I believe it is the result of a broader linguistic phenomenon: Parasitic Reference. Tissues are called Kleenex; petroleum jelly, Vaseline; bleach, Clorox; etc. to the economic benefit of the specific brands referred to and to the economic detriment of those brands that are ignored by this terminology. The alleged gender-neutral uses of "he," "man," etc. are just further examples of this common phenomenon. A gender-specific term, one that refers to a high-status subset of the whole class, is used *in place of* a neutral generic term. Many of us who deplore the efforts of drug companies to get us to use the brand name rather than the generic name of a product have failed to recognize that the use of "he," "man," etc. in place of "they," "one," "person," or "human" is a similar phenomenon with similar effects. Manufacturers realize that someone sent to buy "the cheapest Clorox" is less likely to return with the equal-strength half price store brand than someone sent to buy the cheapest bleach. And this is true even when the term "Clorox" is intended and understood to be synonymous with "bleach." The failure of "Clorox" to be brand-neutral and the failure of "he" and "man" to be gender-neutral appear to be instances of the same pehnomenon.[13]

Regardless of the intentions of the speakers and hearers, and regardless of their beliefs about the meanings of the terms, if the terms refer parasitically, subjectivity can fail, inferences may not go through, and equivocations will be produced. This is true not merely for brand names but for other terms, such as "he" and "man," whose neutral performances have been advertised by lexicographers but which break down easily even under normal speaking conditions. The existence of Parasitic Reference requires that theories of reference and meaning recognize that the functioning of terms in one context may be affected by their uses in other contexts that are not explicitly present.

NOTES

1. Many people believe this claim, but Robin Lakoff in "Language and Woman's Place," *Language in Society 2 (1973): 45-80,* supports it with an impressive number of gender asymmetries in language whose best explanation appears to be the superior position of one gender in the culture. See also Mary Ritchie Key, *Male/Female Language* (Metuchen, N.J.: Scarecrow Press, 1975); and Casey Miller and Kate Swift, *Words and Women* (Garden City, N.Y.: Anchor Press/Doubleday, 1976).

2. Even if the gender-neutral uses of "he," etc. prevent people from considering women in those contexts, there are some contexts where one does not want to be considered (for example, as a murder suspect). So one has also to show that the disadvantages of not being considered for jobs, awards, and consultation outweigh the advantages of not being considered for criminal activities, punishment, and obligations. Women who oppose the Equal Rights Amendment seem to disagree with other women, not on the actual unequal status of women, but rather on whether the advantages of this status outweigh the disadvantages.

3. Although this terminology was originally applied to phonological distinctions (e.g., the third-person singular of regular verbs is marked with an "s"), it has been extended to the use I cite. See John Lyons, *Introduction to Theoretical Linguistics* (Cambridge: Cambridge University Press, 1971), p. 79.

4. Porter G. Perrin and Karl W. Dykema, in *Writer's Guide and Index to English*, 3rd edition (Glenview, Ill.: Scott, Foresman, 1959), pp. 538-539, 551-552, say: "As we must often refer to nouns that name either or both male and female, the language has developed . . . ways of making up for the lack of an accurate pronoun: The usual way is to use *he* or *his* alone even when some of the persons are female . . . Sometimes when the typical invididuals or the majority of the group referred to would be women, *her* is used in the same way."

5. According to Lyons, *Theoretical Linguistics*, p. 467.

6. Evidence for this is to be found in C. E. Osgood, Suci, and Tannenbaum, *The Measurement of Meaning* (Urbana: University of Illinois Press, 1957), especially pp. 36-62. Unmarked terms tend to be scored more positively by subjects on the semantic differential evaluative scale. But this is not always the case. It is worth remarking that "feminine" receives a higher positive evaluation than "masculine."
7. Eve V. Clark in "What's in a Word? On the Child's Acquisition of Semantics in his First Language," in *Cognitive Development and the Acquisition of Language*, T. E. Moore, ed. (New York: Academic Press, 1973), pp. 65-110, points out that children learn to use the unmarked term of a pair before they learn the marked term.
8. L. Jonathan Cohen, "Can There Be Artificial Minds?" in *Reason and Responsibility*, 2nd ed., Joel Feinberg, ed. (Encino, Calif.: Dickenson Publishing Co., 1971), p. 288.
9. H. Paul Grice, "Logic and Conversation," in *Syntax and Semantics,* vol. 3, Peter Cole and Jerry L. Morgan, eds. (New York: Academic Press, 1975).
10. Bertrand Russell, "On Denoting," *Mind* 13 (1905): 479.
11. *Webster's Third New International Dictionary.*
12. Karl R. Popper, "How I See Philosophy," in *The Owl of Minerva*, Charles J. Bontempo and S. Jack Odell, eds. (New York: McGraw Hill, 1975), p. 48.
13. Elizabeth Lane Beardsley, in "Referential Genderization," *Philosophical Forum* 5 (1973-74): 285-293, calls this phenomenon "linguistic imperialism."

Carolyn Korsmeyer

The Hidden Joke: Generic Uses of Masculine Terminology

Vir. is male and *Femina* is female: but *Homo* is male and female. This is the equality claimed and the fact that is persistently evaded and denied. No matter what arguments are used, the discussion is vitiated from the start, because Man is always dealt with as both *Homo* and *Vir*, but Woman only as *Femina*.[1]

The terms *masculine* and *feminine* are used symmetrically only as a matter of form, as on legal papers. In actuality the relation of the two sexes is not quite like that of two electrical poles, for man represents both the positive and the neutral, as is indicated by the common use of *man* to designate human beings in general; whereas woman represents only the negative, defined by limiting criteria, without reciprocity. . . . It amounts to this: just as for the ancients there was an absolute vertical with reference to which the oblique was defined, so there is an absolute human type, the masculine.[2]

I

From the time that the women's rights movement began to emerge in the late eighteenth century to the present "second

This paper is reprinted from *Feminism and Philosophy*, Mary Vetterling-Braggin, Frederick Elliston and Jane English, eds. (Totowa, N.J.: Littlefield, Adams and Co., 1977) by permission of the publisher and author.

wave" of feminism in the 1960s and 70s, women dissatisfied with conventional roles have confronted the argument that certain aspects of female nature determine to at least a degree their position in society.[3] According to hoary custom, a woman's biologically proper place is with children and in homes, and so the assumption of other kinds of jobs and activities can actually be viewed as "unnatural." In the United States this stereotype is fading now; women are gradually entering lines of work that used to be occupied solely by males, and the traditional view of women is espoused only by the most conservative. Despite significant changes over the past years, however, we are far from a state of sexual equality, and ideas of the limits of woman's "proper place" still persist.

One indicator of lingering sterotypes is language. The common usage of idioms and colloquial expressions concerning women reflects both past and present social conditions of their referents. The sex discrimination that is endemic to certain grammatical conventions is a subject fairly familiar to twentieth-century feminists, who often point out, for example, the confusion and distortion that result from the fact that "man" is used both generically to denote all human beings and specifically to differentiate half of those human beings from the other half. So pervasive is this convention that from many descriptions of human life one might conclude that we are a single-sexed race. Not only can "man" be used to mean "men and women," but "he" can mean "he and/or she." Grammar requires that the pronoun accompanying the neutral "one" be "he," and that where women are not explicitly specified, "he" is also the proper pronoun. Until recently, business letters to unknown heads of companies and offices usually used the greeting "Dear Sirs" or "Gentlemen." Again until recently, any woman objecting that she was left out or unaccounted for by such expressions was greeted with the reply that "of course," "he" in such contexts meant her too. For several years now, feminists have fought and gained against the consistent generic use of masculine terms to designate persons of both sexes.[4]

In a study assessing the extent of the generic use of masculine terms in colloquial speech, Elizabeth Lane Beardsley calls the colloquial or grammatical necessity of sexing a referring term "referential genderization."[5] Although English does contain sex-neutral terms like "person," grammar and colloquial usage make consistent use of neutral terms awkward if not impossible, and when a generic term is needed, it is the masculine that is proper. Beardsley argues that such linguistic conventions have significant influence on concept formation—both general concepts about what it means to be a person, and the self-concepts of individuals.[6] Because of this influence, she argues, we should strive to develop and use sex-neutral terms to take the place of expressions that are now current.

Beardsley concludes her essay with a comment from which I would like to begin my own analysis. She is responding to the possible objection that referential genderization is *not* sexist nor detrimental because it is *parallel* — for every "he" there is a balancing "she"; for every masculine a reciprocal feminine:

> This latter suggestion about RG [referential genderization] shows an egregious failure to recognize the overpowering inclination of human beings to make a differential appraisal wherever they have made a distinction. RG, though it admittedly does not directly prescribe the subordination of one sex to the other or specify which sex should occupy the subordinate position, makes it more likely that some subordination and discriminatory treatment will take place. And, by incorporating sex-distinctions in language, RG helps to provide a conceptual framework useful for rationalizing sex-based discriminatory treatment if (and for whatever complex nonlinguistic reasons) this treatment should develop.[7]

In this paper I would like to consider several aspects of sexist conventions in language as they relate to the "differential appraisal" that occurs with sex-distinguishing terms. I am hesitant to rely on the speculation that there is a "human inclination" to make such appraisals; nor indeed is such a hypothesis necessary, for the roots of this phenomenon can be seen by further extending the analysis of sex-distinguishing expressions. If we search for parallelism or symmetry between masculine and feminine expressions in a variety of contexts, we find that in a significant number of instances, the feminine counterpart of a masculine expression carries a different connotation. Under certain conditions, female-designating terms connote something humorous or cute, trivial or ridiculous, where male-designating terms do not; and I shall appeal to a theory of comedy to help illuminate the significance of these situations. My interest is not only to point out that language reveals sexist practices— customary discriminatory treatment of women. It is also to explore the extent to which linguistic conventions — particularly the generic use of masculine terminology — can be a perpetuator of sexist distinctions, regardless of the intent of the speaker.

II

A woman preaching is like a dog's walking on his hind legs. It is not done well; but you are surprised to find it done at all.[8]

The woman's movement has the distinction of being the only social movement in the history of the United States that is regarded by its opponents as a joke.[9]

Political activity on the part of women and on behalf of women seems to have received a notably regular reaction of smiles and ridicule. Perhaps the most succinct linguistic indication of the lack of seriousness accorded feminism today is summed up in that infamous diminutive, "women's lib."("Suffragette," for a time served the same function during the woman suffrage movement, though it later came to be accepted by feminists themselves.)

Of course, humor is by no means reserved for politically charged situations. It is such a ubiquitous feature of much of women's relations with society that it is preserved in ever-repeated stock expressions: "Don't bother your pretty head about it" (indulgent smile); "The ladies, God bless them!" (hearty laugh); "Thank heavens for little girls, for without them what would little boys do?" (smile and wink). But what is playful and affectionate in one context takes on a tougher character in another, and laughter is a formidable weapon. It may not be quite fair to quote such a notorious misogynist on this score, but Nietzsche's reaction to successful women is illustrative of laughter in its more acid form:

It betrays a corruption of the instincts — quite apart from the fact that it betrays bad taste — when a woman adduces Madame Roland or Madame de Stael or Monsieur George Sand, of all people, as if they proved anything in *favor* of "woman as such." Among men these three are the three *comical* women as such — nothing more! — and precisely the best involuntary *counterarguments* against emancipation and feminine vainglory.[10]

Extremes of sentiment such as those expressed by Dr. Johnson and Nietzsche are comparatively rare, but we should not quickly conclude that the phenomenon displayed is rare. If we look for more than outright derision, if we examine situations where no misogynistic intent exists, if we extend our investigation of the "comical" to include any circumstances which induce a less serious atmosphere than might be expected to accompany a man in the same circumstances—then we have ample evidence of situations which become shaded with comedy when a woman is introduced into the picture. Furthermore, consider the ease with which the eipthet "male chauvinist" has made its way into public banter. The term was coined to apply to someone who exhibited condemnable prejudice and social practice, but now it is not uncommon to hear men being called "male chauvinist pigs" as a joke. (Compare the sobering effect of "racist.")

The various ridiculing or bantering reactions to women are more than an annoyance. They serve to show us how indeed there is little parallelism, little symmetry, between the concepts of male and female. If the pronouns "he" and "she" (and related sex-distinguishing terms and the contexts in which they occur) were really parallel, serving only to designate persons of different sex and not to carry significantly different connotations, then one should be able to say the same kinds of things about a "he" as about a "she." We would expect statements not directly related to sex and biology to have parallel colloquial usage, such that the sorts of things regularly said about males and about females would be interchangeable, and such that no shift in connotation would be evident.

This sort of test obviously relies on common, expected usage and not on actual grammatical rules, on what "sounds right" and what "sounds funny," and on an intuitive assessment of the connotations of various terms and idioms. Consequently, conclusions drawn on this subject are likely to be open to some degree of argument, and, for that matter, to a certain amount of historical relativism. Language analysis of this sort is rather like scanning an aerial photograph for evidence of ruined cities beneath, and occasionally one may mistake a ditch for a canal. Despite these conditions, however, it is not hard to demonstrate that in a significant number of contexts there is little or no parallel connotation between male-denoting and female-denoting terminology.

Some of the most obvious instances which illustrate this point are a result of the contemporary social position of women—or, more accurately, the contemporary popular stereotype of that position. Since women in that major occupation called "housewife" devote a great deal of their energies to a home and a family, we are accustomed to descriptions of the following sort:

> Mrs. George Hollander has recently been elected president of the tri-city chapter of the PTA. The wife of one of the community's

most respected bankers, Mrs. Hollander's wide smile and fashionable figure are familiar to many residents of Belledowns who are regular attendants at the bi-annual Community Council picnics. She will devote her first energies this fall to investigating the recent violence at the city's two junior high schools.

These sorts of things, of course, *could* be said about Mr. Hollander, for he is also married, has distinctive physical characteristics, and wears clothes. But it is unlikely that these features would be singled out for special mention; certainly they would not be stressed. Dorothy Sayers wittily inverts the situation and demonstrates how odd it sounds when descriptions of men are cast in the same mold as descriptions which are common of women. For example:

> Professor Bract, although a distinguished botanist, is not in any way an unmanly man. He has, in fact, a wife and seven children. Tall and burly, the hands with which he handles his delicate specimens are as gnarled and powerful as those of a Canadian lumberjack, and when I swilled beer with him in his laboratory, he bawled his conclusions at me in a strong, gruff voice that implemented the promise of his swaggering moustache.[11]

The parody is evident, but the point is well made: We regularly think of women in contexts which stress directly or indirectly their sexual nature, and this custom underscores the fact that a large part of their social relations involve what are ultimately sexual functions. Their family connections and marital status, their appearance and dress, the "femininity of their manner" are all accepted aspects of descriptions of women in newspapers and magazines. These aspects are clearly not evenly paralleled in contexts involving men, for if they were, we would hardly laugh at the tables Sayers has turned.

We do not laugh at similar descriptions of women, for we have grown accustomed to them. But is it the case that they connote nothing humorous at all, or nothing akin to humor? I would argue that in fact this common way of speaking about women contains the germs of humor, and that it helps explain the full significance of referential genderization and like sex-based modes of expression. It also helps explain, I think, why ridicule and humor remain a prime weapon in the battle against women's equality.

Let us expand our check for parallel connotations between masculine and feminine terms by gathering a sample of some of the ways men and women engaged in the same or similar activities:

Male Term	Female Term in Common Usage	Neutral Term
I. singer	singer	singer
teacher	teacher	teacher
II. actor	actress	
launderer	laundress	
III. chairman	chairwoman, Madame chairman	chairperson
Congressman	Congresswoman	Representative
policeman	policewoman	officer
IV. fisherman		
V. driver	woman driver	driver
wrestler	lady/woman wrestler	wrestler
professor	female/woman professor	professor
doctor	lady/woman doctor	doctor
cop	lady cop	cop
VI. bachelor	spinster, bachelorette	
traffic cop	meter maid	
riveter	Rosie the riveter	riveter
airplane race	powder puff derby	airplane race
VII. male prostitute	prostitute	prostitute
male nurse	nurse	nurse
male secretary	secretary	secretary
househusband	housewife	
VIII. welfare recipient	welfare mother	welfare recipient
worker	working mother	worker
janitor	maid, cleaning lady	

Clearly there are a number of different ways that we speak of persons engaged in various activities. Some do and some do not specify the sex of the person, and of those that do, some do and some do not specify it in a way that seems particularly important. Though there may well be more, I have isolated eight groups of expressions. The first three either do not specify the sex of the referent or do so without any significant difference in connotation between terms used for males and those used for females. (Not surprisingly, those terms which either make no distinction or indicate it in the suffix all pertain to occupations in which women are customary participants.) Terms in group III must add an adjunct like "-woman" or "-person" in order to accommodate female participants, and although some tongue-tied awkwardness may be encountered with the first use of a newly minted term, still no (lasting) difference in connotation exists. Group IV can contain no such differences because terms like this have only one form, but it seems peripheral to this study and is of interest only in passing.

It is the last four groups that are of special interest. Group V, it seems to me, contains terms which really need no specification of sex either according to grammar or by reason of idiomatic ease, though they frequently do receive such specification. Although the neutral term is also the one used for males, females are denoted equally well by the same term without any discomfort or confusion of expression. The fact that frequently their sex is also mentioned no doubt has to do with the fact that women are a minority in those occupations, but the important feature of the combination expression is the subtle shift in connotation that can occur with the addition of the feminizing adjunct "-woman" or "-lady." This shift is not always immediately noticeable, but it is clearly present in cases like "woman driver" or "lady cop," and "lady (or female) wrestler." An expression so formed connotes something slightly comical, lighthearted, or cute, in a way that those in the male column do not. (In almost every case, adding the adjunct "-lady" to a term, as opposed to "-woman," is a sign of an added humorous dimension. The same holds true with the suffix "-ette" as opposed to "-ess," I would imagine because the former is used to form a diminutive as well as a feminized term.) Because almost any noun denoting an occupation can take a qualifying adjunct, group V no doubt could contain the largest collection of terms on this list.

With the terms in group VI the shift in connotation is quite obvious. They are similar to those in group V, although the female-designation is established more descriptively. Once again, in a number of those cases where the masculine and the neutral terms are identical (as with "riveter"), the same term could be used to denote a woman in the same occupation. The feminized expressions in common use are humorous-sounding, cartoonish, or cute. Probably the most dramatic difference in connotation — though it is by no means a uniformly humorous one — exists between "bachelor" and "spinster." Although "bachelor" can be used in contexts where its connotation is grim or lonely or sad, it can also be used to connote someone free, debonair, independent, and enviable. "Spinster" has invariably the former connotation, hence the coining of the coy "bachelorette" (not "bacheloress," note) to connote the independent, sexually desirable female.

With the exception of sex-neutral terms, in groups I-VI, the standard term designating a person in a particular occupation, has been male. "Chairwoman" (or "Madame Chairman," which is actually a contradiction) and "actress" are variations on standard forms. With the terms in group VII, however, the female-designating term (at least in the U.S. in this generation) is the standard one, with the male-specifying term being the departure from the norm. If a shift in connotation occurs only because a term is used in a way that deviates from the standard expression or context, then we would expect a similar shift in connotation to be noticeable with the male-designating terms in this group. But with the exception of "househusband," which is used invariably in a jocular way, none of the male variations on the standard themes connote anything odd or cute. (In fact, some may even carry more dignity than the standard female forms.) Therefore, it seems that more than just unusual usage is responsible for the comical connotations evident in groups V and VI.

Group VIII contains terms which are not humorous in either form, but which are similar to the others in that the term used for the female specifies sex in a way which that for the male does not. I shall return to these terms later.

In summary, although there is a trend towards using neutral terms more and more ("chairperson" and "firefighter," for example), such changes are far from universal. It is still true that colloquial practices very often trivialize the terms used to refer to women by connoting something slightly cute or funny, underscoring the fact that "he" and "she" in various contexts are in fact not parallel.

III

It is clear that the humor that frequently awaits women, particularly those engaged in non-traditional occupations, is of some significance to the full achievement of sexual equality. What more can we make of it? Why is comedy a ready attendant to expressions involving women? Do these expressions have anything in common with other circumstances which cause laughter? What *are* the circumstances which cause laughter? This last question of course opens up an avenue of inquiry that reaches far beyond the scope of this paper, but we can at least begin here to make some fair guesses about the comical nature of certain female-designating expressions.

Perhaps the immediate explanation that comes to mind is that it is our experience that is at fault. Our limited associations regarding the tasks women usually perform are rather narrow, and so we are surprised into a smile when we think of a woman in the ranks of wrestlers or hockey players. Expressions indicating out-of-the-ordinary circumstances subtly startle one. Therefore, it would stand to reason that as women in fact broaden their scope of activity, language will catch up with social and political change and feminized expressions will no longer be humorous.

This probably is the case with some of the expressions discussed above. It seems likely to be true of those in group III in particular, and it is probably responsible for the fact that any peculiarity of connotation that may arise with the initial use of "chairperson" or "Congresswoman" is short-lived. However, militating against this as a total explanation is the fact that the terms in group VII (in which the male form is a deviation from the standard female form for an occupation customarily associated with women) suffer no connotation shift.

Is there, then, more to the story? Is language only a passive partner in the asymmetry between expressions concerning men and women? I suggest that not only do we customarily associate women with particular activities, thereby mentally restricting their scope, but the notion of what it is to be a woman is limited as well. As this limitation is reflected in language, "woman" and "she" have a more limited connotation than "man" and "he."

Proceding on this hypothesis, can we continue speculation about the comic and the source of laughter that is directed at women? At this point it is helpful to enlist the aid of a classic theory of laughter, that of Henri Bergson. Some elements of his extensive theory suggest a way of understanding these modes of speaking about women, and in the process, of understanding the full significance of referential genderization and the generic use of the masculine. Admittedly, Bergson is concerned primarily with comedy as a literary and theatrical genre, and it is arguable that he has exhausted all the sources and types of the comic or has noted all the causes of laughter.[12] However, it is by no means necessary to accept all of a theory in order to profit by it, and quite apart from his larger philosophy, some of his observations have an intuitive correctness and are particularly congenial to our analysis.

Bergson's remarks about the context in which laughter occurs are relevant to an understanding of the political effect of ridicule as a weapon. Laughter, he claims, occurs in situations where the spectators are relatively uninvolved, at least temporarily, with the subject of their mirth. In his words, the comic demands "something like a momentary anaesthesia of the heart."[13] Whether or not all instances of laughter follow this design, certainly this is a component of the ridicule which serves a political purpose in the chivalrous resistance to "women's lib." It keeps sympathy at a distance and allows one to dismiss the subject of laughter as not deserving serious consideration.

The conditions that foster laughter in response to women are illuminated by two related Bergsonian concepts: rigidity and inversion. Bergson is particularly famous for his vitalism, his anti-materialistic theory of human nature. His notion that the laughable is the appearance of the purely physical or mechanical, the not-quite-human, is intimately connected to this idea. Whereas the fully human is flexible and elastic and vital, that which is laughable exhibits a mechanical inflexibility, a *rigidity*. The simplest example of this is the banana peel beloved of slapstick comedy: the human body does not accommodate itself to the unexpected, and, like a machine running amuck, it involuntarily flounders, causing laughter. Such situations direct attention to clumsy physicality, allowing spectators to regard the unfortunate subject as a thing, an object.[14] Our emotions are temporarily suspended, and we are preoccupied with the ridiculous physical situation. "Any incident is comic that calls our attention to the physical in a person, when it is the moral side that is concerned."[15]

Slapstick exploits a physical kind of rigidity; there are also forms of character rigidity in comic situations, one of which Bergson terms "inversion." Here laughter arises in reaction to the kind of circumstance which we might call by the more contemporary term "role-reversal." Whenever a character is cast in a role with built-in limitations, a violation of those limits and adoption of an opposite role creates a situation in which we laugh.

> Picture to yourself certain characters in a certain situation: if you reverse the situation and invert the *roles*, you obtain a comic scene . . . Thus, we laugh at the prisoner at the bar lecturing the magistrate; at a child presuming to teach its parents; in a word, at everything that comes under the heading of 'topsyturvydom.'[16]

The idea that laughter can be stimulated when an inherent rigidity is exposed in its object, that the assumption of a non-traditional role can be perceived as comically 'inverted,' suggests a way of understanding the humorous connotations surrounding women. It is clear that our concept of woman carries with it implicit limitations, such that it does not wholly belong in contexts which are not regarded as "feminine." Consequently, when a woman acts contrary to "rigid" sterotype, the results can be seen as laughable, especially by an audience so predisposed. Moreover, linguistic convention itself, not merely customary associations, helps perpetuate this state of affairs. What better way to ensure such limitation than to reserve female-designating terms, as a grammatical convention, only for people whose sex is specifically noted? ("Where sex is not specified, use 'he.' ") The extension of the masculine in its generic use to cover general situations involving all of humanity, and the reservation of feminine terms only for situations where sex is specified, would seem to guarantee the perpetuation of non-parallel connotations for "he" and "she," "man" and "woman," and related expressions. The use of "she" always remains the tacit exception to the rule — the specifically mentioned, deviating case.

It stands to reason that this convention also guarantees that when feminized terms are used, a disproportionate attention will be directed to the sexual character of the referent. A term which also has generic usage connotes "person"; one which is used to specify persons according to sex connotes "person who is remarkable for a physical feature." "He" is bound to be more flexible, more natural in a multitude of contexts, than "she."[17] This is surely at least a partial explanation for the shift in connotation, slight though it may be, that occurs when one qualifies a person engaged in a particular occupation with the adjunct "woman" or "lady" (group V). Nothing the person does changes, nor is there an accompanying mocking description (as there may be in group VI). But specifying the subject in this way calls attention to her physical character, diverting attention from the occupation or activity itself. As Simone de Beauvoir says, "The term 'female' is derogatory not because it emphasizes woman's animality but because it imprisons her in her sex."[18]

In this regard, of course, expressions connoting the comic are only the tip of the iceberg. Perhaps they are the most noticeable linguistic indicators of the asymmetry between masculine and feminine expressions, but they are by no means the only ones, nor the most pernicious, as a consideration of group VIII makes evident. Two of the most common terms in current usage are "welfare mother" and "working mother" — expressions which not only call attention to the sex of their referents, but define them in relation to their offspring as well. The tendency to think of women who work as "working wives" or "working mothers" should make one sceptical about the ultimate reforming effect of recent encouragements to "get women out of the house." Such endeavors, while they may alleviate the problems of individuals, are unlikely to do much damage to traditional stereotype because the stereotype of woman is formed in relation to the stereotype of man; extending the activities of people who remain "working mothers" will do little to repair the asymmetry that now exists between "woman" and "man." Let us look at language again: Would a man say "I have a career and a family too"? This statement might well be true of him, but only his wife is likely to express the situation in that way. So it is with the well-intentioned husband who "helps with the housework." Does his wife help with the housework too? No, she simply does it. She is a "working wife and mother," whose very name indicates that this is her job, not as part of the supporting crew, but in the starring role.

Our way of talking about women, whether blatantly sexist or not, continues to promote a notion of female nature that is quite out of balance with that of the male, for it continues to identify a woman primarily in terms of her sex. Sexist conventions in language may be all the more tenacious because their effects are not conscious. If you accuse someone of being sexist when he or she is just speaking the King's English, that person is likely to respond with understandable indignation. But the situation is discriminatory nonetheless. So long as this disparity exists in language, equality is yet distant, and since in Bergsons's terms this situation continues to be one in which "the physical over-shadows the moral," it is to be expected that humor and ridicule will be waiting in the wings.

Insofar as generic usage of masculine terms perpetuates our limited or "rigid" concept of woman, and by extension, of person, the increasing use of neutral terms or expressions mentioning both males and females where "persons in general" are concerned should have more than a cosmetic effect. It is clear by now that in some ways language is not always the intransigent foe that one might have thought, for new usage can supplant the old with comparative ease. Certainly the battle for sexual equality neither begins nor ends with language, but it is encouraging that there is one barrier that is relatively easily scaled. However, to conclude on a cautionary note, perhaps the ease with which this barrier falls should make us a little suspicious.

NOTES

1. Dorothy Sayers, "The Human Not-Quite-Human," in *Masculine/ Feminine*, eds. Betty Roszak and Theodore Roszak, (New York: Harper and Row, 1969), p. 117.
2. Simone de Beauvoir, *The Second Sex*, H. M. Parshley, trans. (New York: Knopf, 1953), p. xv.
3. For views at both ends of the chronological spectrum, see Rousseau, *Emile*, (1762), and Steven Goldberg, *The Inevitability of Patriarchy* (New York: William Morrow, 1973).
4. Accompanying this argument against the generic use of masculine terminology has been a campaign to rid textbooks and children's reading matter of material reflecting only stereotyped occupations for men and women. These efforts have had a noticeable effect: McGraw Hill Company has issued extensive guidelines requiring elimination of sexist language from their publications, and many states now have anti-sex discrimination rules for school materials.
5. Elizabeth Lane Beardsley, "Referential Genderization," *Philosophical Forum*, Vol. V., Nos 1-2 (1973-74):285-93 I have also made use of some of Beardsley's other terminology, such as "sex-neutral" and "sex-distinguishing" to refer to terms which respectively do not and do indicate the sex of a referent.

   Occasionally, I use "masculine expressions" and "feminine expressions" as shorthand for "expressions which indicate that their subject is male" and "expressions which indicate that their subject is female."
6. Throughout this paper I am sharing Beardsley's assumption that language — what one can and cannot say — is an important factor in concept formation and transmission. (Cf. Beardsley, pp. 287, 291.)
7. Beardsley, *op. cit.*, p. 291.
8. Samuel Johnson, 31 July, 1763, in James Boswell, *Life of Johnson*.
9. Roberta Salper, introduction to *Female Liberation*, (New York: Knopf 1972), p. 3.

   Ridicule is not reserved for political movements involving only women, (witness the effect of political cartoons), but the women's movement and women in general receive a disproportionate share of jokes and jibes. (We might also note that the visibility of the gay movement has opened the door for frequent veiled homosexual jokes on prime time T.V.) The threat women post to the established order cannot always be distanced with ridicule, however, as the venomous reactions of many sports institutions testifies.
10. Friedrich Neitzsche, "Woman De-Feminized," in Roszak and Roszak, *op. cit.*, p. 5.
11. Sayers, *op. cit.*, p. 118.

12. Cf. Wylie Sypher, editor's introduction to *Comedy*, (Garden City, N.Y.: Doubleday, 1956.)

13. Henri Bergson, "Laughter," in *Comedy*, ed. Sypher, p. 64. Although Bergson did not intend to extend his comments to include the view that laughter can be an ally of reaction and tradition, some of his observations are amenable to this extension:

    "Laughter is, above all, a corrective. Being intended to humiliate, it must make a painful impression on the person against whom it is directed. By laughter, society avenges itself for the liberties taken with it. It would fail in its object if it bore the stamp of sympathy or kindness." (p., 187; cf. p. 148)

    We might compare George Meredith's essay on comedy, written shortly before Bergson's, in which he asserts that great comedy — i.e. comedy that does not rely on prejudice or exploitative human relations for its effect — cannot develop in a society where there is "a state of marked inequality between the sexes." ("An Essay On Comedy", in Sypher, ed., *Comedy*, p. 3; cf. p. 31).

14. Bergson, *op. cit.*, p. 97.

15. *Ibid.*, p. 93.

16. *Ibid.*, p. 121.

17. An explicit affirmation that "she" and "woman" have only specific usage occurred in 1974 during the chartering procedings for the Woman's Studies College at the State University of New York, Buffalo. The chartering committee, concerned about possible sex discrimination on the part of the College, inquired about the consistent use of "woman" and "she" to refer to College participants. It was explained that both terms were being used generically to include both men and women, which drew an appreciative response from the audience but was deemed unacceptable by the administration, despite attempts to specify clearly when the generic use was to obtain.

18. Beauvoir, *op. cit.*, p. 1.

Eleanor Kuykendall

Feminist Linguistics
in Philosophy

A prevailing version of linguistics, the Extended Standard
Theory, offers the paradigm of the solitary, rational speaker
who follows, unaware, the complex grammatical rules which
linguists formulate explicitly. This ideal, rational speaker is, of
course, uninfluenced by culture. Feminism, on the other hand,
argues that cultural definitions of gender often conflict with the
ideal of individual and autonomous preception and action. As a
political perspective, feminism proposes that we who experience
these clashes between cultural and individual definitions of
gender can become self-reflectively aware of them, so as to
change our perceptions and actions, including our speech acts.
Feminism also proposes that we can become aware of the
assumptions of people who speak to us.

  According to the Extended Standard Theory, the very notion
of a feminist linguistics is a contradiction in terms, for feminism
above all proposes cultural, and linguistics individual, descriptions of grammars and explanations of the speaker's understanding of these grammars. And the Extended Standard Theory
disclaims attempts to contribute to the speaker's self-reflective
knowledge as inappropriate to science. However, critics of the
Extended Standard Theory, while they refrain from offering
paradigms of the speaker-hearers of these grammars while
awaiting further research in psychology, do propose alternative

conceptions of the grammatical, of the speaker's knowledge of language, and of the relationship between the two. According to these alternative models of linguistic theory, feminist linguistics is at least possible, though a unified description of its method has yet to be formulated.

The following remarks are a proposal for such a formulation, and for its application to philosophy. Feminist philosophy examines the effect of presuppositions of gender on other theoretical discussions, such as those of power and obligation. Feminist linguistics in philosophy would examine ways in which the speaker's intelligence is bewitched by means of presuppositions of gender in language, or by means of presuppositions of gender which are conveyed in uses of language. Like Wittgensteinian analysis the application of feminist linguistics to philosophy is a kind of therapy, and like Austinian analysis it attempts to lay bare the realities speakers use words to talk about, by examining the words themselves. Feminist linguistics proposes that uses of words help constitute the world in which speakers act.

It appears to me that three methodological assumptions are essential to the development of feminist linguistics, and I will discuss each of them in turn with special emphasis on the last. The first is that presuppositions of gender in the structure of language, as well as its meaning and its uses, are cultural, rather than individual. The second is that the clash between cultural and individual assumptions of gender is pervasive, psychologically real, indicative of an irrationality in linguistic performance which may be found in speakers of either sex, and inadequately explained by assuming an ideally rational speaker whose departures from rationality in practice are of no theoretical interest to linguistics. The third methodological assumption of feminist linguistics, which I will illustrate by considering a number of examples, is that speakers and hearers can become self-reflectively aware of clashes between individual and cultural assumptions of gender by making these clashes explicit.

Feminist linguistics assumes, first, that at least part of the burden for determining the individual's conception of meanings of words, as well as the intelligibility of sentences and texts, must be borne by culture. To cite an example from Hilary Putnam, the meaning of the word 'witch' has changed in the last three hundred years because New Englanders no longer believe that there are real witches who make pacts with Satan.[1] To extend Putnam's example to a case he does not mention, feminist linguistics attempts to show how gender is presupposed as a buried metaphor in the use of terms like 'witch' to refer negatively to powerful women despite official denials of the baneful effects witches formerly were supposed to have had. Sometimes feminist linguistics is presented as a radical therapy which shocks the intelligence into recognizing its unacknowledged presuppositions of gender by reversing their usual order, as in Mary Daly's proposal that women are "possessed by a demonic power within the psyche — the masculine subject."[2]

In rejecting the paradigm of the isolated speaker, whose influence by culture is not considered, feminist linguistics proposes that even unacknowledged presuppositions of gender which have been labeled idiosyncratic variations of individual style be communalized and labeled explicitly as such with two pragmatic devices, which I call Female and Male Markers, or ♀ and ♂ Markers. These markers indicate when gender is presupposed in syntax, meaning, pronunciation, or mixtures of these. Under such an analysis 'witch,' in the preceding passage, is Female-Marked, and 'man,' in the following passage from Edmund Husserl's last work, is Male-Marked: " . . . In general the world exists not only for isolated men but for the community of men; and this is due to the fact that even what is straightforwardly perceptual is communalized."[3] Analysis of this passage as gender-marked leads the reader to consider alternatives, such as "In general the world exists not only for isolated persons but for the community of persons; and this is due to the fact that even what is straightforwardly perceptual is communalized," or even "In general the world exists not only for isolated women but for the community of women; and this is due to the fact that even what is straightforwardly perceptual is communalized." What is remarkable about this kind of gender-marked sentence is that changing it provides a basis for communalizing the notion of the understanding of langauge in the analysis that follows. As Sartre remarked in making his own transition between a philosophy based on the perceptions of an isolated subject and a philosophy placing subjects in a community, " 'Human relations' are in fact inter-individual structures whose common bond is language and which *actually* exist at every moment of History. Isolation is merely a particular aspect of these relations."[4]

Proposing that human relationships are inter-individual structures whose common bond is language challenges the Cartesian paradigm of the ideally isolate speaker, the solitary subject in doubt of its own existence and indifferent to that of others. This proposal also challenges the Cartesian assumption of the speaker's idealized rationality, or ability to reject contradiction. These idealizations of the speaker's isolation and rationality depart from the evidence of actual uses of language, in which speakers not only fail to reject contradiction but may even perceive the opposite. These apparent failures of rationality in performance, which linguists adhering to the Extended Standard Theory treat as irrelevant to descriptions of an idealized speaker's rationality, actually affect and are affected by the linguist's construct of idealized rationality, or competence, in subtle ways.

For example, clashes between individual and social perceptions of gender appear as contradictions when words like 'brotherhood' are explicitly classified as both gender-neutral (as in a group of union members) and male-marked (as in one's relationship to a male sibling). A semantic theory which assumes the ideally isolate, rational speaker can explain such cases, however, only as variations in the individual speaker's understanding of the use of 'brotherhood' and not as a contradiction between two distinct meanings of the word.[5] When speakers vacillate between referring only to males as brothers, and referring to females who identify with the male gender as brothers, the implicit assumption of male bonding in the second use of 'brotherhood' is overlooked and confusions that arise are treated as having no part in the semantic structure of the language.

Yet similar confusions arise even when neither sex nor gender enters into analyses of word meaning or sentence structure, and even in discussions of logical relations that are independent of word meaning, or even, we might suppose, of the structure of language. For example the cognitive psychologist P. C. Wason conducted a series of experiments demonstrating a pattern of error in subjects' performance of a complex task—applying exclusive disjunction, which states that either one of two sentences may be true, but not both. The subjects were presented with four diagrams, which were identified in the article as a black diamond, a white diamond, a black circle, and a white circle. The subjects were told that in this group of four designs there was a particular shape and a particular color such that any of the four designs which has one, and only one, of these features, was called a THOG. They were also told that the black diamond was a THOG and asked to say which of the other three designs, if any, was a THOG. Many subjects failed.

In attempting to account for their errors the experimenter points out that applying the general description of the THOG to the paradigm, the black diamond, leads to two inferences. One is that blackness and diamondhood cannot both be features possessed by any other design that could be a THOG. The other inference is that neither blackness nor diamondhood can be features of any other design called a THOG. It follows that if the black diamond is a THOG then the white circle can be a THOG, but neither the black circle nor the white diamond could be THOGs. Nevertheless sixty-five per cent of the wrong solutions were the mirror image of the correct one—claims that the black circle or white diamond were THOGs—although the probability of this kind of wrong answer is one in twenty-seven. The subjects appeared to fare no better when the example was changed to a real-life situation which did involve gender, as in interpreting THOGhood to be exemplified by being either female or under thirty-five, but not both.

The subjects in the THOG experiment erred because they could not separate their perceptions of shape from their perceptions of color and recombine them in accordance with the terms of the experiment. The experimenter proposes that they may be freed from their mistakes by being asked to state the shapes and colors of the designs they wrongly chose as THOGs (being black and circular or white and a diamond) and to compare their wrongly chosen examples with the general rule that THOGhood consists in having at least one, but not both, of the particular features of THOGhood. Thus if the black diamond is a paradigm of THOGhood, the black circle and the white diamond could not be, for they would either possess both of the features of THOGhood or neither of them. So the experimenter proposes that subjects can be made aware of their errors in applying a general syntactic rule, exclusive disjunction, by making their answers explicit and seeing that the characteristics of their answers contradict both the requirements of the general rule and the description of the paradigm, the black diamond.[6]

It appears, however, that two aspects of the experimenter's presentation influenced the subjects' ability to apply a general rule in practice. The experimenter acknowledges the first, that exclusive disjunction is actually two general rules stated as one.

In this experiment the two general rules state, respectively, that a design is either black or white and either a diamond or a circle; and that no THOG can have both the characteristic color and the characteristic shape associated with THOGs. The second aspect of the experimenter's presentation, which he does not consider in analyzing the subjects' errors, is that he identified the designs both by names, such as 'black diamond' and by descriptions, such as 'black' and 'diamond.' The subjects had to make the transition between identifying a figure with a single phrase, such as 'black diamond,' and analyzing that identification as two descriptions, such as 'black' and 'diamond.' Not only was the general rule used to pick out the example complex in structure; identifying, or picking out, the examples was a process requiring the subject not only to refer to it, but also to describe it using the same words. This second problem suggests that subjects can correct their answers by seeing how the examples they chose contradict the requirements of the general rules only if they can also recognize that the examples were picked out by complex identifying descriptions not made explicit in the experiment.

In an analogous way, perceptions of gender in language both conflict with and are described in conflicting ways by theories of language which idealize the speaker's rationality as the speaker's unanalyzed competence to reject contradiction. If any figure is both black and a diamond, it may be truly referred to as 'black' and 'diamond.' But it is falsely named by either of its separate descriptions, taken alone. And if any person is both a male sibling and a friend he may be both truly referred to and described as 'brother.' If he is a friend but not a male sibling he can be referred to, as a courtesy, as 'brother,' but not described truly as such unless kinship in the family and kinship in the community can be distinguished. If a person is a friend but not a sibling her description, as a courtesy, as 'brother' is inconsistent not only with her absence of family relationship but also with her sex. It is an unjustified convention of the Extended Standard Theory, I suggest, to assume the speaker's ideal rationality in both identifying and describing black diamonds and brothers and to treat departures from standard descriptions as aberrations of the speaker's rationality in performance, or mere matters of individual style.

These examples begin to show, then, that tying characterizations of the speaker's rationality exclusively to syntax and sharply separating discussions of syntax from discussions of meaning and use, as the Extended Standard Theory proposes, fails to capture what is essential to a speaker's rationality. According to the model of linguistic competence, which is the speaker's idealized rationality, presented by the Extended Standard Theory, a sentence that is intelligible to an ideally rational speaker is also grammatical, or ordered in accordance with logical principles which the linguist attempts to state. But linguistic theory has recently begun to recognize, in opposition to the methodological principle which ties descriptions of rationality to syntax, cases in which syntax alone fails to capture either the notions of intelligibility to the speaker or grammatical correctness. According to an earlier view of Noam Chomsky, which posits the paradigm of the essentially rational speaker, syntactic theory alone should be able to predict the ungrammaticality of sentences like 'Nine of my three friends are linguists,' since rational speakers find such sentences unacceptable. More recent work has suggested that a semantic restriction has to be introduced into syntax, or else invoked after syntactic transformations have already been completed, to rule out this kind of ungrammatical sentence. "Phonological perturbations" too, affect syntax. For example 'John is the person I want to succeed' can be a transformation either of 'I want to succeed John' or 'I want John to succeed,' so that the surface structure of 'John is the person I want to succeed' is ambiguous. On the other hand 'John is the person I wanna succeed' can be interpreted only as a transform of 'I wanna succeed John,' and not of 'I wanna John to succeed.'[7]

The discovery of cases in which intelligibility structure and grammaticality cannot be explained by syntactic structure alone suggests that discussions of the speaker's knowledge of the language, and abstract discussions of grammaticality, have to be separated. Indeed, some linguists have proposed that speakers who find deviant or "irrational" grammatical structures acceptable help bring about language change, as in an increasing acceptance of such sentences as 'Will the person with the New York license plate please move their car?'[8] The process of language change exemplified in acceptance of the plural pronoun to make a gender-neutral reference in the singular suggests that social change can be perceived in transitions between what was, and what now is, considered intelligible, so that abstract discussions of grammatical structure which fail to consider language change fail to capture the notion of what is understandable to the rational speaker.

Feminist linguistics attempts (as the Extended Standard Theory does not) not only to describe clashing assumptions of gender in language as they bear on assessments of the speaker's rationality, but also to make self-reflective knowledge of these clashes available to speakers. If persons of either sex can drive cars, for example, feminist linguists will perceive a cultural assumption in a sentence like 'Will the person with the New York license plate please move his car' which is inconsistent with the assumption that the driver could be female. Changing the language to make the plural 'their' refer to the singular is a kind of therapy forcing speakers to acknowledge the contradiction between an implicitly assumed general rule which posits gender-neutral reference and specific applications of the rule which refer to only one gender. This is an example, among many that I will examine in passages that follow, whose analysis helps speakers become self-reflectively aware of their presuppositions of gender and of clashing presuppositions of other sorts which carry hidden presuppositions of gender. It should not be supposed, though, that identifying Female and Male gender Markers in English, as in the examples of 'brotherhood' or the use of 'he' to refer to females, equates Male-Marked uses of language with dominance, power, assertiveness, or seriousness; or Female-Marked uses of languages with deference, powerlessness, nonassertiveness, or nonseriousness, as some linguists have suggested. The Male and Female Markers permit these sociolinguistic interpretations of their use only when they clash, or cancel each other, and the cancellations can be reversed. Some of these cancellations, however, are illustrated in the complex examples which follow.

The gender markers easiest to describe are not complex and present no clashes between individual and cultural assumptions of gender. They include cases like 'mother' and 'father' (at least as applied to biological or adoptive parents), or cases in which an amalgam of syntax with semantics, phonology, or even pragmatics need not be considered. Linguists who reject the possibility of such amalgams can thereby eliminate all but trivial examples from consideration. Even so, relatively pure examples of gender-marked language remain for reflective analysis.

1. There appear, however, to be no such clear cases in English syntax. For example there is no specific verb ending

which is marked for the female or male speaker of English as
there is for Japanese, nor is there any specific word order
prescribed invariably for female or male speakers such that
sentences produced by speakers of one sex are unacceptable, or
analyzed as ungrammatical, if uttered or written by speakers of
the opposite sex.

2. Among the clear examples of semantic gender markers
which are used to refer to ('sister') or by women to describe
('mauve,' 'ecru') are many in which presuppositions of gender
occur together in the same phrase or sentence with presuppositions of the opposite gender or of gender-neutrality. For example 'woman doctor,' 'male nurse,' and 'male model' are marked
respectively as ♀♂,♂♀, and ♂♀, and the presupposition of the first
gender marker cancels the presupposition of the second.
Recognition that 'firemen' and 'chairman' are marked for the
male gender led to the coinage of the gender-neutral
'firefighter,' 'chairperson,' and 'chair.'[9] Acceptance of new
coinages may be inferred when a previously implicit presupposition of gender is made explicit, cancelling the presupposition of
gender-neutrality in the new coinage, as in 'woman
homemaker.'[10]

3. Phonologists have recently observed characteristics of the
speaker's voice that are not entirely determined by biology, such
as pitch. The sex of the adult speaker can usually be identified by
the biologically determined range of the speaker's voice, but this
can be varied. Sally McConnell-Ginet has pointed out that
female speakers often adopt a pattern of constant pitch and
changing loudness, perhaps to maintain the audience's attention, but that they appear to adopt this pattern unconsciously.[11]
Men speaking to children, like day-care teachers, or to women
with whom they wish to express solidarity, can also be observed
adopting patterns of constant pitch and changing loudness.
Therefore both pitch and loudness can be chosen by speakers of
either sex to mark the utterance for either gender.

Far more difficult cases to analyze in English involve
sentences in which an apparently gender-neutral syntactic construction appears to be complicated or cancelled, or
amalgamated with semantic and phonological markers so that it
is not clear which speech act is being attempted, or whether the
speaker is clearly committed to carrying out any speech act at
all. Robin Lakoff has proposed that hedged sentences like 'I
want to ask whether it's time to go,' and indirect syntactic con-

structions like 'It's time to go, isn't it?' for 'Let's go,' which are used to carry out what linguists now call indirect speech acts, constitute a woman's language for speakers of English.[12]

If these examples do not stand up to scrutiny as cases of gender-marked language, as I have argued elsewhere,[13] they fail to do so because Lakoff erroneously claims that women's uses of tag questions and other sorts of indirect speech acts constitute women's nonassertiveness and nonseriousness, when in fact they can be used assertively and seriously by speakers of either sex. Speakers of both sexes employ indirect speech acts in exchanges which can be used to dominate, as in insulting a professor by praising her charm but ignoring her wit; or to defer, as in praising a professor for his wit but ignoring his lack of charm. The confusions that arise are complicated by the need to examine whole texts, or whole conversations, to discover what speakers or writers intend to do. Linguists, by contrast, usually take the sentence as their largest unit of analysis and their inability to recognize these confusions or to contribute to the speaker's self-reflective awareness of them is a consequence of their methodological decision to examine only sentences.

Even when only single sentences are studied, however, two kinds of confusion arise. I want to consider these two kinds of confusion for the example of insulting, in which cultural presuppositions of gender are often covertly directed against women.

1. Confusion arises, first, because insulting is a speech act whose *name*, 'insult,' cannot be used in its first-person form to carry out the speech act of insulting.[14] So 'I insult you' cannot be used to insult you, and 'I insult that you are an intellectual lightweight' cannot be used to insult either, although the complement of the sentence, 'You are an intellectual lightweight,' can be used to insult. A non-academic speaker might even be able to claim that no insult was intended, creating a double bind in which what appears to be the intention of the message clashes with what the speaker says the intention is.

2. The second kind of confusion arises in the sort of communication H. P. Grice calls an "implicature" and J. J. Katz calls an "insinuation." For example a colleague implicates or insinuates that a woman is an intellectual lightweight by saying that she is charming. The speaker may or may not be conscious of intending to insinuate that the woman is stupid, but in any case the speaker can deny intending to insinuate that the woman is stupid.[15] The result of this confusion, which is a violation of

Grice's conversational maxim of manner which requires speakers to be clear, is that once again the speaker can create a double bind by denying that what appears to be the intention of the message — to insult — is its intention.

In both cases speakers are in a position comparable to that of subjects who had difficulty with the THOG problem and who could not reconcile their application of the general rule to the identifications and descriptions of the particular examples they used the rule to pick out. But speakers who insult in either of the two ways just described may be perfectly aware that they are doing it, so that the duality of their intention creates a double bind for the audience that is no problem for the speaker at all, if the speaker both intends to insult and to deny that an insult is intended. The hearer's problem is to get the speaker to acknowledge that an insult was intended, in order to deal with it on more general grounds. For example if a referee finds a point made in a colleague's paper 'charming,' that can be taken to implicate that the referee does not take the paper seriously, perhaps because of the topic or the author's sex. The author has the recourse of presenting arguments requiring the referee to take the topic seriously, perhaps by showing that the referee has overlooked points that are critical to the development of the topic, or by attacking the referee's sexism directly. The latter course is ineffective, however, as long as the referee is in a position to argue that his remarks are relevant to the paper's topic.

An appropriate strategy to adopt is to find a way of making the referee's intentions explicit, so that he can no longer appear to be arguing rationally both that his remarks are relevant and that he does not intend to insult. Linguists have been impeded in describing such a process as anything but an extra-linguistic or pragmatic matter because they confine themselves to the description of the grammaticality of sentences, rather than texts or conversations in which such sentences occur. But the problem of rendering the speaker's intentions explicit can still be made manageable, in the cases I will now analyze, by restating the conversation or written argument as a single sentence, or sentences, in which the referee's arguments are presented explicitly as his statements of felicity conditions, or restrictions on the appropriateness of their use. So, for example, if anyone promises to do something without actually being able to do it, the speech act of promising is infelicitous and the infelicity can be exposed by examining the oddity of a sentence like 'I promise to meet you on the Boston Common at five o'clock, but of course I'll be in San Francisco until four.' The sentence is self-defeating, if not unintelligible, because the second clause describes a condition that makes fulfillment of the first impossible.

To turn to a more complex example, an analysis of an academic paper whose insult is not explicit may be made explicit by rewriting the referee's remarks as a single sentence or sentences used to carry out indirect speech acts whose reasons are presented as subordinate clauses, as in:

1. Let me say that I find the paper incoherent, because the author does not make the relevant distinctions.
*2. Let me say that I find the paper incoherent, because as head of the personnel committee I am entitled to make that assessment.
3. I regret to say that I find the paper badly argued, because the author neglects the important counter-examples of Hitler's and Stalin's mothers in claiming that motherhood and homemaking are activities without effect in the political sphere.

In the second sentence, according to an analysis of a different example given by Alice Davison, the felicity condition given in the subordinate clause modifies the performative verb used as a hedge, 'say,' rather than the performative verb actually used to give the assessment, 'find.' That is, the reason clause modifies a sentence which has the surface form of an imperative, when the actual illocutionary force of the sentence is an evaluation.[16] In consequence the second sentence is ungrammatical in that the clause presenting the speaker's reasons is incorrectly placed in the sentence.

The third sentence, however, remains a problem. If it should be taken as grammatical, it is troublesome in other ways. By implicating that a discussion of two of the world's more questionable political figures is relevant to discussing the question of a mother's political influence, the author of the sentence implicates both that women must act indirectly and that the effects of their acts are evil, which can be taken as an insult. Although I know of no way to give a direct linguistic analysis of such an example, I suggest that the insinuator can sometimes be persuaded to restate the implicature more directly as a felicity condition of a sentence like:

4. I regret to say that I find the argument incoherent, because it neglects the important point that women are ultimately indirect agents in the acts of their sons.

This example cannot be attacked as ungrammatical, but the sexist assumption on which the referee bases his evaluation is made explicit, so that it can be analyzed directly, perhaps as an *argumentum ad feminam*.

The process of attempting to render the intentions of such communications explicit carries with it the hazard that the insinuator may have sufficient political power to continue imposing his conception of what is relevant and defensible even when this contradicts the assumptions of feminism. I do not know of any way to demonstrate anything like the ungrammaticality of this kind of sexism in argumentation, and present it as an unresolved problem for feminist linguistics and more generally for speech act theory. The irrationality of such arguments was, of course, first noticed by Aristotle.

Speakers-hearers of both sexes engage in the sorts of indirect speech acts and insinuation I have just discussed, in which they can deny what they appear to be using the sentence to do, so that there is nothing about double-binding in indirect speech acts, *per se*, that is marked for gender. When tokens of sentences used to carry out such speech acts are embedded in texts or conversations, however, and the contradictory intentions of the speaker can be made explicit, the clash can be subjected to feminist analysis.

I conclude by speculating on the implications of the examples I have just discussed for the development of feminist linguistics as a methodology, and for its application to philosophy.

First, I have suggested some very serious difficulties with applying existing linguistic methodology to feminist issues. It seems likely that the competence model, which ties grammaticality to syntax and identifies grammaticality with rationality, will have to be given up, or that at least discussions of abstract grammaticality be separated from discussions of the speaker's knowledge of the language. The idealization of the *individual* speaker's knowledge of the language will also have to be given up, for a feminist linguistic methodology requires a social conception of the speaker's knowledge of the language.

Second, the philosophical uses to which a feminist linguistic methodology could be applied will result in the development of the speaker-hearer's self-reflective awareness of what is actually going on when sentences are used to carry out speech acts. The development of such self-reflective awareness will lead not only to a heightened awareness of presuppositions of gender, but also to a clearer perception of what it is to intend to do something in and by saying something.

Finally, an increase in the speaker-hearer's self-reflective awareness of presuppositions of gender and conflicting intentions to do something in and by saying something may lead in time to the development of new philosophical theories. One such new theory might propose replacing a notion of power as the ability to dominate and compel the desired respose with a notion of power as the ability to become self-reflectively aware of one's own intentions, and those of others, so as to be able to exercise one's competence directly.[17]

NOTES

1. "The Meaning of 'Meaning'," in *Language, Mind, and Knowledge*, Keith Gunderson, ed. (Minneapolis: University of Minnesota Press, 1975), pp. 170-171.

2. *Beyond God the Father* (Boston: Beacon Press, 1973), p. 50.

3. *The Crisis of European Sciences and Transcendental Phenomenology*, David Carr, trans. (Evanston: Northwestern University Press, 1970), p. 163.

4. *Critique of Dialectical Reason*, Alan Sheridan-Smith, trans. (London: NLB, 1976), p. 99.

5. Arnold M. Zwicky and Jerrold M. Sadock, "Ambiguity Tests and How to Fail Them," in *Syntax and Semantics*, IV, John M. Kimball, ed. (New York: Academic Press, 1975), pp. 4-10.

6. P. C. Wason, "Self Contradictions," in *Thinking: Readings in Cognitive Science*, P. N. Johnson-Laird and P. C. Wason, eds. (Cambridge: University Press, 1977), pp. 126-128.

7. Paul Postal, "Linguistic Anarchy Notes," in *Syntax and Semantics, VII: Notes from the Linguistic Underground*, James D. McCawley, ed. (New York: Academic Press, 1976), p. 127; Noam Chomsky, *Reflections on Language* (New York: Pantheon Books, 1975), pp. 78-117; and Joan Bresnan, "A Realistic Transformational Grammar," in *Linguistic Theory and Psychological Reality,* Morris Hale, Joan Bresnan, and George A. Miller, eds. (Cambridge: MIT Press, 1978), p. 42. citing an unpublished observation by Larry Horn.

8. T. G. Bever, J. M. Carroll, and R. Hurtig, "Analogy or Un-grammatical Sequences that are Utterable and Comprehensible are the Origins of New Grammars in Language Acquisition and Linguistic Evolution," in *An Integrated Theory of Linguistic Ability,* Thomas G. Bever, Jerrold J. Katz, and D. Terence Langendoen, eds. (New York: Crowell, 1976), p. 162. See also Virginia Valian, "Linguistics and Feminism," in *Feminism and Philosophy*, Mary Vetterling-Braggin, Frederick Elliston, and Jane English, eds. (Totowa, N. J.: Littlefield-Adams, 1977), pp. 163-164.

9. But their use to refer only to women is a rejection of the new coinage. See Cheris Kramer, Barrie Thorne, and Nancy Henley, "Perspectives on Language and Communication," *Signs,* III (Spring, 1978): 648.

10. As in N. R. Kleinfield, "A. T. & T. Gets Customer Opinions By Phone," *New York Times*, July 31, 1978, D3.

11. "Intonation in a Man's World," *Signs,* III (Spring, 1978): 558.

12. *Language and Woman's Place*, (New York: Harper Colophon Books, 1975).

13. "Breaking the Double Binds," *Language and Style,* XII (1979).

14. The sentence 'I insult you easily' has been suggested to me by Linda Patrik as a counterexample. But this seems to me to be a description of other speech acts rather than a name of one presently engaged in.

15. H. P. Grice, "Logic and Conversation," in *Syntax and Semantics, III: Speech Acts*, Peter Cole and Jerry Morgan, eds. (New York: Academic Press, 1975), pp. 41-58; and Jerrold J. Katz, *Propositional Structure and Illocutionary Force* (New York: Crowell, 1977), pp. 193-194. I discuss this topic also in my "Assertive Power," *New York Review of Women's Studies*, I (1979).

16. "Indirect Speech Acts and What to Do with Them, "in Cole and Morgan, *op. cit.,* p. 164.

17. Earlier versions of this paper were read at The National Workshop Conference on Teaching Philosophy, Union College, Schenectady, New York, August 9, 1978 and at Women and Society: a Symposium, St. Michael's College, Winooski, Vermont, March 25, 1979. Thanks to those audiences and to Pamela J. Annas, Peter M. Brown, Stanley Gutman, Ingrid J. Lorch, and Janet Farrell Smith for comments.

Jane Duran

Gender-Neutral Terms

Recent articles in philosophy of language have attempted to come to grips with the notion of a masculine term functioning neutrally. Until a few years ago, the unspoken assumption prevalent in general English usage had been that such terms could be used in a neutral sense: grammars and manuals of style indicated that the masculine pronoun "he" was more-or-less interchangeable with "one." In her paper "The Myth of the Neutral 'Man'," Janice Moulton has argued that there is no genuinely neutral use of such terms, while Caroline Korsmeyer has argued in another piece that there may be such a use, but that part of the effect of neutral usage is to create an aura of discredibility around some straightforwardly feminine terms. I will argue that neither Moulton's nor Korsmeyer's thesis is entirely correct as it stands; that there is gender-neutral usage of masculine terms, and that such usage may not always function in marked contrast to that of designated feminine terms where such terms exist.

Moulton's general line of argument is that terms like "man" and "he" are not really functioning neutrally when purporting to refer to both genders of the human race. In other words, it is Moulton's position that the usage of such terms is not merely an effect of sexism, but rather a cause of it; her argument is that " . . . however innocently and neutrally they are intended, the words 'he,' 'man,' etc., may not function as genuine gender-neutral terms; that their use is unavoidably somewhat gender-specific; and that male gender specific descriptions make it difficult to recognize that descriptions in that context could apply to a female."[1]

Moulton notes at the outset that the question of whether or not patently masculine terms can have a gender-neutral use does not revolve around the fact that they obviously have at least some uses which are not gender-neutral. She cites the fact that many terms, such as "tall" and "wide," can be used in senses which do not necessarily imply that the referents are tall or wide. Such terms are referred to as "unmarked" when used in the sense where no expectation of tallness or width is created. The question is, then, are there unmarked usages of "he," "man," and "his"? That is, is it possible to use those terms in such a way that no expectation with regard to gender is created?

In arguing that the answer to the latter question is "no," Moulton remarks that the use of a marked term — "short," for instance, as opposed to the unmarked "wide" — frequently carries with it a pejorative connotation. Shortness and narrowness may be perceived — in many contexts — as being of less value than tallness and width. (That this is not necessarily the case for all contexts may readily be seen by constructing a few examples. Certain very fine pieces of wire used in the making of a watch, to cite one instance, would have narrowness as a notable attribute. In this context, the asking of the question "How narrow is it?" would not seem to have any pejorative connotation whatsoever. The reader may construct other examples.[2]) In any case, as Moulton notes, if "he" and "man" were indeed similar to the unmarked adjectives "tall' and "wide," and if it were the case that they have somewhat more positive associations than, say, "she" and "woman," these associations might constitute some kind of explanation of their recurrent use. But the important question remains: Given a current theory of meaning, such as Grice's,[3] wherein *intent* and *recognition of intent* are the keys to the meaning of an utterance, how can it plausibly be argued that "he" and "man" do not have gender-neutral meanings? In other words, if in uttering "Neanderthal man was a hunter," I intend that the utterance include both the subsets of Neanderthal males and Neanderthal females, and if my audience recognizes my intent, how could I have failed to give the term "man" a gender-neutral meaning?

Moulton addresses the topic as follows: "In order to show that 'man' and 'he' and like terms are not really neutral, I propose to show that it is not enough that one intend a term to have a particular meaning for it to have that meaning; that intended neutral uses of 'he,' and 'man,' etc. can fail to be neutral; and that such failures have implications for all other allegedly neutral uses."[4] But surely the fact that an intended use can fail is not a criterion for whether or not the terms are in fact — or can be — really neutral. On Grice's theory of meaning — which seems to be the paradigm for the discussion — "*A* must intend to induce by *x* [an utterance] a belief in an audience, and he must also intend his utterance to be *recognized* as so intended." [Emphasis mine.][5]

Failure of recognition by the audience may on some level be the failure of the utterer — it may simply be the case that his or her statement was incomprehensible, and that no reasonably intelligent listener, under ordinary conditions, could have been expected to recognize the intent. On a finer level of discrimination, however, it may be the failure of the audience. To take another leaf from Grice, conversational implicature should not fail between two intelligent adults unless some sort of violation of the logic of conversation has taken place.[6] If I make inquiries of a friend regarding my acquaintance Julia's performance in her new job, I am warranted in making an inference from the reply, "Well, she just received the pink slip this morning." Indeed, I am not only warranted in making the inference, the logic of conversation requires that I make it. The inference that her performance was somehow unsatisfactory is that which I was intended to make by the utterer, and the belief that her performance was unsatisfactory is a belief that the utterer intended that I acquire, and that I recognize as being intended. The notions of recognition of intent and conversational implicature may justifiably be carried over into our analysis of statements like "Neanderthal man was a hunter," since, as Moulton herself remarks, " . . . however the use of a term gets started, it would seem that if it was intended a certain way when used, and understood that way by others, then, on any available theory of meaning, that's what it means."[7]

Analysis of some of the sentences used by Moulton to attempt to show that speakers' intentions to use the terms gender-neutrally may fail — and thus show that the terms are not really gender neutral — is rendered more interesting and precise by the application of the Gricean concepts mentioned above. One of Moulton's first examples is the sentence "She's the best man for the job," concerning which she remarks that it would be a rare person who could utter it without irony.[8] This is certainly true currently, but it has not always been the case. Within recent memory, such sentences were uttered — and without undue irony — whenever the relatively rare situation of a woman's being given a job almost always previously held by men occurred. Although the use of the word "man" in this context does not have the impact of the word in the phrase "Neanderthal man," it is not implausible to think that (at least a few years ago) the utterer could have intended that the entire phrase be interpreted as "She's the best person for the job," and could reasonably have expected the intent to be recognized. Certainly, "She's the best man for the job" is not a paradigm for cases where "man" can be used to cover both male and female human beings. Moreover, it is clearly possible that on this usage — which would now be rare or tongue-in-cheek — failure of recognition of intent might be ascribed to the fault of the utterer rather than to that of the audience. But failure of recognition of intent may occur with the usage of any term or utterance, however neutral. If it occurs with the use of incontrovertibly neutral terms like "person" or "one," we may ascribe it to the unimaginativeness or stupidity of the listener. Mere failure of recognition of intent, in and of itself, is not the proper criterion for whether or not a term may legitimately be considered to be neutral, as I have already argued.

Moulton notes that Russell's analysis of the proposition "I met a man" (" 'I met x and x is human' is not always false") does not take into account the importance of context. ("Russell did not notice that 'man' is not used neutrally in his context."[9]) But "man" is used neutrally in Russell's context — as a paradigmatic utterance, it is clear that the term "man" is intended to apply to all human beings. We experience anxiety when a 5-year-old girl returns late from school and says "I met a man" because we know that she is too young, in ordinary circumstances, to have come across the subtleties of gender ambiguity and neutrality in utterances, and that her statement must refer to a grown male. (Unless, of course, she is a prodigy who has already read Russell!) Here context gives the listener enough information for her to distinguish the intent and for her to recognize it as such.

Moulton's strongest argument begins with her claim that if " . . . it can be shown that a familiar and paradigmatic example of a gender-neutral use of 'man' or 'men' is not really neutral at all . . . then . . . it can be argued that there is no real gender-neutral meaning of those terms."[10] Her prime example is the textbook syllogism.

All men are mortal
Socrates is a man
Therefore Socrates is mortal

Moulton argues that replacement of the middle term by "Sophia is a man" makes it "false or insulting," and that " . . . it is not taken to mean that Sophia is a member of the human species."[11] But surely this is not necessarily the case. If "men" is taken as "human beings" — which is the acknowledged intent — "Sophia is a man" may sound *odd*, but not necessarily either false or insulting. By the same token, if "men" has as its referent the set of all human beings (and if that set may be thought of as the union of the two sets of men and women) the syllogism in its original form is neither invalid nor equivocal. It merely means that any object in the union of the two subsets may satisfy the predicate and be used to create a true middle term. The syllogism quoted above is not "just like"[12]

All banks are closed on Sunday.
The Outer Banks are banks.
Therefore the Outer Banks are closed on Sunday.

"The Outer Banks are banks" is humorous: the intent is a pun. It is inconceivable that the meanings can genuinely be equivocated because the referents of the two uses of the five-letter word "banks" are understood to be different. Not so the word "men" as it appears in the original syllogism, if it is understood on the first mention as meaning "human beings."

Moulton concludes her argument by citing the phenomenon of "Parasitic Reference": Just as all tissue has come to be called Kleenex, and all bleach Clorox, so, it is argued, all human beings have come to be referred to by the terms ordinarily used to designate specifically male human beings. This may well be the case; it may also be true that the use of such terminology is at least mildly prejudicial to tissues not Kleenex, to bleach not Clorox and to human beings not male. Although many or even most of the putatively gender-neutral usages of obviously male terminology may not be taken gender-neutrally, this does not show that the intended gender-neutral use of such terms before an audience *recognizing* the intent is not gender-neutral.

Since it may readily be agreed that the overall effect of the continual attempted gender-neutral use of masculine terms is harmful, and even potentially harmful in the cases where it succeeds, Caroline Korsmeyer's analysis of the difference between gender-neutral usage (a phenomenon she accepts) and the usage of specific sex-linked terms (particularly female ones) is stimulating.

Korsmeyer argues that there is only an apparent parallelism between gender-neutral terms, or masculine terms functioning as such, and their feminine counterparts.[13] She remarks: "We regularly think of women in contexts that stress directly or indirectly their sexual nature and this custom underscores the fact that a large part of their social relations involve what are ultimately their sex-related functions . . . . These aspects are clearly not evenly paralleled in contexts involving men . . . "[14] The larger argument is that the process of referential genderization, that is, the process by which a referent is standardly given the pronoun "he" or some other masculine pronoun unless there is specific reason not to, has insidious significance. If the two sets of terms — the masculine/gender-neutral and the feminine — are not really parallel, or equivalent in effect, then a subtle value judgment is being made when the feminine term is used.

Korsmeyer has a taxonomy of terms which she cites as providing evidence, in varying degrees, of the nature of the lack of parallelism in the use of these terms. In some cases, there simply is no standard female term to use in referring to a woman's having a certain occupation. "Driver" and "wrestler" are cited: Here the male term is also gender-neutral, and, as Korsmeyer notes, it does not sound odd to use these terms to refer to women who happen to have these occupations. The problematic area arises when, for some occupations, an attempt is made to create a feminine term — "lady driver" and "lady wrestler" have, Korsmeyer argues, "slightly comical, lighthearted or cute" connotations.[15] In some cases, the effect of using the feminine term is still more deleterious — "Rosie the riveter" and "powder puff derby" are "cartoonish." The net effect, of course, is that it would seem that a woman is complimented in some sense if she is not referred to by these terms (it might be an accolade to insist that an extremely capable woman race driver be referred to by the term "driver," as are her male counterparts). This may, in fact, very well be the case. It is noteworthy that in Korsmeyer's taxonomy, only a few of the female terms have anything like full standing: "actress," "laundress" and "chairwoman" seem to have no connotations worse than those attached to their male equivalents, but they certainly are exceptions. The same may be said of the hoary "aviatrix" — although the term is no longer in common usage, we are reluctant to say that Amelia Earhart was demeaned by the term. Korsmeyer notes: "I suggest not only that we customarily associate women with particular activities, thereby mentally restricting their scope, but that the notion of what it is to be a woman is limited as well. As the limitation is reflected in language, 'woman' and 'she' have a more limited connotation than 'man' and 'he'."[16] And it is, of course, the fact that mention of "she," or use of the female term, is restricted to the deviant case that is at the heart of the problem. For if the gender-neutral term is associated, however faintly, with the male, then the paradigm term indicates in some sense that a genuine article of its type — a genuine driver, professor or doctor — has at least some masculine qualities. To the extent that the driver, professor or doctor does not have masculine qualities the designation may become inappropriate, and it is at this point that the female designation (which may well be more or less overtly humorous) is called in. The qualities of seriousness, learnedness and so forth (traditionally masculine) which may at some level attach to the term "professor" certainly can carry over to include a woman professor who is perceived to be substantially like the mentally-held stereotype of the male professor. As the woman deviates from the stereotype (as she becomes more stereotypically feminine) the term becomes less and less appropriate — and finally humorous: We can imagine a comedy skit wherein Charo or Marilyn Monroe is given the role of "professor."

Certainly, the generic usage of masculine terms, particularly when the feminine counterparts are retained for effect, perpetuates stereotyped notions of what it means to be a "doctor," "driver" and so forth. And yet it is equally clear that there are at least some terms which are genuinely gender-neutral and which have no feminine counterparts: "singer" and "teacher" are among those cited by Korsmeyer. At the same time, a few of the feminine terms, such as "actress," seem to have no negative connotations pertaining solely to their status as feminine terms.

This paper has attempted to argue that there are gender-neutral usages of terms which are also masculine — "he" and "man." Given a Gricean theory of meaning, it would seem that at least some of the intended usages will carry over through recognition and that the terms will have a gender-neutral meaning in a given context. By the same token, there are at least some gender-neutral terms which seem to have no connotations of masculinity, although they are frequently used to apply to males, *e.g.*, Korsmeyer's "singer" and "teacher."

It may well be the case that the larger problem for the gender-neutral use of masculine terms is one of intent. It may be that the speaker fails to make his or her intent obvious by providing insufficient or ambiguous context, or that a term is used deliberately so that a humorous one can follow it, thereby casting the term originally used in a different light. The use of gender-neutral terms — if they are to be kept gender-neutral — requires a keen awareness of context and a reservoir of good faith.

NOTES

1. Janice Moulton, "The Myth of the Neutral 'Man', " in *Feminism and Philosophy*, Mary Vetterling-Braggin *et al*, eds. (Totowa, N.J.: Littlefield, Adams and Co., 1977), p. 126 (p. 102 in this volume).
2. Moulton herself makes note of this, p. 130 (p. 105 in this volume).
3. H.P. Grice, "Meaning," *Philosophical Review*, LXVI, no. 3 (July 1957).
4. Moulton, *op. cit.*, p. 131 (p. 107 in this volume).
5. Grice, *op. cit.*, p. 383.
6. H.P. Grice, "Logic and Conversation," in *Syntax and Semantics,* vol. 3, Peter Cole and Jerry L. Morgan, eds. (New York: Academic Press, 1975).
7. Moulton, *op. cit.*, p. 131 (p. 107 in this volume).
8. *Ibid.*, p. 132 (pp. 108 in this volume).
9. *Ibid.*, p. 133 (p. 109 in this volume).
10. *Ibid.*
11. *Ibid.*
12. *Ibid.*
13. Caroline Korsmeyer, "The Hidden Joke: Generic Uses of Masculine Terminology," in *Feminism and Philosophy*, Mary Vetterling-Braggin *et al,* eds. (Totowa, N.J.: Littlefield, Adams and Co., 1977), p. 142 (p. xxx in this volume).
14. *Ibid.*, p. 143 (p. 121 in this volume).
15. *Ibid.*, p. 145 (p. 123 in this volume).
16. *Ibid.*, p. 147 (p. 125 in this volume).

Elizabeth Lane Beardsley

Degenderization

I have defined the term "genderization" elsewhere as "the linguistic practice of requiring a sex-distinction in discourse about human beings, in such a way that to disregard the sex-distinction produces a locution which is incorrect . . . or inappropriate. . . ."[1] Not surprisingly, there has proved to be considerable divergence of opinion concerning the criteria used for determining whether a locution is "inappropriate."

In this paper I shall discuss certain expressions whose status as genderized has been a matter of dispute. I shall be concerned here, not with expressions defined in terms of a sex-distinction (S-D terms), but rather with expressions which, though not defined as S-D, have nevertheless been charged by some with possessing some feature that renders their application to members of one sex or the other inappropriate. These latter expressions, while admittedly not S-D, are held to fall short of full sex-neutral (S-N) status.[2] They can be said to exhibit "secondary genderization," and to present problems for ordinary language. That is to say, they call for "degenderization," so that language may cease to reinforce sexist beliefs and practices in our society.

In what follows I want to single out for examination one group of expressions that have been regarded by some as falling short of full S-N status and hence as candidates for degenderization. In Section I, I shall discuss the question whether these particular expressions should be said to be genderized at all. In Section II, I shall consider the relative merits of alternative tactics for degenderization, to be used wherever it is deemed to be needed.

I

The class of expressions to be examined in this paper consists of nouns ending in the syllable "-man." Since controversy has centered largely on one such noun, it will serve sell as a focus for discussion. The word is "chairman." Some language-users call for its replacement by "chairperson," while others firmly resist this move. The dispute has been conducted at so informal a level that the assumptions of the disputants have been articulated rarely, if ever. It is instructive, however, to try to formulate them.

The partisans of "chairperson" evidently believe that "chairman" carries a sufficient taint of genderization to make it objectionable. They have not argued, so far as I know, that the word is *defined* in terms of a sex-distinction. Presumably they would accept as faithful to common usage an ordinary dictionary definition such as *"chairman:* one who presides over an assembly, meeting, etc."[3] It is the ending "-man" that is deemed to carry the full force of the alleged genderization; and the ending has evidently not been powerful enough to produce a word that is S-D by definition.

We must ask whether it can simply be taken for granted that "-man" used as an ending violates the S-N character in words in which it appears. Those who would degenderize "chairman" will reply that "-man" has the grammatical status of a suffix, i.e., that it is rule-linked with a distinction of some sort. What could this be, they will ask, but a distinction of sex? Here the partisans of "chairperson" may be invited to look again at the definition of "chairman" quoted above. Those who accept this definition can provide an alternative account of "-man" as a suffix--one, moreover, that is congruent with the definition of the total word: "-man" is here a suffix of agency. A "chairman," i.e., is "one who chairs." The S-N definition of "chairman" is not in conflict with its ending, since the ending itself has a S-N force, denoting not sex but agency.

Two objections (at least) will be raised to what has just been said. First, that since the notion that there can be a geniunely S-N use of the word "man" is a "myth,"[4] the notion that "-man" can be used as a suffix of S-N agency is likewise mythical. Arguments developed about *words*, however, do not entail conclusions about *suffixes*. Accordingly, those who argue that the purportedly S-N use of the words "man" and "he" is self-defeating[5] may without inconsistency argue that "-man" can be used as a S-N suffix. No one can claim that S-D words have been pressed into service as suffixes in an even-handed fashion, of course — but that is another matter.

A second possible objection to my account of "-man" as a suffix is that, given the pervasive assumption in our society that agents are male, the construal of the ending "-man" as a suffix of agency does not really eliminate the secondary genderization of "chairman." To deal fully with this objection is not possible here, but certain points may be noted.

For many purposes, it is indeed illuminating to point out the extent to which the agent/patient distinction has been linked to the male/female distinction. Without understanding this, readers of contemporary feminist literature are very likely to misunderstand certain themes, such as the justification of violence. A recent article by the usually perceptive moral critic Henry Fairlie demonstrates this misunderstanding.[6]

For our present purpose, however, the question is how best to deal with the link in language between agency and maleness. The total avoidance of "-man" as a suffix of agency is based on a perception of the link as too strong to break. Other techniques of linguistic reform are based on an assumption that the link can be broken. It is now time to examine these other techniques, i.e., to discuss tactics for degenderization.

II

One tactic would be to allow as a suffix of agency only those endings which, considered as words, are S-N. This is, of course, the tactic of those who would replace "chairman" by "chairperson." Let us call this the tactic of "reconstructive degenderization" (RD).

A second tactic would be to show contextually, wherever possible, that a word ending in "-man" is being applied to a female. This linguistic tactic, to be maximally effective, may require real-world efforts aimed at enlarging, e.g., the class of female chairmen to be spoken of; but since these efforts can be justified on other grounds they need not be faulted in the present connection. Let us call the tactic of increasing the frequency of explicit application of "chairman" to females the tactic of "contextual degenderization" (CD). Note that this tactic has a use for preventing genderization as well as for combatting it where it exists. Thus even those who argue, as I have done in

Section I, that "chairman" does not exhibit either primary or secondary genderization may support CD as a preventive measure for this term.

There are words which though not genderized either by definition or by some syntactical feature such as a suffix, have acquired a kind of mock-genderized status by being applied almost exclusively to members of one sex. An example is "nurse." These words may be said to exhibit "tertiary genderization." When a man is a nurse, he is said to be a "male nurse." Contextual degenderization of "nurse" would, if skillfully and persistently used, obviate the felt need for expressions like "male nurse" (or "woman doctor").

A fundamentally different approach to the problem of how to weaken the link between agency and maleness would be to introduce for every activity-word ending in "-man" a parallel word ending in "-woman." This approach is plainly not a tactic for degenderization at all, but rather for a genderization that would be more equitable than what we now have. Let us call this the method of "parallel genderization" (PG). Even if its appallingly cumbersome features could be tolerated, its inferiority to degenderization (by whatever tactic) seems clear. The rationale for degenderization is the thesis that in much discourse about human beings, sex-distinctions are simply unnecessary and irrelevant. Parallel genderization may seem to promote equity, but the claim that equity will in the long run be better served by degenderization is not open to serious dispute.

Now, given that degenderization is desirable where genderization is deemed to exist, the choice of tactics remains. The advantages of CD over RD seem to me very clear.

English does not provide a suitably colloquial S-N ending to replace "-man." The use of "-person" as a suffix is cumbersome. Far worse, it debases moral discourse by undermining the distinction between "person" as "human being" and "person" as "moral agent and bearer of moral rights."[7] The latter concept is too important to risk cheapening it by talk of "chairpersons." Moreover, the clarification and preservation of a concept of moral personhood will do more to rectify any injustices done to members of the second sex than will any other philosophic enterprise.

CD has the advantage of not being cumbersome, and the advantage of risking no damage to the concept of personhood. It also bids fair to be an effective tactic for degenderization. Even in the case of words defined in terms of a sex-distinction it is a powerful linguistic device. Consider, for example, the recent news stories reporting that a female Russian dancer returned home to "a hero's welcome." (A recent headline in the *Yale Alumni Magazine* proclaimed "Phyllis Curtin to Be New Master at Branford College."[8]) Finally, consider the growing practice of referring to distinguished female stage performers as "actors." Here one must note wryly that lists of "best performances" may yield to degenderization rather slowly. Should we say that, even though all dramatic performers can (and should) be classified as "actors," different standards of excellence are required for appraising "best actors" and "best actresses"? This is a question that merits further discussion.[9]

The process of contextual degenderization is one that must be carried on over time, and at any given moment there will be some words for which it will be judged to have succeeded and some for which it will not. (It is worth keeping in mind that this process has stricken from the language such words, in common use a century ago, as "poetess" and "sculptress.") The chief thesis of this paper is that where genderization (of either primary or secondary form) is deemed to be present, CD should be tried. For some of us, "chairman" is not a genderized term. Its ending is no more noticeable than the ending of a surname such as "Silverman" or "Chapman" (even though it is true for proper nouns as well as for general nouns that etymology encapsulates social history).

Those who can attend to the ending of "chairman" only by making a direct effort may be tempted to charge the partisans of "chairperson" with being excessively literal. One thinks of a witty and tough-minded character in a recent crime novel who, when told she was a "godsend," replied, "Please, no mythology."[10] To the statement, "We need a new chairman," the reply "Please, no sexism" would not be regarded as a joke by many today. But perhaps it should be, and in this paper I have tried to show which steps toward producing that climate of opinion ought to be taken, and which ought not.

NOTES

1. E. L. Beardsley, "Traits and Genderization," in *Feminism and Philosophy*, Mary Vetterling-Braggin, Fred Elliston, and Jane English, eds. (Littlefield, Adams & Co.: Totowa 1977), p. 117.
2. These terms and abbreviations were introduced in my "Referential Genderization," *Philosophical Forum*, 5 (1973-74): 285-93.
3. This definition is taken from the *American Heritage Dictionary*.
4. See Janice Moulton, "The Myth of the Neutral 'Man'," in *Feminism and Philosophy*, *op. cit.*, pp. 124-37.
5. I argue this in "Referential Genderization."
6. See his "On the Humanity of Women," *The Public Interest*, 23 (1971): 16-32.
7. An important treatment of this distinction is given by A. I. Melden in *Rights and Persons*, (Oxford, England: Blackwell International, 1977). See also Mary Anne Warren "On the Moral and Legal Status of Abortion," in T. Mappes and J. Zembaty, eds. *Social Ethics*, (New York: McGraw Hill), pp. 17-23.
8. *Yale Alumni Magazine*, June 1979, p. 23.
9. Genderization in its "characterizing" mode seems to be involved here; see my "Traits and Genderization."
10. This exchange is quoted by Newgate Calendar in his review of Roger L. Simon, *Peking Duck*, in *The New York Times Book Review*, July 22, 1979, p. 17.

Terms Describing Sexual Intercourse

Robert Baker

"Pricks" And "Chicks": A Plea For "Persons"

There is a school of philosophers who believe that one starts philosophizing not by examining whatever it is one is philosophizing about but by examining the words we use to designate the subject to be examined. I must confess my allegiance to this school. The import of my confession is that this is an essay on women's liberation.

There seems to be a curious malady that affects those philosophers who, in order to analyze anything, must examine the way we talk about it. They seem incapable of talking about anything without talking about their talk about it — and, once again, I must confess to being typical. Thus I shall argue, first, that the way in which we identify something reflects our conception of it; second, that the conception of women embedded in our langauge is male chauvinistic; third, that the conceptual revisions proposed by the feminist movement are confused; and finally, that at the root of the problem are both our conception of sex and the very structure of sexual identification.

I. IDENTIFICATION AND CONCEPTION

I am not going to defend the position that the terms we utilize to identify something reflect our conception of it; I shall simply explain and illustrate a simplified version of this thesis. Let us assume that any term that can be (meaningfully) substituted for x in the following statements is a term used to identify something: "Where is the x?" "Who is the x?" Some of the terms that can be substituted for x in the above expressions are metaphors; I shall refer to such metaphors as metaphorical identifications. For example, southerners frequently say such things as "Where did that girl get to?" and "Who is the new boy that Lou hired to help out at the filling station?" If the persons the terms apply to are adult Afro-Americans, then "girl" and "boy" are metaphorical identifications. The fact that the metaphorical identifications in question are standard in the language reflects the fact that certain characteristics of the objects properly classified as boys and girls (for example, immaturity, inability to take care of themselves, need for guidance) are generally held by those who use identifications to be properly attributable to Afro-Americans. One might say that the whole theory of southern white paternalism is implicit in the metaphorical identification "boy" (just as the rejection of paternalism is implicit in the standardized Afro-American forms of address, "man" and "woman," as in, for example, "Hey, man, how are you?").

Most of what I am going to say in this essay is significant only if the way we metaphorically identify something is not a superficial bit of conceptually irrelevant happenstance but rather a reflection of our conceptual structure. Thus if one is to accept my analysis he must understand the significance of metaphorical identifications. He must see that, even though the southerner who identifies adult Afro-American males as "boys" feels that this identification is "just the way people talk"; but for a group to talk that way it must think that way. In the next few paragraphs I shall adduce what I hope is a persuasive example of how, in one clear case, the change in the way we identified something reflected a change in the way we thought about it.

Until the 1960s, Afro-Americans were identified by such terms as "Negro" and "colored" (the respectable terms) and by the more disreputable "nigger," "spook," "kink," and so on.

Recently there has been an unsuccessful attempt to replace the respectable identifications with such terms as "African," and "Afro-American," and a more successful attempt to replace them with "black." The most outspoken champions of this linguistic reform were those who argued that nonviolence must be abandoned for Black Power (Stokely Carmichael, H. Rap Brown), that integration must be abandoned in favor of separation (the Black Muslims: Malcolm X, Muhammad Ali), and that Afro-Americans were an internal colony in the alien world of Babylon who must arm themselves against the possibility of extermination (the Black Panthers: Eldridge Cleaver, Huey Newton). All of these movements and their partisans wished to stress that Afro-Americans were different from other Americans and could not be merged with them because the difference between the two was as great as that between black and white. Linguistically, of course, "black" and "white" are antonyms; and it is precisely this sense of oppositeness that those who see the Afro-American as alienated, separated, and nonintegratable wish to capture with the term "black." Moreover, as any good dictionary makes clear, in some contexts "black" is synonymous with "deadly," "sinister," "wicked," "evil," and so forth. The new militants were trying to create just this picture of the black man — civil rights and Uncle Tomism are dead, the ghost of Nat Turner is to be resurrected, freedom now or pay the price, the ballot or the bullet, violence is as American as cherry pie. — The new strategy was that the white man would either give the black man his due or pay the price in violence. Since conceptually a "black man" was an object to be feared ("black" can be synonymous with "deadly," and so on), while a "colored man" or a "Negro" was not, the new strategy required that the "Negro" be supplanted by the "black man." White America resisted the proposed linguistic reform quite vehemently, until hundreds of riots forced the admission that the Afro-American was indeed black.

Now to the point: I have suggested that the word "black" replaced the word "Negro" because there was a change in our conceptual structure. One is likely to reply that while all that I have said above is well and good, one had, after all, no choice about the matter. White people are identified in terms of their skin color as whites; clearly, if we are to recognize what is in reality nothing but the truth, that in this society people are conscious of skin color, to treat blacks as equals is merely to identify them by their skin color, which is black. That is, one might argue that while there was a change in words, we have no reason to think that there was a parallel conceptual change. If the term "black" has all the associations mentioned above, that is unfortunate; but in the context the use of the term "black" to identify the people formerly identified as "Negroes" is natural, inevitable, and, in and of itself, neutral; black is, after all, the skin color of the people in question. (Notice that this defense of the natural-inevitable-and-neutral conception of identification quite nicely circumvents the possible use of such seemingly innocuous terms as "Afro-American" and "African" by suggesting that in this society it is *skin color* that is the relevant variable.)

The great flaw in this analysis is that the actual skin color of virtually all of the people whom we call "black" is not black at all. The color tones range from light yellow to a deep umber that occasionally is literally black. The skin color of most Afro-Americans is best designated by the word "brown." Yet "brown" is not a term that is standard for identifying Afro-Americans. For example, if someone asked, "Who was the brown who was the architect for Washington, D.C.?" we would not know how to construe the question. We might attempt to read "brown" as a proper name (Do you mean Arthur Brown, the designer?"). We would have no trouble understanding the sentence "Who was the black (Negro, colored guy, and so forth) who designed Washington, D.C.?" ("Oh, you mean Benjamin Banneker.") Clearly, "brown" is not a standard form of identification for Afro-Americans. I hope that it is equally clear that "black" has become the standard way of identifying Afro-Americans not because the term was natural, inevitable, and, in the context, neutral, but because of its occasional synonymy with "sinister" and because as an antonym to "white" it best fitted the conceptual needs of those who saw race relations in terms of intensifying and insurmountable antonyms. If one accepts this point, then one must admit that there is a close connection between the way in which we identify things and the way in which we conceive them — and thus it should be also clear why I wish to talk about the way in which women are identified in English.[1] (Thus, for example, one would expect Black Muslims, who continually use the term "Black *man*" — as in "the black *man's* rights" — to be more male chauvinistic than Afro-

Americans who use the term "black *people*" or "black *folk.*")

II. WAYS OF IDENTIFYING WOMEN

It may at first seem trivial to note that women (and men) are identified sexually; but conceptually this is extremely significant. To appreciate the significance of this fact it is helpful to imagine a language in which proper names and personal pronouns do not reflect the sex of the person designated by them (as they do in our language). I have been told that in some oriental languages pronouns and proper names reflect social status rather than sex, but whether or not there actually exists such a language is irrelevant, for it is easy enough to imagine what one would be like. Let us then imagine a language where the proper names are sexually neutral (for example, "Xanthe"), so that one cannot tell from hearing a name whether the person so named is male or female, and where the personal pronouns in the language are "under" and "over." "Under" is the personal pronoun appropriate for all those who are younger than thirty, while "over" is appropriate to persons older than thirty. In such a language, instead of saying such things as "Where do you think *he* is living now?" one would say such things as "Where do you think *under* is living now?"

What would one say about a cultural community that employed such a language? Clearly, one would say that they thought that for purposes of intelligible communication it was more important to know a person's age grouping than the person's height, sex, race, hair color, or parentage. (There are many actual cultures, of course, in which people are identified by names that reflect their parentage; for example, Abu ben Adam means Abu son of Adam.) I think that one would also claim that this people would not have reflected these differences in the pronominal structure of their language if they did not believe that the differences between unders and overs was such that a statement would frequently have one meaning if it were about an under and a different meaning if it were about an over. For example, in feudal times if a serf said, "My lord said to do this," that assertion was radically different from "Freeman John said to do this," since (presumably) the former had the status of a command while the latter did not. Hence the conventions of Middle English required that one refer to people in such a way as to indicate their social status. Analogously, one would not distinguish between pronominal references according to the age differences in the persons referred to were there no shift in meaning involved.

If we apply the lesson illustrated by this imaginary language to our own, I think that it should be clear that since in our language proper nouns and pronouns reflect sex rather than age, race, parentage, social status, or religion, we believe one of the most important things one can know about a person is that person's sex. (And, indeed, this is the first thing one seeks to determine about a newborn babe — our first question is almost invariably "Is it a boy or a girl?") Moreover, we would not reflect this important difference pronominally did we not also believe that statements frequently mean one thing when applied to males and something else when applied to females. Perhaps the most striking aspect of the conceptual discrimination reflected in our language is that man is, as it were, essentially human, while woman is only accidentally so.

This charge may seem rather extreme, but consider the following synonyms (which are readily confirmed by any dictionary). "Humanity" is synonymous with "mankind" but not with "womankind." "Man" can be substituted for "humanity" or "mankind" in any sentence in which the terms "mankind" or "humanity" occur without changing the meaning of the sentence, but significantly, "woman" cannot. Thus, the following expressions are all synonymous with each other: "humanity's great achievements," "mankind's great achievements," and "man's great achievements." "Woman's great achievements" is not synonymous with any of these. To highlight the degree to which women are excluded from humanity, let me point out that it is something of a truism to say that "man is a rational animal," while "woman is a rational animal" is quite debatable. Clearly, if "man" in the first assertion embraced both men and women, the second assertion would be just as much a truism as the first.[2] Humanity, it would seem, is a male prerogative. (And hence, one of the goals of woman's liberation is to alter our conceptual structure so that someday "mankind" will be regarded as an improper and vestigial ellipsis for "humankind," and "man" will have no special privileges in relation to "human being" that "woman" does not have.[3])

The major question before us is, "How are women conceived of in our culture?" I have been trying to answer this question by talking about how they are identified. I first considered pronominal identification; now I wish to turn to identification through other types of noun phrases. Methods of non-pronominal identification can be discovered by determining which terms can be substituted for "woman" in such sentences as "Who is that woman over there?" without changing the meaning of the sentence. Virtually no term is interchangeable with "woman" in that sentence for all speakers on all occasions. Even "lady," which most speakers would accept as synonymous with "woman" in that sentence, will not do for a speaker who applies the term "lady" only to those women who display manners, poise, and sensitivity. In most contexts, a large number of students in one or more of my classes will accept the following types of terms as more or less interchangeable with "woman." (An asterisk indicates interchanges acceptable to both males and females; a plus sign indicates terms restricted to black students only. Terms with neither an asterisk nor a plus sign are acceptable by all males but are not normally used by females.)

A. NEUTRAL TERMS: *lady, *gal, *girl (especially with regard to a co-worker in an office or factory), * + sister, *broad (originally in the animal category, but most people do not think of the term as now meaning pregnant cow)

B. ANIMAL: *chick, bird, fox, vixen, filly, bitch (Many do not know the literal meaning of the term. Some men and most women construe this use as pejorative; they think of "bitch" in the context of "bitchy," that is, snappy, nasty, and so forth. But a large group of men claim that it is a standard nonpejorative term of identification — which may perhaps indicate that women have come to be thought of as shrews by a large subclass of men.)

C. PLAYTHING: babe, doll, cuddly

D. GENDER (association with articles of clothing typically worn by those in the female gender role): skirt, hem

E. SEXUAL: snatch, cunt, ass, twat, piece (of ass, and so forth), lay, pussy (could be put in the animal category, but most users associated it with slang expression indicating the female pubic region), + hammer (related to anatomical analogy between a hammer and breasts). There are many other usages, for example, "bunny," "sweat hog," but these were not recognized as standard by as many as ten percent of any given class.

The students in my classes reported that the most frequently used terms of identification are in the neutral and animal classifications (although men in their forties claim to use the gender classifications quite a bit) and that the least frequently used terms of identification are sexual. Fortunately, however, I am not interested in the frequency of usage but only in whether the use is standard enough to be recognized as an identification among some group or other. (Recall that "brown" was not a standardized term of identification and hence we could not make sense out of "Who was the brown who planned Washington, D.C.?" Similarly, one has trouble with "Who was the breasts who planned Washington, D.C.?" but not with "Who was the babe (doll, chick, skirt, and so forth) who planned Washington, D.C.?")

Except for two of the animal terms, "chick" and "broad" — but note that "broad" is probably neutral today — women do not typically identify themselves in sexual terms, in gender terms, as playthings, or as animals; *only males use nonneutral terms to identify women.* Hence, it would seem that there is a male conception of women and a female conception. Only males identify women as "foxes," "babes," "skirts," or "cunts" (and since all the other nonneutral identifications are male, it is reasonable to assume that the identification of a woman as a "chick" is primarily a male conception that some women have adopted).

What kind of conception do men have of women? Clearly they think that women share certain properties with certain types of animals, toys, and playthings; they conceive of them in terms of the clothes associated with the female gender role; and, last (and, if my classes are any indication, least frequently), they conceive of women in terms of those parts of their anatomy associated with sexual intercourse, that is, as the identification "lay" indicates quite clearly, as sexual partners.

The first two nonneutral male classifications, animal and plaything, are *prima facie* denigrating (and I mean this in the literal sense of making one like a "nigger"). Consider the animal classification. All of the terms listed, with the possible exception of "bird," refer to animals that are either domesticated for servitude (to *man*) or hunted for sport. First, let us consider the term "bird." When I asked my students what sort of birds might be indicated, they suggested chick, canary (one member, in his forties, had suggested "canary" as a term of identification), chicken, pigeon, dove, parakeet, and hummingbird (one member). With the exception of the hummingbird, which like all the birds suggested is generally thought to be diminutive and pretty, all of the birds are domesticated, usually as pets (which reminds one that "my pet" is an expression of endearment). None of the birds were predators or symbols of intelligence or nobility (as are the owl, eagle, hawk, and falcon); nor did large but beautiful birds seem appropriate (for example, pheasants, peacocks, and swans). If one construes the bird terms (and for that matter, "filly") as applicable to women because they are thought of as beautiful, or at least pretty, *then there is nothing denigrating about them.* If, on the other hand, the common properties that underlie the metaphorical identification are domesticity and servitude, then they are indeed denigrating (as for myself, I think that both domesticity and prettiness underlie the identification). "Broad," of course, is, or at least was, clearly denigrating, since nothing renders more service to a farmer than does a pregnant cow, and cows are not commonly thought of as paradigms of beauty.

With one exception all of the animal terms reflect a male conception of women either as domesticated servants or as pets, or as both. Indeed, some of the terms reflect a conception of women first as pets and then as servants. Thus, when a pretty, cuddly little chick grows older, she becomes a very useful servant — the egg-laying hen.

"Vixen" and "fox," variants of the same term, are the one clear exception. None of the other animals with whom women are metaphorically identified are generally thought to be intelligent, aggressive, or independent — but the fox is. A chick is a soft, cuddly, entertaining, pretty, diminutive, domesticated, and dumb animal. A fox too is soft, cuddly, entertaining, pretty, and diminutive, but it is neither dependent nor dumb. It is aggressive, intelligent, and a minor predator — indeed, it preys on chicks — and frequently outsmarts ("outfoxes") men.

Thus the term "fox" or "vixen" is generally taken to be a compliment by both men and women, and compared to any of the animal or plaything terms it is indeed a compliment. Yet considered in and of itself, the conception of a woman as a fox is not really complimentary at all, for the major connection between *man* and fox is that of predator and prey. The fox is an animal that men chase, and hunt, and kill for sport. If women are conceived of as foxes, then they are conceived of as prey that it is fun to hunt.

In considering plaything identifications, only one sentence is necessary. *All the plaything identifications are clearly denigrating since they assimilate women to the status of mindless or dependent objects.* "Doll" is to male paternalism what "boy" is to white paternalism.

Up to this point in our survey of male conceptions of women, every male identification, without exception, has been clearly antithetical to the conception of women as human beings (recall that "man" was synonymous with "human," while "woman" was not). Since the way we talk of things, and especially the way we identify them, is the way in which we conceive of them, any movement dedicated to breaking the bonds of female servitude must destroy these ways of identifying and hence of conceiving of women. Only when both sexes find the terms "babe," "doll," "chick," "broad," and so forth, as objectionable as "boy" and "nigger" will women come to be conceived of as independent *human beings*.

The two remaining unexamined male identifications are gender and sex. There seems to be nothing objectionable about gender identifications per se. That is, women are metaphorically identified as skirts because in this culture, skirts, like women, are peculiarly female. Indeed, if one accepts the view that the slogan "female and proud" should play the same role for the women's liberation movement that the slogan "Black is beautiful" plays for the black-liberation movement, then female clothes should be worn with the same pride as Afro clothes. (Of course, one can argue that the skirt, like the cropped-down Afro, is a sign of bondage, and hence both the item of clothing and the identification with it are to be rejected — that is, cropped-down Afros are to Uncle Tom what skirts are to Uncle Mom.)

The terms in the last category are obviously sexual, and frequently vulgar. For a variety of reasons I shall consider the import and nature of these identifications in the next section.

III. MEN OUGHT NOT TO THINK OF WOMEN AS SEX OBJECTS

Feminists have proposed many reforms, and most of them are clearly desirable, for example, equal opportunity for self-development, equal pay for equal work, and free day-care centers. One feminist proposal, however, is peculiarly conceptual and deeply perplexing. I call this proposal peculiarly conceptual because unlike the other reforms it is directed at getting people to think differently. The proposal is that *men should not think of women (and women should not think of themselves) as sex objects*. In the rest of this essay I shall explore this nostrum. I do so for two reasons: first, because the process of exploration should reveal the depth of the problem confronting the feminists; and second, because the feminists themselves seem to be entangled in the very concepts that obstruct their liberation.

To see why I find this proposal puzzling, one has to ask what it is to think of something as a sex object.

If a known object is an object that we know, an unidentified object is an object that we have not identified, and a desired object is an object that we desire, what then is a sex object? Clearly, a sex object is an object we have sex with. Hence, to think of a woman as a sex object is to think of her as someone to have sexual relations with, and when the feminist proposed that men refrain from thinking of women in this way, *she is proposing that men not think of women as persons with whom one has sexual relations*.

What are we to make of this proposal? Is the feminist suggesting that women should not be conceived of in this way because such a conception is "dirty"? To conceive of sex and sex organs as dirty is simply to be a prude. "Shit" is the paradigm case of a dirty word. It is a dirty word because the item it designates is taboo; it is literally unclean and untouchable (as opposed to something designated by what I call a curse word, which is not untouchable but rather something to be feared — "damn" and "hell" are curse words; "piss" is a dirty word). If one claims that "cunt" (or "fuck") is a dirty word, then one holds that what this term designates is unclean and taboo; thus one holds that the terms for sexual intercourse or sexual organs are dirty, one has accepted puritanism. If one is a puritan and a feminist, then indeed one ought to subscribe to the slogan *men should not conceive of women as sexual objects*. What is hard to understand is why anyone but a puritan (or, perhaps, a homosexual) would promulgate this slogan; yet most feminists, who are neither lesbians nor puritans, accept this slogan. Why?

A word about slogans: Philosophical slogans have been the subject of considerable analysis. They have the peculiar property (given a certain seemingly sound background story) of being obviously true, yet obviously false. "Men should not conceive of women as sex objects" is, I suggest, like a philosophical slogan in this respect. The immediate reaction of any humanistically oriented person upon first hearing the slogan is to agree with it — yet the more one probes the meaning of the slogan, the less likely one is to give one's assent. Philosophical analysts attempt to separate out the various elements involved in such slogans — to render the true-false slogan into a series of statements, some of which are true, some of which are false, and others of which are, perhaps, only probable. This is what I am trying to do with the slogan in question. I have argued so far that one of the elements that seems to be implicit in the slogan is a rejection of women as sexual partners for men and that although this position might be proper for a homosexual or puritanical movement, it seems inappropriate to feminism. I shall proceed to show that at least two other interpretations of the slogan lead to inappropriate results; but I shall argue that there are at least two respects in which the slogan is profoundly correct — even if misleadingly stated.

One plausible, but inappropriate, interpretation of "men ought not to conceive of women as sex objects" is that men ought not to conceive of women *exclusively* as sexual partners. The problem with this interpretation is that everyone can agree with it. Women are conceived of as companions, toys, servants, and even sisters, wives and mothers — and hence not exclusively as sexual partners. Thus this slogan loses its revisionary impact, since even a male chauvinist could accept the slogan without changing his conceptual structure in any way — which is only to say that men do not usually identify or conceive of women as sexual partners (recall that the sexual method of identification is the least frequently used).

Yet another interpretation is suggested by the term "object" in "sex object," and this interpretation too has a certain amount of plausibility. Men should not treat women as animate machines designed to masturbate men or as conquests that allow men to "score" for purposes of building their egos. Both of these variations rest on the view that to be treated as an object is to be treated as less than human (that is, to be treated as a machine or a score). Such relations between men and women are indeed immoral, and there are, no doubt, men who believe in "scoring." Unfortunately, however, this interpretation — although it would render the slogan quite apt — also fails because of its restricted scope. When feminists argue that men should not treat women as sex objects, they are not *only* talking about fraternity boys and members of the Playboy Club; they are talking about all males in our society. The charge is that in our society men treat women as sex objects rather than as persons; it is this universality of scope that is lacking from the present interpretation. *Nonetheless, one of the reasons that we are prone to assent to the unrestricted charge that men treat women as sex objects is that the restricted charge is entirely correct.*

One might be tempted to argue that the charge that men treat women as sex objects is correct since such a conception underlies the most frequently used identifications, as animal and plaything; that is, these identifications indicate a sexual context in which the female is used as an object. Thus, it might be argued that the female fox is chased and slayed if she is four-legged, but chased and laid if she is two. Even if one admits the sexual context *implicit* in *some* animal and plaything identifications, one will not have the generality required; because, for the most part, the plaything and animal identifications themselves are nonsexual — most of them do not involve a sexual context. A pregnant cow, a toy doll, or a filly are hardly what one would call erotic objects. Babies do not normally excite sexual passion; and anyone whose erotic interests are directed toward chicks, canaries, parakeets, or other birds is clearly perverse. The animals and playthings to whom women are assimilated in the standard metaphorical identifications are not symbols of desire, eroticism, or passion (as, for example, a bull might be).

What is objectionable in the animal and plaything identifications is not the fact that some of these identifications reflect a sexual context but rather that — regardless of the context — these identifications reflect a conception of women as mindless servants (whether animate or inanimate is irrelevant). The point is not that men ought not to think of women in sexual terms but that they ought to think of them as human beings; and the slogan *men should not think of women as sex objects* is only appropriate when a man thinking of a woman as a sexual partner automatically conceives of her as something less than human. The point about *sex objects* is not merely that it is inappropriate for a man, when, for example, listening to a woman deliver a serious academic paper, to imagine having sexual intercourse with the woman; it is inappropriate, of course, but much in the same way that it is inappropriate to imagine playing tennis with the speaker. The difference between a tennis partner and a sex partner is that whereas there is nothing degrading about a woman's being thought of as a tennis partner, there seems to be something *degrading* about her being thought of as a man's sex partner in our society — at least outside of the circumscribed context of a love relationship. (Note that it would be inappropriate, but not necessarily degrading to the woman, for a man in the audience to imagine courting the woman, having an affair with the woman, or marrying the woman; it does degrade the woman for the man to mentally undress the woman, or imagine an act of sexual intercourse between them.) The reason why unadorned sexual partnership is degrading to the female is that in this relationship the female is conceptualized, and treated not merely as a mindless thing productive of male pleasure, but as an *object* in the Kantian sense of the term — as a person whose autonomy has been violated. Or, to put the point differently, the reason why it is degrading for a woman to be conceptualized as a sexual partner is because *rape* is our paradigm of unadorned sexual intercourse.

IV. OUR CONCEPTION OF SEXUAL INTERCOURSE

Consider the terms we use to identify coitus, or more technically, the terms that function synonymously with "had sexual intercourse with" in a sentence of the form "A had sexual intercourse with B." The following is a list of some commonly used synonyms (numerous others that are not as widely used have been omitted, for example, "diddled," "laid pipe with"):

> screwed
> laid
> fucked
> had
> did it with (to)
> banged
> balled
> humped
> slept with
> made love to

Now, for a select group of these verbs, names for males are the subjects of sentences with active constructions (that is, where the subjects are said to be doing the activity); and names for females require passive constructions (that is, they are the recipients of the activity — whatever is done is done to them). Thus, we would not say "Jane did it to Dick," although we would say

"Dick did it to Jane." Again, Dick bangs Jane, Jane does not
bang Dick; Dick humps Jane, Jane does not hump Dick. In contrast, verbs like "did it with" do not require an active role for
the male; thus, "Dick did it with Jane and Jane with Dick."
Again, Jane may make love to Dick, just as Dick makes love to
Jane; and Jane sleeps with Dick as easily as Dick sleeps with
Jane. (My students were undecided about "laid." Most thought
that it would be unusual indeed for Jane to lay Dick, unless she
played the masculine role of seducer-agressor.)

The sentences thus form the following pairs. (Those noncon-
joined singular noun phrases where a female subject requires a
passive construction are marked with a cross. An asterisk indicates that the sentence in question is not a sentence of English
if it is taken as synonymous with the italicized sentence heading
the column.[4]

>*Dick had sexual intercourse with Jane*
> Dick screwed Jane +
> Dick laid Jane +
> Dick fucked Jane +
> Dick had Jane +
> Dick did it to Jane +
> Dick banged Jane +
> Dick humped Jane +
> Dick balled Jane (?)
> Dick did it with Jane
> Dick slept with Jane
> Dick made love to Jane

>*Jane had sexual intercourse with Dick*
> Jane was banged by Dick
> Jane was humped by Dick
> *Jane was done by Dick
> Jane was screwed by Dick
> Jane was laid by Dick
> Jane was fucked by Dick
> Jane was had by Dick
> Jane balled Dick (?)
> Jane did it with Dick
> Jane slept with Dick
> Jane made love to Dick

*Jane screwed Dick
*Jane laid Dick
*Jane fucked Dick
*Jane had Dick
*Jane did it to Dick
*Jane banged Dick
*Jane humped Dick

These lists make clear that within the standard view of sexual intercourse, males, or at least names for males, seem to play a different role than females, since male subjects play an active role in the language of screwing, fucking, having, doing it, and perhaps, laying, while female subjects play a passive role.

The asymmetrical nature of the relationship indicated by the sentences marked with a cross is confirmed by the fact that the form "__ed with each other" is acceptable for the sentences not marked with a cross, but not for those that require a male subject. Thus:

Dick and Jane had sexual intercourse with each other
Dick and Jane made love to each other
Dick and Jane slept with each other.
Dick and Jane did it with each other
Dick and Jane balled with each other (*?)
*Dick and Jane banged with each other
*Dick and Jane did it to each other
*Dick and Jane had each other
*Dick and Jane fucked each other
*Dick and Jane humped each other
*(?)Dick and Jane laid each other
*Dick and Jane screwed each other

It should be clear, therefore, that our language reflects a difference between the male and female sexual roles, and hence that we conceive of the male and female roles in different ways. The question that now arises is, "What difference in our conception of the male and female sexual roles requires active constructions for males and passive for females?"

One explanation for the use of the active construction for males and the passive construction for females is that this grammatical asymmetry merely reflects the natural physiological asymmetry between men and women: the asymmetry of "to screw" and "to be screwed," "to insert into" and "to be inserted into." That is, it might be argued that the difference between masculine and feminine grammatical roles merely reflects a difference naturally required by the anatomy of males and females. This explanation is inadequate. Anatomical differences do not determine how we are to conceptualize the relation between penis and vagina during intercourse. Thus one can easily imagine a society in which the female normally played the active role during intercourse, where female subjects required active constructions with verbs indicating copulation, and where the standard metaphors were terms like "engulfing" — that is, instead of saying "he screwed her," one would say "she engulfed him." It follows that the use of passive constructions for female subjects of verbs indicating copulation does not reflect differences determined by human anatomy but rather reflects those generated by human customs.

What I am going to argue next is that the passive construction of verbs indicating coitus (that is, indicating the female position) can *also* be used to indicate that a person is being harmed. I am then going to argue that the metaphor involved would only make sense if we conceive of the female role in intercourse as that of a person being harmed (or being taken advantage of).

Passive constructions of "fucked," "screwed," and "had" indicate the female role. They also can be used to indicate being harmed. Thus, in all of the following sentences, Marion plays the female role: "Bobbie fucked Marion"; "Bobbie screwed Marion"; "Bobbie had Marion"; "Marion was fucked"; "Marion was screwed"; and "Marion was had." All of the statements are equivocal. They might literally mean that someone had sexual intercourse with Marion (who played the female role); or they might mean, metaphorically, that Marion was deceived, hurt, or taken advantage of. Thus, we say things as "I've been screwed" ("fucked," "had," "taken," and so on) when we have been treated unfairly, been sold shoddy merchandise, or conned out of valuables. Throughout this essay I have been arguing that metaphors are applied to things only if what the term *actually* applies to shares one or more properties with what the term *metaphorically* applies to. Thus, the female sexual role must have something in common with being conned or being sold shoddy merchandise. The only common property is that of being harmed, deceived, or taken advantage of. *Hence we conceive of a person who plays the female sexual role as someone who is being harmed* (that is, "screwed," "fucked," and so on).

It might be objected that this is clearly wrong, since the unsignated terms do not indicate someone's being harmed, and hence we do not conceive of having intercourse as being harmed. The point about the unsigned terms, however, is that they can take both females and males as subjects (in active constructions) and thus *do not pick out the female role.* This demonstrates that we conceive of sexual roles in such a way that only females are thought to be taken advantage of in intercourse.

The best part of solving a puzzle is when all the pieces fall into place. If the subjects of the passive construction are being harmed, presumably the subjects of the active constructions are doing harm, and, indeed, we do conceive of these subjects in precisely this way. Suppose one is angry at someone and wishes to express malevolence as forcefully as possible without actually committing an act of physical violence. If one is inclined to be vulgar one can make the sign of the erect male cock by clenching one's fist while raising one's middle finger, or by clenching one's fist and raising one's arm and shouting such things as "screw you," "up yours," or "fuck you." In other words, one of the strongest possible ways of telling someone that you wish to harm him is to tell him to assume the female sexual role relative to you. Again, to say to someone "go fuck yourself" is to order him to harm himself, while to call someone a "mother fucker" is not so much a play on his Oedipal fears as to accuse him of being so low that he would inflict the greatest imaginable harm (fucking) upon that person who is most dear to him (his mother).

Clearly, we conceive of the male sexual role as that of hurting the person in the female role — but lest the reader have any doubts, let me provide two further bits of confirming evidence: one linguistic, one nonlinguistic. One of the English terms for a person who hurts (and takes advantage of) others is the term "prick." This metaphorical identification would not make sense unless the bastard in question (that is, the person outside the bonds of legitimacy) was thought to share some characteristics attributed to things that are literally pricks. As a verb, "prick" literally means "to hurt," as in "I pricked myself with a needle"; but the usage in question is as a noun. As a noun, "prick" is a colloquial term for "penis." Thus, the question before us is what characteristic is shared by a penis and a person who harms others (or, alternatively, by a penis and by being stuck by a needle). Clearly, no physical characteristic is relevant (physical characteristics might underlie the Yiddish metaphorical attribution "schmuck," but one would have to analyze Yiddish usage to determine this); hence the shared characteristic is nonphysical; the only relevant shared non-physical characteristic is that both a literal prick and a figurative prick are agents that harm people.

Now for the nonlinguistic evidence. Imagine two doors: in front of each door is a line of people; behind each door is a room; in each room is a bed; on each bed is a person. The line in front of one room consists of beautiful women, and on the bed in that room is a man having intercourse with each of these women in turn. One may think any number of things about this scene. One may say that the man is in heaven, or enjoying himself at a bordello; or perhaps one might only wonder at the oddness of it all. One does not think that the man is being hurt or violated or degraded — or at least the possibility does not immediately suggest itself, although one could conceive of situations where this was what was happening (especially, for example, if the man was impotent). Now, consider the other line. Imagine that the figure on the bed is a woman and that the line consists of handsome, smiling men. The woman is having intercourse with each of these men in turn. It immediately strikes one that the woman is being degraded, violated, and so forth — "that poor woman."

When one man fucks many women he is a playboy and gains status; when a woman is fucked by many men she degrades herself and loses stature.

Our conceptual inventory is now complete enough for us to return to the task of analyzing the slogan that men ought not to think of women as sex objects.

I think that it is now plausible to argue that the appeal of the slogan "men ought not to think of women as sex objects," and the thrust of much of the literature produced by contemporary feminists, turns on something much deeper than a rejection of "scoring" (that is, the utilization of sexual "conquests" to gain esteem) and yet is a call neither for homosexuality nor for puritanism.

The slogan is best understood as a call for a new conception of the male and female sexual roles. If the analysis developed above is correct, our present conception of sexuality is such that to be a man is to be a person capable of brutalizing women (witness the slogans "The marines will make a man out of you!" and "The army builds *men*!" which are widely accepted and which simply state that learning how to kill people will make a person more manly). Such a conception of manhood not only bodes ill for a society led by such men, but also is clearly inimical to the best interests of women. It is only natural for women to reject such a sexual role, and it would seem to be the duty of any moral person to support their efforts — to redefine our conceptions not only of fucking, but of the fucker (man) and the fucked (woman).

This brings me to my final point. We are a society preoccupied with sex. As I noted previously, the nature of proper nouns and pronouns in our language makes it difficult to talk about someone without indicating that person's sex. This convention would not be part of the grammar of our language if we did not believe that knowledge of a person's sex was crucial to understanding what is said about that person. Another way of putting this point is that sexual discrimination permeates our conceptual structure. Such discrimination is clearly inimical to any movement toward sexual egalitarianism and virtually defeats its purpose at the outset. (Imagine, for example, that black people were always referred to as "them" and whites as "us" and that proper names for blacks always had an "x" suffix at the end. Clearly any movement for integration as equals would require the removal of these discriminatory indicators. Thus at the height of the melting-pot era, immigrants Americanized their names: "Bellinsky" became "Bell," "Burnstein" became "Burns," and "Lubitch" became "Baker.")

I should therefore like to close this essay by proposing that contemporary feminists should advocate the utilization of neutral proper names and the elimination of gender from our language (as I have done in this essay); and they should vigorously protest any utilization of the third-person pronouns "he" and "she" as examples of sexist discrimination (perhaps "person" would be a good third-person pronoun) — for, as a parent of linguistic analysis once said, "The limits of our language are the limits of our world."

NOTES

1. The underlying techniques used in this essay were all developed primarily by Austin and Strawson) to deal with the problems of metaphysics and epistemology. All I have done is to attempt to apply them to other areas; I should note, however, that I rely rather heavily on metaphorical identifications, and that first philosophy tends not to require the analysis of such superficial aspects of language. Note also that it is an empirical matter whether or not people do use words in a certain way. In this essay I am just going to assume that the reader uses words more or less as my students do; for I gathered the data on which words we use to identify women, and so on, simply by asking students. If the reader does not use terms as my students do, then what I say may be totally inapplicable to him. The linguistic surveys on which this article is based were done on samples of student language at Wayne State University (Detroit) and Wayne County Community College (inner city centers: Detroit) during the 1970-71 academic year. A number of surveys conducted by students at Union College in 1973, and 1974 indicate different usages. Whereas in the first survey active female constructions for verbs indicating sexual intercourse (e.g. 'Jane laid Dick') were regarded as deviant, later surveys found these constructions to be acceptable. This may be explained by differences in the class structure (since Union College students are predominately white upper middle class, while WSU students are lower middle class and the WCCC students were from the black inner city), or by some more pervasive changes in conception of the woman's role.

2. It is also interesting to talk about the technical terms that philosophers use. One fairly standard bit of technical terminology is "trouser word." J. L. Austin invented this bit of jargon to indicate which term in a pair of antonyms is important. Austin called the important term a "trouser word" because "it is the use which wears the trousers." Even in the language of philosophy, to be important is to play the male role. Of course, the antifeminism implicit in the language of technical philosophy is hardly comparable to the male chauvinism embedded in commonplaces of ordinary discourse.

3. Although I thought it inappropriate to dwell on these matters in the text, it is quite clear that we do *not* associate many positions with females — as the following story brings out. I related this conundrum both to students in my regular courses and to students I teach in some experimental courses at a nearby community college. Among those students who had not previously heard the story, only native Swedes invariably resolved the problem; less than half of the students from an upper-class background would

get it (eventually), while lower-class and black students virtually never figured it out. Radical students, women, even members of women's liberation groups fared no better than anyone else with their same class background. The story goes as follows: A little boy is wheeled into the emergency room of a hospital. The surgeon on emergency call looks at the boy and says, "I'm sorry I cannot operate on this child; he is my son." The surgeon was not the boy's father. In what relation did the surgeon stand to the child? Most students did not give any answer. The most frequent answer given was that the surgeon had fathered the boy illegitimately. (Others suggested that the surgeon had divorced the boy's mother and remarried and hence was not legally the boy's father.) Even though the story was related as a part of a lecture on women's liberation, at best only 20 percent of the written answers gave the correct and obvious answer — the surgeon was the boy's mother.

4.   For further analysis of verbs indicating copulation see "A Note on Conjoined Noun Phrases," *Journal of Philosophical Linguistics*, vol. 1, no. 2, Great Expectations, Evanston, Ill. Reprinted with "English Sentences Without Overt Grammatical Subject," in Zwicky, Salus, Binnick, and Vanek, eds., *Studies Out in Left Field: Defamatory Essays Presented to James D. McCawley* (Edmonton: Linguistic Research, Inc., 1971). The puritanism in our society is such that both of these articles are pseudo-anonymously published under the name of Quang Phuc Dong; Mr. Dong, however, has a fondness of citing and criticizing the articles and theories of Professor James McCawley, Department of Linguistics, University of Chicago. Professor McCawley himself was kind enough to criticize an earlier draft of this essay. I should also like to thank G.E.M. Anscombe for some suggestions concerning this essay.

Janice Moulton

Sex and Reference

I

In this essay I shall discuss the infrequency of female orgasms in sexual intercourse. I shall claim that concern about this infrequency embodies a confusion about the concept of sexual intercourse. The confusion is reflected in our language and in other widespread, although factually unsubstantiated, beliefs about sexual intercourse.[1]

Hardly anyone today denies that women are capable of orgasms, even as capable as men when sufficiently stimulated. Kinsey says: "In general females and males appear to be equally responsive to the whole range of physical stimuli which may initiate erotic reactions . . . and the specific data show that the average female is no slower in response than the average male when she is sufficiently stimulated and when she is not inhibited in her activity."[2] The key words are "sufficiently stimulated." Although women have the same capacity for orgasm as men, they reach orgasm far less frequently during sexual intercourse.[3]

Invariably, suggestions for increasing the possibility of female orgasms focus on releasing inhibitions of the female, prolonging intercourse, or stimulating the female before intercourse. However, these methods often create new problems. Direct stimulation of the female before intercourse usually ceases when intercourse begins. If these procedures fail, the woman may be considered sexually inadequate, or the man sexually incompetent. Sexual activity, instead of being a source of pleasure and enjoyment, is treated as a complicated and difficult skill, something not to be enjoyed, but mastered. Often the female is advised to fake orgasm (men, the marriage manuals point out, obviously cannot fake it and so could never be under an obligation to try).[4] Faking relieves the obligations of the male but certainly does not solve the problems of the female. The old disparity between the frequency of male and female orgasms remains, to which the need for deception has been added.

In spite of this disparity, many people who are interested in orgasm for the female still rely on sexual intercourse as the main or only method of interpersonal sexual stimulation.[5] The continued belief, despite the facts, that intercourse is the appropriate sexual activity to bring about the orgasms of both male and female involves a conceptual confusion. Sexual intercourse is an activity in which male arousal is a necessary condition, and male satisfaction, if not also a necessary condition, is the primary aim. Despite this, sexual intercourse is thought by many to be an activity that involves (or ought to) both male and female equally. But female arousal and satisfaction, although they may be concomitant events occasionally, are not even constituents of sexual intercourse.

II

Our language mirrors this confusion. Grammatically, polite expressions for sexual intercourse tend to be symmetric, giving the impression that what A does to B, B likewise does to A. Yet their definitions give a different picture. Although both male and female genitals are mentioned, the activity is characterized solely in terms of the *male* responses that constitute it.

Most expressions for sexual intercourse have the symmetry of other relations, like "shaking hands with," "being a sibling of" and "dancing with."[6] If a woman has sexual intercourse with a man, then it follows from the meaning of the terms that he has had sexual intercourse with her. If he has gone all the way with her, then, logically, she has gone all the way with him. Since so many of the expressions for intercourse exhibit this symmetry, one might be led to expect that he and she are equally involved in this activity. Thus, if a male orgasm is a primary aim and usual constituent of the activity, it would seem that a female orgasm should be an aim and constituent too.

The exceptions, the expressions for sexual intercourse that are not symmetric, are significant in that they are vulgar. If he fucked her, it does not follow that she has fucked him, but only that she has been fucked by him. The grammar of the word "fuck" does not imply that he and she are equally involved in the activity.[7]

Acceptable expressions for sexual intercourse are symmetric; unacceptable expressions usually are not. Thus the grammar reflects the expectations of many people that if sexual intercourse is considered a decent and nice thing to do, men and women are likely to find it equally satisfying; and if it is considered a vulgar, dirty experience, they will not. This contrast reinforces the idea that a man and a woman *should*, if they are decent and nice, find this activity equally pleasurable. The belief is further reinforced by the slang use of the vulgar expressions such as "fuck" and "screw" to mean take advantage of, deceive, and injure. Thus, the grammar of these expressions invites us to believe that sexual intercourse, if it does not involve deceit and injury, is an activity that pertains to both parties equally. Viewed as an activity in genetics, sexual intercourse does involve both parties equally. But as an activity for producing pleasure, it is not an equal opportunity experience.

III

What purports to be a mutually pleasurable activity, what is politely expressed in terms of a symmetric relation, in fact results in far fewer orgasms for women than for men. The reasons for this become obvious when we consider the definitions of expressions for sexual intercourse.

For sexual subjects dictionaries are usually barren sources. However, *Webster's Third New International Dictionary of the English Language* gives a definition under "coitus," and refers one to this word for all synonymous expressions. Coitus is defined as "the act of conveying the male semen to the female reproductive tract involving insertion of the penis in the vaginal orifice followed by ejaculation."[8] If we look up "ejaculation" we find "the sudden or spontaneous discharging of a fluid (as semen in orgasm) from a duct"; and for "orgasm": "the climax of sexual excitement typically occurring toward the end of coitus."

According to these definitions the male orgasm is a necessary condition for sexual intercourse (coitus). To many people the only necessary condition of sexual intercourse is penetration;

coitus interruptus is still coitus. But male orgasm is such a regular and expected part of sexual intercourse that the *Webster's Third* definition is widely accepted. For example, the law, which defines rape in terms of penetration, requires the presence of semen in the vaginal tract as *evidence* of the penetration. (Of course, this is because the testimony of the victim is not considered sufficient. If the law thought victims of other crimes were as likely to be liars, it might require other evidence to substantiate the charge. Significantly, for this paper, although many people object to the way rape victims are treated by the law, to my knowledge no one has objected to the semen test on the grounds that male orgasm is not an invariable aspect of rape.)

Thus, although there are exceptions, sexual intercourse is widely accepted as a process that is brought to a conclusion by the male orgasm. Physiologically it is usually impossible to continue intercourse after male orgasm. Thus, any discussion of the female orgasm during sexual intercourse is actually a discussion of the female orgasm before or during the male orgasm. Once the male orgasm occurs, sexual intercourse ends. This puts an arbitrary restriction on the period during which the female orgasm may occur. In addition, sexual intercourse formally begins when the primary focus for sexual stimulation in the male (the penis) is inserted in a container particularly well suited to bring about the male orgasm (the vaginal orifice). Although the dictionary merely says that sexual intercourse "involves" this insertion, anything prior to this insertion is termed "foreplay" or "preliminaries"; the real thing does not begin until the insertion occurs.[9]

The important point to notice is that this activity, which is described by verbs that are logically symmetrical, is in fact *defined* exclusively in terms of *male* stimulation by contact with the female, leading to (or at least aiming at) *male* orgasm. Thus, discussions of the female orgasm during sexual intercourse amount to discussions of the female orgasm after the source of *male* stimulation is placed in its container and before or during the *male* orgasm. The female locus of stimulation and the female orgasm are not even part of the definition of sexual intercourse. From this view, one might wonder why anyone ever thought the female orgasm had anything to do with sexual intercourse, except as an occasional and accidental co-occurrence. Sometimes the telephone rings, too.

IV

Some claims about the nature of sexual behavior can be seen as attempts to explain the asymmetry between male and female orgasms. Ignoring the definition of sexual intercourse, they assume that sexual intercourse would ordinarily involve the mutual pleasure of both male and female, and blame the inadequacies of the participants when it does not.

The claim about vaginal orgasms says, in effect, that for sexual intercourse to be a mutually pleasurable activity, the anatomical source of female stimulation must be the container that stimulates the male, and if it is not, there is something wrong with the female. The claim does not deny that women have orgasms for which the clitoris is the anatomical source. But such orgasms, it is claimed, (1) are not very good and (2) indicate immaturity.[10] In childhood masturbation the anatomical source may be the clitoris, but in sexual intercourse it should become the vagina. Significantly, no analogous difference between the locus of stimulation in masturbation and intercourse is claimed for the male. Nor is it claimed that a male must mature to experience an intense orgasm during intercourse.

The claim about vaginal orgasms contradicts physiological evidence. All female orgasms share the same physiological characteristics; all may result in contractions of the vagina, but direct stimulation of the clitoral area produces more intense and rapid orgasms.[11]

It might be argued against this evidence that orgasm is not mainly a physiological, but a psychological, state. However, psychological (introspective) data are not allowed as falsifications by this claim for the superiority of vaginal orgasms. If a woman denies having orgasms produced by vaginal stimulation, her report can be discredited by the claim that she is fixated in childhood and does not experience a real orgasm because of her lack of sexual maturity. If a woman reports that vaginal orgasms are less intense than clitorally oriented ones, according to the claim, she does not know what a vaginal orgasm is. If it is less intense than a clitoral orgasm, it could not be a vaginal orgasm, which by definition is the more intense.

Psychologically the above claim is untestable; physiologically it is groundless. What purpose does this myth serve? It gives an account that hails sexual intercourse as a mutually pleasurable activity despite the facts against it. It also gives an explanation for this discordance with the facts: the female may still be more interested in the childish, self-centered sexual pleasures of masturbation and not mature enough to enjoy intercourse. The supposed symmetry of sexual intercourse presupposes this maturity; the facts are sometimes otherwise.

Another such claim is that in the best sexual experiences the male and female orgasms occur simultaneously. There is little specific physiological evidence to support this. In fact there is a loss of perceptual awareness that accompanies orgasm.[12] Thus, with simultaneous orgasms, neither participant is very aware of what is happening to the other. Part of the reason for interpersonal sexual activity is to enjoy the pleasure given to the other person. But with simultaneous orgasms one is less able to appreciate the partner's experience because one is overwhelmed by one's own.

What rationale supports this widely believed claim about simultaneous orgasms?[13] Sexual intercourse is an event that regularly and expectedly culminates in the male orgasm. So if the female orgasm happened at the same time, then intercourse would have culminated in a female orgasm too. Simultaneous orgasms would provide the female's orgasm with the same status as the male's and would guarantee that sexual intercourse really had been a mutual activity. If people only did it right, sexual intercourse would merit the symmetry of its polite expressions.

V

Once it is recognized that sexual intercourse is an activity characterized in terms of male arousal and orgasm, for which female arousal and orgasm is irrelevant, the disparity between male and female orgasms in sexual intercourse should not be a problem. The disparity would be reduced if the standard sexual activity were a process characterized by the arousal and satisfaction of both sexes, rather than, as it is now, the process of sexual intercourse.[14] When sexual intercourse occurs, the male must be sexually aroused and regularly is orgasmic. If this activity included the same responses for the female, everything would be fine. But, as we know, it does not. The whole problem arises from trying to produce a female orgasm as a useful by-product of a process aimed at producing the male orgasm. And this attempt arises from the belief that the process will be, or should be, a mutually pleasurable activity involving both partners equally.

VI

One might object to blaming a conceptual confusion for the infrequency of female orgasms in sexual intercourse. It may be agreed that for most people sexual intercourse begins with stimulation of the male and ends with the male orgasm. But the objection would claim that this is the result of a male-oriented society. The contrast between grammar and definition may exist, but that too is the result of a male-oriented culture.

If the discrepancy in orgasm attainment were simply the result of male orientation, sexual intercourse could be represented as something to be initiated and carried out solely by the male for his own pleasure, with or without the use of the female. No one would be concerned about female orgasms at all.

It might be diplomatic to misrepresent sexual intercourse as a mutually pleasurable activity, a pretense that would help keep women in their place. One would not expect such deception to fool anyone acquainted with the facts. Yet many people (both male and female) believe that sexual activity should provide maximum satisfaction for both parties, recognize that women reach orgasm in intercourse far less often than men, and yet, thinking that sexual intercourse is a symmetric activity, continue to believe that it should provide the same sort of satisfaction for both sexes. If there were no conceptual confusion, then those who were only concerned with male satisfaction in sexual activity between males and females could restrict that activity to intercourse, while those concerned with female satisfaction as well would not be so restricted.

VII

Perhaps the nature of the confusion can be best brought out by an analogy. Let us imagine a culture in which the women prepared all the food and spoon-fed it to the men, but fed none to themselves. And suppose this feeding activity was described as if it were a mutual activity, that is, by expressions that indicated symmetric relations. This custom would be described by expressions such as "have feeding behavior with." Logically it would follow that if he had feeding behavior with her, then she had feeding behavior with him. Despite this symmetry and the universal and frequent practice of feeding behavior, a great many women in this culture suffered from malnutrition. Instead of changing or expanding the custom, so that women got a chance to eat too, the society attributed the malnutrition to biological differences. It was argued that women's bodies were not as able to be nourished as were men's. Malnutrition was considered a consequence of a sex-linked congenital defect. Experts claimed that women, unlike men, could not be satisfied with mere hunger-satiation anyway. Instead, the satisfaction women derived from feeding behavior was in the warmth and closeness of a meaningful relationship.

Educated women introduced variations of feeding behavior that included spoon-licking while cooking. This was called "foretaste." Men often encouraged it, although it was rarely continued when feeding behavior began. Other women relied on self-feeding to survive, but this was frowned on by the whole community as perverted, antisocial behavior. The influence of custom was so strong that few believed that women in the kitchen together might feed each other. It was commonly thought that women who fed each other did so only because they could not get men to feed. No one ever thought they did it to get food.

Gourmet cookbooks claimed that in truly gourmet feeding both male and female got nourished together. However, since only one spoon was used in feeding behavior, simultaneous nourishment was very unusual. Even when it was managed most of the food spilled and neither party got very much.

Nutrition manuals argued that since feeding behavior *should* be a mutual activity, the female *should* receive nourishment through the spoon that feeds the male, and if she did not, there was something inadequate about her. The books did not deny that a female could be nourished through her mouth. But such nourishment, they claimed, (1) is not very satisfying and (2) indicates immaturity. In childhood self-feeding, the focus of feeding satisfaction may be the mouth, but in mature feeding behavior, it should become the spoon. Of course, the locus of nourishment in the male was not thought to be different in mature feeding behavior from that of childhood self-feeding.

In this imaginary culture the problem of how to provide nourishment for the female during feeding behavior is beset with the same conceptual difficulties as the problem in our culture of how to provide orgasm for the female during sexual intercourse. Attributing either problem to basic anatomic differences between men and women is absurd. It is not anatomic differences that account for female malnutrition in the feeding-behavior culture. The female is just not getting enough food. Note that a larger female would not get enough food just by getting the same amount of food as a smaller male. What counts as "enough" varies with the individual.

Similarly, it is not anatomical differences that account for lack of female orgasms during sexual intercourse. The female is just not getting enough stimulation.

VIII

It is often said that for women the sympathy and understanding expressed in sexual relations is more satisfying than an orgasm.[15] Many critics of physiological research claim that it ignores these psychological aspects of sexual behavior. Now of course these psychological aspects are important. They are the whole reason for engaging in interpersonal sexual activity rather than masturbation. But if a woman spends the time and energy to produce someone else's orgasm, with the understanding that she is participating in a mutual activity, it is only fair that her partner do the same for her. If she has to be satisfied with sympathy and understanding alone, then so should her partner.

IX

Sexual activities, as with most social behaviors, are stylized, deriving much of their immutability from the language that describes them. For each new generation of humans, lacking the instinctual control of other species, the "rediscovery" of sexual activity is greatly influenced by information carried by spoken and written language. There is a big difference between pointing out a conceptual confusion and its remedy and actually changing the behavior that the confusion helps maintain. To do the latter it is necessary to change the concept of the standard sexual activity to one that involves the arousal and satisfaction of all participants. That involves changing the romantic looks and smiles that now convey "I'm interested in sexual intercourse with you" so that they convey "I'm interested in our both having a satisfying sexual experience together."

NOTES

1. This essay does not question the sociological data of Kinsey or Masters and Johnson. Nor does it raise any epistemological questions concerning their data, since I assume that knowledge about the sexual pleasure of others is just as possible as knowledge about any other feelings. And I assume that women are just as able as men to know about their own feelings of sexual pleasure.

2. Alfred Kinsey et al., *Sexual Behavior in the Human Female* (Philadelphia: W. R. Saunders, 1953), p. 163.

3. According to Kinsey's research "something between 36 and 44 percent of the females in the sample had responded to (experienced) orgasm in a part but not all of their coitus in marriage. About one-third of those females had responded only a small part of the time, and the other third had responded a major portion of the time, even though it was not a hundred percent of the time . . ." (*ibid.*, p. 375). That is, fewer than 14 percent managed to have orgasms a major portion of the time, while over 56 percent had never had an orgasm during coitus. Objections to Kinsey's statistics [cf. Abram Kardiner, *Sex and Morality* (London: Routledge & Kegan Paul, 1955), p. 73] claim that his percentages of female orgasms during intercourse are much too *high*, giving women expectations that could never be met. Yet men, with rare exceptions, experience orgasms in sexual intercourse every time, without special techniques or partner skill.

4. Eustace Chesser, *An Outline of Human Relationships* (London: William Heinemann, Ltd., 1959), p. 66: " . . . the misfortune of premature (preceeding the female's orgasm) ejaculation is extremely common. It cannot be too strongly emphasized that intercourse is more beset with difficulties for a man than a woman. A woman may take no pleasure in it for a variety of reasons, but if she cares deeply for her husband, she can pretend."

5. The popularity of David Reuben's book *Any Woman Can* (have an orgasm in intercourse) shows that (1) it is widely known that many women do not have orgasms, and (2) many people who are interested in orgasm for the female think of sexual intercourse as the appropriate sexual activity.

6. A selection of verbs and verb phrases for sexual intercourse from the *Dictionary of American Slang* and from *Webster's Third New International Dictionary* include the taboo: "screw," "lay," "fuck," and "ball"; the slang: "do it (with)," "make," "make it (with)," "go all the way," and "give it to"; more acceptable expressions: "mate," "copulate," "couple," "have sex," "engage in coitus," and "sleep with"; expressions for intercourse outside marriage: "fornicate," "commit adultery"; and expressions for intercourse on a regular basis: "have an affair," "shack up," "have a relationship."

7. It has even been claimed that it is ungrammatical for "fuck" to have a female subject (cf. Robert Baker, " 'Pricks' and 'Chicks': A Plea for 'Persons'," herein, pp. 176). However, the *Dictionary of American Slang* says about "lay": "As most taboo words, this is primarily used by, but not restricted to use by, males" (p. 313). My experience supports the latter source.

8. Even this definition is incorrect. If the male semen is deliberately prevented by a condom from entering the female reproductive tract, it would still be an act of coitus. A more accurate definition might be: That act involving insertion of the penis in the vaginal orifice followed by ejaculation.

9. In the standard coital position sexual stimulation of the penis actually prevents similar stimulation of the primary area of sexual stimulation of the female. [William Masters and Virginia Johnson, *Human Sexual Response* (Boston: Little, Brown and Co., 1966), p. 60].

10. Kardiner, p. 67; Noel Lamare, *Love and Fulfillment in Woman* (New York: Macmillan, 1957), p. 21; Sigmund Freud, "The Transformation of Puberty," in *The Basic Writings of Sigmund Freud*, trans. A.A. Brill (New York: Random House, 1938), pp. 613-4; and Freud, "Female Sexuality," in *Collected Papers*, vol. 5, ed. J.V. Strachey (London: Hogarth Press, 1953), p. 252.

11. Masters and Johnson, *Human Sexual Response, op. cit.,* pp. 59, 66-7.

12. *Ibid.,* p. 135.

13. After orgasm the genital areas of both sexes may become over-sensitive, so that continued stimulation is painful. Simultaneous orgasms would avoid this problem, but at the cost of delicate and difficult timing that often diminishes the intensity of the orgasm. More important, I suspect, is that the loss of awareness actually encourages the support for simultaneity, as it provides an ideal time for the faking recommended by the marriage manuals. The male is excused from not knowing and can ask "Did you?" when at any other time the answer would be obvious to him.

14. For some people this change might result in no variation of physical behavior. This is not a recommendation for any particular sort of physical behavior — let that be the province of physiologists — but a recommendation that the physical behavior engaged in, whatever it is, fit (or try to fit) this description: A process that involves the arousal and satisfaction of all participants equally.

15. Eustace Chesser, *Is Chastity Outmoded?* (London: William Heinemann, Ltd., 1960), p. 88.

Stephanie Ross

How Words Hurt:
Attitude, Metaphor,
And Oppression

An old nursery rhyme assures us that "Sticks and stones may break my bones/But names can never hurt me." Yet many philosophers claim that words *can* hurt. They argue that ordinary language is sexist and that sexist language oppresses women. For example, Elizabeth Beardsley has drawn attention to referential genderization (RG) which occurs "whenever a speaker who is saying something about human beings must make distinctions based on sex on pain of saying something linguistically incorrect."[1] She claims that RG increases sexual distinctions, and thereby "helps to provide a conceptual framework useful for rationalizing sex-based discriminatory treatment."[2] Robert Baker claims that

> any movement dedicated to breaking the bonds of female servitude must destroy our ways of identifying and hence of conceiving of women . . . Contemporary feminists should advocate the utilization of neutral proper names and the elimination of gender from our language.[3]

I would like to thank my colleagues James Doyle, Ronald Munson, and Henry Shapiro for comments on an earlier draft of this paper.

I believe these claims are sound, but to my knowledge no philosopher has provided a satisfactory account of *how* words hurt. Certainly words can be used to taunt and defame, to voice threats and instill fear, to express discriminatory edicts and tyrannical decrees. Yet none of these possibilities explains the particular charge that our ordinary, everyday ways of talking about women are sexist and oppressive. Some writers suggest that the oppressive aspects of ordinary language are etymological: certain words have roots which are denigrating and offensive to women. Yet most of us are unaware of the etymologies of the words we use. How can historical facts of which both speakers and listeners are unaware transform their words into vehicles of oppression?

In this paper I shall offer an account of how words can hurt. I shall begin by sketching a theory which doesn't work — the theory of etymological oppression. I shall argue that the ancient roots of ordinary English words cannot — by themselves — make those words oppressive. Then I shall turn to a closely related phenomenon which does perpetuate sexism in language. This is the phenomenon of metaphoric identification. Robert Baker first charted the relations between metaphor and sexism in his paper " 'Pricks' and 'Chicks': A Plea for 'Persons'."[4] I shall extend Baker's analysis by proposing a link between metaphor and attitude. Briefly, I claim that metaphors often express attitude, and that the metaphors implicit in sexist language express attitudes of contempt and disdain towards women. To support this claim I shall examine some attitude-measurement devices used by social scientists. I shall also point out a structural similarity which makes metaphor an apt vehicle for the expression of attitude. Thus I hope to show that the nursery rhyme with which I opened is mistaken. Words can hurt, and one way they do is by conveying denigrating or demeaning attitudes.

I. ETYMOLOGICAL ECHOES?

In an angry article in the *New York Times*, Barbara Lawrence traces the etymology of the verb *to fuck* to the German *ficken* meaning "to strike," to the Latin *fustis*, meaning "a staff or cudgel," and to the Celtic *buc*, meaning "a point, hence, to pierce."[5] She goes on to discuss the etymology of the verb *to screw* and to point out what a painful and mutilating activity screwing is:

> Consider what a screw actually does to the wood it penetrates . . .
> The verb, besides its explicit imagery, has antecedent associations
> to "write on," "scratch," "scarify," and so forth — a revealing
> fusion of a mechanical or painful action with an obviously deni-
> grated object.[6]

Lawrence suggests that these two words oppress women because
of the brutal and denigrating imagery implicit in their
etymology. While I agree that both words are offensive, I believe
that neither one oppresses in virtue of its etymology. And of
the two, only "screw" offends in virtue of its associated imagery. In what follows I shall argue that the possibility of
etymological oppression is not genuine. And in the next section I
shall show that the facts cited by Lawrence are relevant to a different sort of explanation of how words hurt.

Consider the case for etymological oppression. If women are
oppressed by etymological aspects of the words used to describe
them, then words must somehow carry their etymologies along
with them. The words' current meanings must in some way or
other resonate with etymological echoes. This possibility isn't
altogether absurd. As root words are transformed and travel
from language to language, they undoubtedly preserve certain of
their semantic and orthographic features. Otherwise we couldn't
re-identify versions of the same word, or attribute a common
ancestry to different words in different languages. The proponent of etymological oppression must hold in addition that these
etymological echoes help fix a word's current meaning and that
knowing a word's etymology helps us to understand that meaning. Just such a claim is made by Wilfred Funk in the introduction to his book *Word Origins:*

> To know the past of an individual helps us to understand him
> better. To know the life history of a word makes its present mean-
> ing clearer and more nearly unforgettable.[7]

The final step in the argument for etymological oppression must
show how a word linked to roots which are offensive or insulting
can oppress those it is used to describe.

A formalized version of the argument I have been sketching
might go as follows:

> (1) The etymologies of our words contribute to their
> current meanings.

(2) The statements we make about people, places, etc., are determined in part by the etymological echoes carried by our words.

(3) Many words used to describe sexual activities are derived from roots which insult or belittle women.

(4) Language can be a vehicle of oppression.

Therefore (5) Sexist language oppresses women.

A few comments are in order about premise (4). So far I have spoken quite loosely about hurt, offense, and oppression, but these really are quite different notions. In Chapter Two of his book *Social Philosophy*, Joel Feinberg discusses hurt, harm, and knowledge. Noting that the legal tradition defines harm as the invasion of an interest,[8] Feinberg argues that hurt is a species of harm. He claims that one can be harmed unknowingly,[9] but he upholds the maxim "What a person doesn't know can't hurt him." Thus Feinberg characterizes hurts as those special harms of which the victim is necessarily aware. Assault and battery is a hurt, while undetected burglary or undiscovered adultery count as harms.

The distinction between offense and oppression parallels what Feinberg draws between hurt and harm.[10] One can be oppressed unknowingly but offense requires (logically or conceptually) the awareness and acknowledgement of its victim. Feinberg classes offense *and* oppression as harms, noting that offenses are usually harms of a relatively trivial kind.[11] Given this background, one might object to premise (4) of the argument sketched above by claiming that language can offend but not oppress. I believe there *are* situations in which language alone can be a vehicle of oppression. For instance, when our way of referring to a given group of people perpetuates degrading stereotypical views about them.[12] But since a thorough investigation of the concept of oppression is beyond the scope of this paper, I shall remain agnostic on the question of whether language can oppress as well as offend. To refute the theory of etymological oppression, I shall argue against the specific possibility of words oppressing in virtue of their etymology. Even if premise (4) turns out to be false, I intend my argument to block the weaker claim that language offends, insults, or hurts in virtue of etymological details. My claim is this: if a particular word's etymology in unknown to its speaker and hearer, then it cannot facilitate oppression *or* glorification. On the other hand, if the insulting aspect of a word's meaning is a matter of current public knowledge, then it is both ideal and misleading to claim that the word oppresses in virtue of its etymology.

Consider the ways in which a word's meaning might be related to that of the words from which it arose. Some words are imported into our language unchanged, or else have a meaning very close to that of their ancestors. For example, our word "bane" meaning a curse or poison is a modern version of the Old English and Middle High German words "bana" and "bane" meaning death or murder; our word "copulate" comes directly from the Latin "copulare" meaning to fasten together, link, or couple. Other words inherit meaning from their ancestors in a less straightforward way. For instance, the word "faint" comes from the Old French "feindre" meaning to feign. While not all fainting spells are feigned, some of them are suspect, and this might help to explain the derivation. Another example is the term "tryst." Mr. Funk explains that "tryst," which today refers to lovers' clandestine meetings, originally signified a station in hunting where the huntsman lay in wait for his prey.[13] This twist in "tryst's" history is not entirely mysterious, for love and romance do resemble blood-sports in a number of ways. All three can involve cunning, guile, pursuit, and pain; all three can have a victim. As a final example of an etymological twist, consider the word "pretty." This term is descended from the Old English "praettig," meaning tricky, wily, and crafty. Here again the present-day meaning of a word seems almost to reverse that of its ancestor. "Praettig" picked out people of whom one had to be wary; "pretty" picks out people upon whom it is pleasant to gaze.

What are we to make of these word histories? Every word can be related in one way or another to its ancestors. In some cases, meaning and orthography are inherited directly, in others the word histories involve more confusing and convoluted transformations.[14] But how does this bear on the claim that etymology can be a vehicle of oppression? Return to Lawrence's first example, the word "fuck." Its derivation from the terms "ficken," "buc," and "fustis" (to strike, to pierce, a cudgel) seems relatively straightforward. All three ancestors convey images of injury and force. When applied to a sexual context, these images characterize intercourse in a way which devalues the woman's role.[15] Thus a proponent of etymological oppression might claim that the etymological details cited by Lawrence resonate in every use of the word "fuck" and that these echoes account for the oppressive force of that word.

I don't find this analysis convincing. I agree with Lawrence that "fuck" often offends. Yet I am not a philologist; I do not know Latin or Celtic; I did not (until reading Lawrence's article) know anything about the history of the word. For these reasons I believe that my offense is prompted not by the word "fuck"'s past history, but by our present-day classification of that word as vulgar and offensive. However, these considerations do not fully refute the theory of etymological oppression. For oppression does not require the awareness or co-operation of its victims. Consider the following example. Many feminists claim that men oppress women by treating them as sex-objects. Perhaps American women are all oppressed by *Playboy* magazine. A feminist might argue that *Playboy* oppresses women by purveying a debilitating image of their abilities, interests, and goals. Yet guilt or responsibility is difficult to assign. In publishing *Playboy*, Hugh Hefner is merely trading on attitudes already prevalent throughout our society. Moreover, these attitudes are held by women as well as men. Women who buy *Cosmopolitan* are, in a sense, studying up on how to become Playmates. Thus the oppression perpetuated by *Playboy* and similar publications is not something of which its victims are aware, for many women adopt the very attitudes which are oppressing them.

I take this example to show that lack of awareness does not suffice to establish lack of oppression.[16] Returning to the linguistic case, does lack of etymological knowledge equally fail to refute the charge of etymological oppression? I think not. The two cases are importantly different. While (political) oppression can proceed without the knowledge or co-operation of its victims, successful communication requires awareness on the part of participants. The theory of etymological oppression requires that etymological details facilitate oppression *by* facilitating communication — in particular, by fixing the meanings of certain words. Yet this latter task cannot be achieved by semantic details for which speaker and hearer remain ignorant. Thus the case for etymological oppression crumbles.

Let me clarify my argument. Ordinarily, verbal communication occurs when a person uses words to convey information — or misinformation — thoughts, and feelings. And an act of communication succeeds only if the hearer understands the message sent her way. A characterization of everyday verbal communication — that is, of communication in its ordinary conversational context — might go as follows:

(A) The speaker intends to communicate with the hearer and intends to do so by securing the hearer's recognition of that intention.

(B) The hearer believes there to have been an attempt at communication and believes certain information to have been conveyed by the speaker's words.

(C) This information is conveyed in virtue of the semantic properties of the speaker's words.[17]

My claim about etymological oppression is this: etymological facts unknown to speaker and hearer cannot facilitate the standard sort of communication defined by conditions (A) — (C). These conditions rule out cases where language is not used at all (screams, purrs, and cooings) as well as cases where the speaker's words do not convey information in virtue of their standard meaning (cases where a speaker's beliefs or attitudes are inferred from her tone of voice; cases where a speaker's utterance in a language one doesn't understand provides crucial information, e.g. that the enemy is approaching).[18] If the theory of etymological oppression is to apply in the remaining situations, then etymological details must facilitate oppression by somehow fixing the standard meanings of words. Yet etymological details do not play such a role. First of all, such details do not determine the meanings of a speaker's words. Of course there is a sense in which a word's history does determine the present meaning of that word. But it is entirely trivial: a word's present meaning is whatever meaning is at the end of its etymological history. As we saw above, a word's meaning can be related in many different ways to that of its ancestors. The great range of possibilities here — from 'same meaning' to 'no discernible meaning relation at all' — undercuts any attempt to systematically relate present meaning to etymology. Secondly, etymological details play no role in determining whether conditions (A) — (C) have been fulfilled. If a word's present meaning diverges from that of its ancestors, then semantic details about the latter are irrelevant to explaining what the word is now standardly used to convey. While if the word's present meaning and that of its ancestors coincide, it is unnecessary and misleading to invoke the latter (by hypothesis unknown) in explaining communication. Successful communication is sufficiently explained by the requirement that speaker and hearer both know the present-day meanings of the speaker's words. Knowledge of etymological details is not needed.

We could of course recast the theory of etymological oppression to meet these objections. A new theory might make reference to subliminal etymological oppressive effects, and so on. But such a theory would be even less plausible than its predecessor. I have pursued the theory of etymological oppression at length in order to show that non-semantic features of a word (e.g. being a vehicle of oppression) cannot be explained by appeal to etymology. Nonetheless, I believe that the facts Lawrence cited about the words "fuck" and "screw" are important. In the remainder of this paper I shall develop an alternative account of why such words oppress. My account will show the relevance of the information Lawrence provides.

II. METAPHORICAL IDENTIFICATION

Return to Lawrence's two examples, "fuck" and "screw." We agree that both these words are insulting and that both are classed as impolite. In addition, I have argued that "fuck" does not offend women because of its etymological ties to "ficken," "fustis," and "buc." Most speakers are unaware of these ties. They find the term offensive because they know it is classed as offensive by their fellow speakers.[19] I believe the offensiveness of "screw" can be explained quite differently, and this is shown even in Lawrence's summary reference to its "revealing fusion of a mechanical or painful action with an obviously denigrated object." The difference here is that most of us are aware of these aspects of screws. Even if we haven't given much thought to screwing as a method of fastening (as opposed to nailing or glue-ing) we can immediately acknowledge the correctness of Lawrence's claims. A screw is hard and sharp; wood by contrast is soft and yielding; force is applied to make a screw penetrate wood; a screw can be unscrewed and reused but wood — wherever a screw has been embedded in it — is destroyed forever. Once we marshall these everyday facts about screw and screwing, their ramifications become clear. When the verb *to screw* is used to describe sexual intercourse, it carries with it images of dominance and destruction. The woman's role in intercourse is similar to that of wood destroyed by the screw which enters it.[20] Additional echoes are carried by a further use of the verb *to screw* in financial contexts. To screw someone in this sense is to wring her dry, to practice extortion.

Metaphor is the device at work here. The use of the verb *to screw* to describe sexual intercourse invites us to view this latter activity in terms drawn from carpentry and mechanics. As noted above, many facts about screws and screwing are applicable to the new realm as well. And this is just what we should expect of an apt metaphor. But "screwing" is not a fresh, new label for intercourse. This use of the term is accepted, though deemed coarse and impolite. Thus we are dealing here with a dead metaphor — an established use of the word "screw" which has additional depth and resonance because it associates the two realms of sex and mechanics. The central claim I want to make in this paper is that metaphors of this sort are our primary vehicles for conveying attitudes. The offensiveness of the verb *to screw* is rooted in the attitude it conveys toward the female role in intercourse, and this attitude can be specified by attending to the details of the metaphor. None of the claims I shall make are tied to any one theory of metaphor. While there is much debate about the nature of metaphorical truth, the paraphrasability of metaphors, and so on, I shall skirt these issues. I trust that my positive claims about metaphor will apply to any reasonable account of that trope.

The relation between sexism and metaphor has been charted ably by Robert Baker in his article " 'Pricks' and 'Chicks': A Plea for 'Persons'." I want to expand on his work by showing in detail how metaphors can serve to express attitudes. But let me first outline Baker's position. Baker claims that the way in which we identify something reflects our conception of it.[21] This claim is not controversial. It may even be tautological on some readings of "concept." However, the identifications Baker focusses on throughout his paper are metaphorical ones. This enlivens things because metaphors are not finitely paraphrasable. Since their implications can be spun out at length, the identifications they convey are comparably complex.

To establish his claim, Baker first considers racial identifications. He compares the differing conceptions of blacks conveyed by the four lables "Negro," "colored," "Afro-American," and "black." In the course of his discussion, he imagines the

remarks "Where did that girl get to?" and "Who is the new boy
that Lou hired to help out at the filling station?" voiced by white
Southerners, and then comments:

> If the persons the terms apply to are adult Afro-Americans, then
> 'girl' and 'boy' are metaphorical identifications. The fact that the
> metaphorical identifications in question are standard in the
> language reflects that certain characteristics of the objects properly
> classified as boys and girls (for example, immaturity, inability to
> take care of themselves, need for guidance) are generally held by
> those who use the identifications to be properly attributable to
> Afro-Americans.[22]

Baker's acknowledgement that these metaphors are standard
usage is important, for it establishes that the metaphors in question are dead metaphors. The Southerners who use them do not
first think long and hard about race relations, then consciously
construct metaphors which reveal the situation. Rather, they use
the terms "boy" and "girl" because these are common curren-
cy. Probably few speakers spell out the implications of these
terms for themselves as Baker has in the passage quoted above.
Nonetheless, these implications are available — at least potentially — to any competent speaker. They resonate in each
metaphorical use of the terms "boy" and "girl" quite unlike the
supposed echoes of "buc," "fustis," and "ficken"
resonatingineach use of "fuck."

This is the important difference between Baker's account of
the offensiveness of certain idioms and the account I proposed
and rejected in Part I of this paper — the implications of dead
metaphors are known or accessible to their speakers, while
etymological details often are not. To see this, note that dead
metaphors are those which have become trite and commonplace.
Tenor and vehicle have been associated so frequently that their
juxtaposition no longer seems fresh or illuminating. Given this
long and public liason, it follows that neither tenor nor vehicle
can be entirely mysterious unless the metaphor was consistently
misunderstood. (One obvious exception to this claim is the use
of metaphor in scientific theories. Here the subject matter is indeed arcane and the presence of metaphor signals that our
understanding is not yet complete. However, these cases needn't
concern us here since our problem is ordinary language and its
power to offend and oppress.) Finally, these comments about
metaphor apply equally to metaphorical identifications. These

are simply cases where instead of a full statement of the metaphor ("A is B") the name or description of the vehicle replaces that of the tenor ("B is ∅ "replaces "A is ∅ ").

Baker takes the account of metaphorical identification which emerges from his discussion of racism and applies it to a second area, that of sexism. He argues that many of our ways of identifying women involve (dead) metaphors which insult and belittle. Among the categories of metaphorical identification he points out are animal terms ("chick," "fox"), toy terms ("doll"), juvenile terms ("babe," "kid," "sis") as well as more explicitly sexual and/or anatomical terms. I believe Baker is right about the force of these terms, though I grant there are certain cases which his account does not explain. For example, his theory does not apply to terms (like "fuck") which offend because we class them as offensive. Nor does it apply to terms which offend by excluding women from consideration. Examples here include general labels like "chairman" and "fireman" as well as the personal pronouns "he" and "his" when used to agree with an antecedent of unspecified gender ("everyone," "someone"). Neither of these examples offends in virtue of metaphorical implications. (However, in keeping with Baker's program we can explain both by reference to a second figure of speech: synecdoche. Both wrongly take part of humanity — the male sex — and use it to stand for the whole. The resulting idioms make it all too easy for women to be overlooked.)

III. ATTITUDE AND METAPHOR

Despite these lacunae, Baker's account fits a sizable number of cases of sexism in language. However, Baker calls our attention to the relation between metaphor and sexism without explaining how this relation fosters the oppression of women. I believe this is a fact in need of explanation. In what follows, I shall extend Baker's program by proposing an account of how metaphorical identifications oppress and offend. I suggest that metaphors often express attitudes. In particular, I suggest that the metaphorical identifications which Baker discusses express contemptuous and disdainful attitudes towards women. To justify this claim, I shall present three sorts of evidence. First, I shall present and discuss a single example, drawn from a novel of Willa Cather. Rather than argue in the abstract that metaphors can express attitudes, I shall examine a particular passage and argue that the best interpretation of it accords with my theory. Next, I shall offer some evidence drawn from social psychology. I shall examine the methods social psychologists employ to test for attitudes and point out the central role played by metaphor. Finally, I shall offer a more abstract argument for my claim, based on 'structural' resemblances between attitude and metaphor.

Consider the following passages from *The Professor's House:*

> He loved his family, he would make any sacrifice for them, but just now he couldn't live with them. He must be alone. That was more necessary to him than anything had ever been, more necessary than his marriage had been in his vehement youth. He could not live with his family again — not even with Lillian. Especially not with Lillian! Her nature was intense and positive; it was like a chiselled surface, a die, a stamp upon which he could not be beaten out any longer. If her character were reduced to an heraldic device, it would be a hand (a beautiful hand) holding flaming arrows — the shafts of her violent loves and hates, her clear-cut ambition.[23]

In these lines Willa Cather details the reactions of her protagonist, Professor Godfrey St. Peter, to the news that his family is returning early from a European tour. The passage tells us a good deal about St. Peter's temperament, loyalties, and needs, his early attachments and his current desires. But my interest is in the Professor's description of his wife, Lillian. Just what is revealed by the simile comparing her nature to a sharp metallic die, or the metaphor imagining her character as a heraldic device? What do we learn about the Professor in learning that *these* are his thoughts?

For a start, we do not learn about the Professor's beliefs. At least not in any straightforward sense. One might object that St. Peter expresses at least the belief that Lillian's character can be represented by a heraldic device of such and such a sort. But little follows from this concession. The Professor uses figurative language to talk about his wife. His beliefs about Lillian herself are of primary interest, not his beliefs about the suitability of various metaphors. And his endorsement of a particular trope does little to reveal his literal beliefs about his wife. This is so in part because metaphors aren't readily paraphrased; also because we rarely resort to metaphor to formulate and communicate our literal (pedestrian) beliefs. Thus, although the Professor's description is revealing, it doesn't reveal his beliefs about Lillian.

Nor does it reveal particular emotions he feels toward Lillian. Granted, the tone of the entire passage is hysterical, and its general topic seems to be love. But neither love nor hysteria characterizes St. Peter's portrait of Lillian. Although the opening sentence of the passage assures us that St. Peter loves his family, his portrait reveals love's absence, or its aftermath. (He remarks later, "Surely the saddest thing in the world is falling out of love — if once one has ever fallen in.") Similarly, although St. Peter seems hysterical and overwrought in this passage, these emotions do not carry over to his description of Lillian. She is not the object of his hysteria. Instead she receives a knowing, considered assessment.

What, then, does the Professor's description convey? I suggest it expresses his attitude towards Lillian. It reveals, first, the Professor's admiration for his wife. The words "intense," "positive," "flaming," and "violent" attest to her strength, while the mention of a heraldic device connotes nobility, privilege, and respect. The assessment is not entirely admiring, however, for many of St. Peter's terms come from the vocabularies of war and technology.[24] Here Lillian is characterized as strong in a more pejorative sense — strength as hardness. The metaphors of die and stamp suggest unyielding resistance, insistent repetition. St. Peter pictures himself weary, beaten, obliterated by her stamp. The mention of a chiselled surface provides further reinforcement, not only with the immediate image of cold stone and hard edges, but also in its muted suggestion of struggle, of an adversary relationship. (Compare chiselling stone with casting bronze, building clay.) In all these metaphors Lillian is protrayed as awesome, strong, stubborn, and dangerous. The final conceit suggests more specific criticisms of her character — the violence of her emotions and the transparence of her ambition.

The two figures of speech St. Peter employs to describe Lillian are thus immensely effective. They convey his admiration and awe, his distaste and defeat. I claim that these features indicate the Professor's attitude towards his wife. What do I mean by an attitude? Examples might include admiration, approval, dislike and disdain. Attitudes are intentional states (in Brentano's sense). Thus they are object-directed; all attitudes are attitudes toward or attitudes about something or other. In addition, attitudes involve beliefs about their objects and convey evaluations of them. If I admire Jane because she is intelligent, capable, and sympathetic, then Jane is the object of my attitude, and my attitude is grounded in my beliefs about her character. Since intelligence, competence, and sympathy are traits we prize, my attitude conveys a favorable evaluation of Jane. Some of my beliefs about Jane might be mistaken. If so, my attitude is misplaced or inappropriate. Attitudes themselves are not classed as true or false. In sum, if we imagine a continuum of psychological states, attitudes occupy an intermediate ground between judgement and belief, on the one hand, and emotions and moods, on the other. Like emotions, attitudes are object-directed, non-propositional, and evaluative. Yet attitudes are less visceral than emotions, less partisan, and less closely tied to distinctive behavioral manifestations. Returning to our example, the Professor's attitude towards Lillian is not conveyed by the bare factual claim that he takes her loves and hates to be violent. Thus it is not merely a belief or judgement about his wife. Nor is it a violent state which has overwhelmed him. The reflective mood of his extended metaphorical description indicates that he is not in the throes of a ravaging emotion. His psychological state lies between these poles.

My claim that metaphors express attitudes must be qualified in several respects. First, I do not claim that *all* metaphors serve this function, nor that they do so in all contexts. I would certainly be at a loss to determine the attitude conveyed by "The camel is the ship of the desert"! My claim is that sometimes metaphors express attitudes. And second, even in those cases where metaphors do convey attitude, I do not claim that we can always specify just which attitude is being expressed. The example discussed above is a case in point. The Professor's attitude towards Lillian is a complex attitude for which we have no standard name. It is not plain awe or unalloyed admiration. Despite our inability to name his attitude, I believe it is correct and illuminating to classify it as such. Finally, attitudes, like emotions and beliefs, can be unconscious. There may well be cases where someone has an attitude, expresses it in various ways (including metaphorical identifications of the attitude-object) yet doesn't know that this is so. Thus we are not always the best authorities about the attitudes we hold, reveal, express. Note that this accords with the claims made in Part I of this paper about knowledge and oppression. We do not always know when we are being oppressed; we can in fact become unwitting collaborators in our own oppression. (I do not, by the way, claim that the attitude St. Peter expresses towards his wife Lillian is a sexist one; it is simply a negative attitude, directed towards a woman.)

IV. METAPHORICAL MEASUREMENT

My brief essay in literary analysis was meant to offer one sort of support for the claim that metaphors often express attitudes. A second part of support comes from a quite different area: present-day social psychology. Attitude is the central concept of this discipline. Much of the research in past decades has centered on means to measure, predict, control, and explain shifts in attitude. My interest lies in a group of attitude measuring devices descended from Osgood's Semantic Differential. These devices — all 'paper and pencil tests' rather than physiological or behavorial (role-play) measures of attitude — suggest further connections between attitude and metaphor.

The Semantic Differential evolved from more general concerns about meaning. While working on the logic of semantic differentiation, Osgood, Suci, and Tannenbaum proposed the notion of a multi-dimensional semantic space. They associated the meaning of each and every concept with a unique location in this space. Their account of semantic space suggested a means for testing and measuring attitudes.[25] The Semantic Differential tests a subject's attitude toward a particular object by first naming that object, then listing a set of paired bi-polar adjectives. Each adjective pair is separated by seven intervals. The subject assigns the attitude object to one of these seven slots, thereby ranking it from -3 to +3 in reference to each adjective pair.

Among the experiments discussed by Osgood *et al.* is one where the Semantic Differential included the six scales good/bad, fair/unfair, valuable/worthless, tasty/distasteful, clean/dirty, and pleasant/unpleasant. A second attitude and belief measuring device — the AB Scales devised by Martin Fishbein — measures attitude with the five scales good/bad, sick/healthy, harmful/beneficial, wise/foolish, and clean/dirty.[26] Consider the use of the Semantic Differential or the AB Scales to measure attitudes. It seems clear that for any candidate attitude-object, some of these adjectives will apply not literally but metaphorically. For instance, suppose both tests are being used to test attitudes towards St. Louis. Here the adjectives "clean" and "dirty" might apply literally, to describe how clean the Sanitation Department keeps the streets, but the pairs "tasty" and "distasteful," "sick" and "healthy" do not. That is, they are not applied on the basis of gustatory experience or the presence of germs. The terms "sick" and "healthy" do have a commonly accepted use when applied to cities, just as the terms "tasty" and "distasteful" (or "tasteless") do when applied to appearance or decor. Because these (extended) uses are commonplace, they count as cases of dead metaphor. Still others of the adjectives mentioned above would apply to St. Louis in ways more straightforwardly metaphorical. For example, talk of wise or foolish cities, and perhaps even of valuable or worthless cities, involves genuine metaphor. The adjectives do not apply literally, nor is such usage so familiar that its initial freshness has faded. Thus "St. Louis is wise" and "St. Louis is valuable" are metaphorical claims. Of course these are not good metaphors; they are not appropriate or enlightening. Yet I believe that their appearance in such devices as the Semantic Differential and the AB Scales is significant, for it indicates that metaphors — even strained and awkward ones — are taken to be a measure of attitude.

This connection between metaphor and attitude is not logically tied to Osgood's theoretical presuppositions. The connection remains plausible even if we dispense with the notion of an n-dimensional semantic space. Let me speculate a little as to why this is so. The adjectives Osgood chooses allow us to measure partisanship in a vaguely quantifiable way. Since the adjectives are paired, each scale permits us to locate two poles and identify one with being "for," the other with being "against." So far this recalls the treatment of attitude put forward by emotive theorists like Ayer and Stevenson. For these writers, attitudes were nothing more than leanings pro or con, for or against. But this picture of attitude is much too faceless. If we have only attitudes for and against, we cannot distinguish among envy, admiration, and awe (all vaguely ways of being 'for' the attitude object). Nor among disdain, dislike, and indifference (all vaguely ways of being 'against' the attitude object). These further nuances are, I believe, captured by the metaphorical application of Osgood's terms. Spelling out in detail the relation between tenor and vehicle (as I did above in the example from Willa Cather) allows us to see a variety of different colors and tints where the emotive theorists give us only the Manichean choice of black and white.[27]

I don't want to claim too much for the Semantic Differential and its relatives. I think in principle there is a difference between e.g. judging something to be very foolish, somewhat valuable, and quite dirty, and judging it to be somewhat foolish, very valuable, and somewhat dirty. However, I don't think it is a difference which we can effectively comprehend as a difference in attitude. That is, I don't claim that from a Semantic Differential or AB Scale with attitude object St. Louis, we can recommend the subject's attitude and determine that it is admiration rather than approval or awe. (Recall the discussion above about identifying particular attitudes on the basis of metaphorical expressions.) Moreover, I believe that there is an alarming lack of consensus within the discipline of social psychology as to just what attitudes actually are. This results in further disagreement as to how they are expressed, how they can be measured, and so on.[28] But I do believe that social psychology's reliance on tests like the Semantic Differential is further *prima facie* evidence for some connection between metaphor and attitude. And I believe that the rather abstract correlation I alluded to above — a correlation between a variety of similarly valenced attitudes and a variety of differently weighted responses along the semantic scales comprising a given attitude measurement device — provides an additional argument for the claim that some metaphors convey attitudes. I shall turn to that next.

V. INTENTIONAL TRANSCENDENCE

My concluding argument for this connection between metaphor and attitude appeals to what I shall (loosely) call structural considerations. I claim that there is an isomorphism between metaphor on the one hand and attitude on the other which makes metaphor a particularly apt vehicle for the expression of attitude. This isomorphism has to do with the logical structure of attitude and metaphor: in particular, with their irreducibility to belief and to literal talk, respectively. I shall call this shared trait intentional transcendence.

Consider one of the central questions about metaphors — their paraphrasability. Can the significance of a metaphor be completely spelled out? In the article "Aesthetic Problems of Modern Philosophy,"[29] Stanley Cavell argues that metaphors are paraphrasable. To prove his point, he proposes the following paraphrase of the metaphor "Juliet is the sun":

Romeo means that Juliet is the warmth of his world; that his day begins with her; that only in her nourishment can he grow. And his declaration suggests that the moon, which other lovers use as emblems of their love, is merely her reflected light, and dead in comparison; and so on.[30]

Cavell's "and so on" is crucial here. He qualifies his claim by noting that metaphors are paraphrasable in a manner "marked by its concluding sense of 'and so on.'"[31] Thus Romeo does not mean that Juliet is like the sun in four respects and four respects only. His metaphor has further significance, further ramifications to be drawn out. For instance, that Juliet is the center of his universe. This richness is what some call the pregnancy of metaphor; it is what I mean by the phrase "intentional transcendence." A number of other writers call attention to this trait. For example, Max Black distinguishes a class of interaction metaphors which cannot be replaced by literal translations without loss of cognitive content.[32] Philip Wheelwright distinguishes two forms of metaphor, one of which — diaphor — creates new meaning through presentational juxtaposition.[33] Nelson Goodman's metaphorical account of metaphor (as the transfer of a schema to an alien realm, where the immigrant sometimes effects new organization and new associations[34]) gives a picture of paraphrase which helps to explain its richness. Alan Tormey's subjunctive theory of metaphor[35] also supports this view. Relations between tenor and vehicle can be spun out indefinitely because we can explore countless crannies of the possible world in which the counterfactual holds.

Consider now intentional transcendence in the psychological realm. Just as metaphors resist collapse into a finite set of literal sentences, so attitudes resist collapse into a finite set of grounding beliefs. All attitudes are belief-dependent. For example, to have an attitude of admiration towards Lauren Bacall, I must hold a number of factual beliefs about her (e.g. that she is the blonde actress in "To Have and Have Not," that she also appears in "Key Largo," that she was Bogart's wife). Such beliefs establish that my attitude is directed towards the proper object. There aren't any particular beliefs about Bacall such that I need to hold *those* beliefs in order to have an attitude directed towards her. I simply must have some collection of beliefs about her, some of which are accurate. [If all my beliefs about Bacall were false and applied instead to Ginger Rogers — e.g. "She's

the brassy redheaded actress who danced with Fred Astaire" —
then my attitude is not an attitude towards Lauren Bacall at all.
It is an attitude towards Ginger Rogers about whom I have (at
least) this false belief: that her name is Lauren Bacall.]

This dependence of attitude upon belief has been ably
documented in the literature.[36] Though some collection of
Bacall-beliefs must be present in order to direct my admiration,
these beliefs do not constitute my attitude. This is so because
many of Bacall's detractors might hold the very same beliefs.
This suggests that there are further beliefs logically involved in
my attitude. In addition to the beliefs which direct my attitude
towards the appropriate object (in this case, Bacall) I hold additional beliefs which determine which attitude it is. Thus, if I
think Bacall acts well, is beautiful and intelligent, then my attitude is one of admiration. If I think her a cheap brassy blonde
with no acting skills, my attitude is instead one of disdain. Note
that my admiration for Bacall does not reduce to this further set
of beliefs about her. First, because other people might admire
her without holding these particular beliefs. And second,
because some might hold these same beliefs without admiring
her. Nor can we reduce admiration to holding a preponderance
of favorable beliefs, nor even to the single belief that its object is
admirable. It is always possible to hold such beliefs about a person (object) yet not admire that person (object).[37]

My point about these attitudes is this: they are no more reducible to the cluster of beliefs which ground them than metaphors
are reducible to the set of sentences which provide a paraphrase.
To proclaim Bacall stunning, quick, and talented is not yet to
admire her; to cite ten ways in which Juliet resembles the sun is
not yet to exhaust Shakespeare's metaphor. Thus metaphors and
attitudes alike have a sort of intentional transcendence which accords them both richness and mystery. And this structural
similarity suggests why metaphorical language might express attitudes more effectively than literal talk *or* wordless gestures.

VI. SUMMING UP

In this paper I have offered an increasingly abstract set of
arguments in response to the question "Can words hurt?" I
began by stating the feminist charge that ordinary language is
sexist and in need of reform. I considered one possible account
of sexism in language — the theory of etymological oppression

— and argued that this theory was not credible. Remaining agnostic on the question of whether words oppress, I proposed an alternative account of many of the cases feminists deem offensive. I claimed — following Robert Baker — that terms of our language often function as (dead) metaphors. I went on to suggest that such metaphors express attitudes rather than literal beliefs. To support this proposal, I offered further information about the nature of attitudes, about the paraphrasability of metaphors, and about the attitude-measurement devices employed by social psychologists. While this resulted in discussion at quite some remove from our initial question, I believe that these disparate pieces fit together to provide a full and convincing account. If correct, my analysis explains not only how metaphorical language can hurt and offend, but also how it can flatter, comfort, and soothe. It does so by conveying the various attitudes which are essential to our evaluations, enthusiasms, prejudices, and passions.

NOTES

1. Elizabeth Beardsley, "Referential Genderization", *Philosophical Forum* 5 (1973-4): 285.
2. *Ibid.*, p. 291.
3. Robert Baker, " ' Pricks' and 'Chicks': A Plea for 'Persons'," in *Philosophy and Sex*, Robert Baker and Frederick Elliston, eds. (Buffalo: Prometheus Books, 1975), pp. 53, 63 (pp. 170, 180 in this volume).
4. Baker, *passim*.
5. Barbara Lawrence, "Four-Letter Words Can Hurt You," in *Philosophy and Sex*, Robert Baker and Frederick Elliston, eds. (Buffalo: Prometheus Books, 1975) p. 32.
6. *Ibid.*, p. 32.
7. Wilfred Funk, *Word Origins and their Romantic Stories* (New York: Wilfred Funk Inc., 1950), p. 2.
8. Joel Feinberg, *Social Philosophy* (Englewood Cliffs: Prentice-Hall Inc., 1973). On page 26, Feinberg lists personality, property, reputation, domestic relations, and privacy among interests.
9. *Ibid.*, p. 27. Feinberg says, "typically, having one's interests violated is one thing, and knowing that one's interests have been violated is another."
10. The parallel breaks down in only one respect. I don't think we would claim that all offenses are a species of oppression; a trivial insult may well be offensive without seriously threatening its target's rights and/or dignity.
11. Feinberg, *op. cit.,* p. 28.
12. Richard Wasserstrom discusses this possibility in his paper "Racism and Sexism" in *Philosophy and Women*, Sharon Bishop and Marjorie Weinzweig eds. (Belmont: Wadsworth, 1979). He states, "We use concepts. Quite often without realizing it, the concepts used take for granted certain objectionable aspects of racist ideology without our being aware of it." (13) Note that when such linguistic habits become widely shared, the victims become accomplices in their own degradation.
13. Funk, *op. cit.,* p. 263.
14. The limiting case is represented by words which mean what they do today because of mistakes and misunderstandings in the past. Here the current meaning of the words bears no logical relation to that of the words from which they are descended.
15. For a more detailed argument along these lines, see Janice Moulton's "Sex and Reference," in this volume pp. 183-193. Moulton argues that our concept of sexual intercourse is defined without reference to female orgasm, and that this fact is reflected in our language.

16. If anyone finds the example implausible as a case of oppression, consider instead a Marxist view of American society, according to which all women are equally oppressed by the capitalist system, whether they are housewives lolling in leisure, waitresses punching a time clock, or executives climbing the corporate ladder.
17. My formulation is indebted to Grice's papers on meaning.
18. Of course, one can use words to perform communicative tasks without relying on the meanings of those words. When Groucho Marx gains entrance to the club by uttering the correct password ("Swordfish?") the effects of his utterance have nothing to do with the ichthyological associations of that word. Compare Searle's example where an American soldier remarks "Kennst du das Land wo die Zitronen bluhen" in order to convince his Italian captors that he is a German officer. [From "What is a Speech Act?" in *The Philosophy of Language* by J. R. Searle, ed. (Oxford: Oxford University Press, 1971), p. 46] Here again, success does not at all depend on the meanings of the words he utters, but on how those words are classified by his audience.
19. I don't believe this is merely a virtus dormativa argument. As Nelson Goodman emphasizes in *Languages of Art*, some aspects of a word's meaning are determined by what that word picks out, others by what words pick *it* out.
20. This image of intercourse is not inevitable. Alternatives have been proposed. For example, Robert Baker has suggested we think of intercourse as an action in which the woman envelops the man. ("Jane engulfed Dick.") Here the imagery suggests intercourse is a gentle and delicate act in which the woman plays an active role. My colleague James Doyle has reminded me that my account of screws is also not an inevitable one, that those familiar with machine screws might, unlike carpenters, find them symbolic of equity and harmonious fit.
21. Baker, p. 45, (p. 161 in this volume).
22. *Ibid.,* p. 46, (p. 162 in this volume).
23. Willa Cather, *The Professor's House* (New York: Grosset and Dunlap, 1925), p.274.
24. Compare Norman Mailer's description of his protagonist Stephen Rojack's marriage in *An American Dream* (New York: The Dial Press, 1965): "I had spent the last year parting company with my wife. We had been married most intimately and often most unhappily for eight years, and for the last five I had been trying to evacuate my expeditionary army, that force of hopes, all-out need, plain virile desire and commitment which I had spent on her. It was a losing war, and I wanted to withdraw, count my dead, and look for love in another land, but she was a great bitch, Deborah, a lioness of the species: unconditional surrender was her only raw meat." (p. 9)

25. Osgood, Suci, and Tannenbaum describe the theoretical background of the Semantic Differential in *The Measurement of Meaning* (Urbana: University of Illinois Press, 1957). As stated above, they identified the meaning of each and every concept with a unique location in semantic space. Semantic scales — defined by pairs of bi-polar adjectives — constitute lines within the semantic space. (p. 25). Osgood *et al.* used factor analysis to determine the underlying axes or dimensions of this space. The three dominant factors were evaluation, potency, and activity. (p. 72). (Osgood, Suci, and Tannenbaum note that semantic space is multidimensional. Additional dimensions were tentatively identified as stability, tautness, novelty, and receptivity. (p. 74). This theoretical suggested a means for testing and measuring attitudes. A subject's attitude towards a particular concept was defined as the projection of a particular point (the location in semantic space identified with the meaning of that concept) onto the evaluative dimension. This projection could be determined by presenting the subject with a number of semantic scales lying along the evaluative dimension. Thus the Semantic Differential.

26. Martin Fishbein, "The AB Scales: An Operational Definition of Belief and Attitude," in *Readings in Attitude Theory and Measurement*, Martin Fishbein, ed. (New York: J. Wiley and Sons, 1967).

27. This is less true for a situation like the Semantic Differential, where the metaphors are presented to the subject ready-made, than for some of the cases Baker documented in his article.

28. I have documented these claims in my dissertation "Attitude and Belief," Harvard University, Nov. 1977.

29. Stanley Cavell, "Aesthetic Problems in Modern Philosophy" in *Must We Mean What We Say?*, (New York: Charles Scribner's Sons, 1969), p. 79.

30. *Ibid.*, pp. 78-79.

31. *Ibid.*, p. 79, in a footnote added in 1968.

32. Max Black, "Metaphor," *Proceedings of the Aristotelian Society*, LV, (1954-5).

33. Philip Wheelwright, *Metaphor and Reality* (Bloomington: Indiana University Press, 1975). pp. 78 ff.

34. Nelson Goodman, *Languages of Art* (Indiana: Bobbs-Merrill Co. Inc., 1968), p. 80.

35. Presented at an aesthetics symposium of the APA.

36. See, for example, David Pears, "Causes and Objects of Some Feelings and Psychological Reactions"; Irving Thalberg, "Emotion and Thought"; and Bernard Williams, "Pleasure and Belief"—all in *Philosophy of Mind*, Stuart Hampshire, ed. (New York: Harper and Row, 1966).

Part III (C)

"Ms."

Michael Levin

Vs. Ms.

Academia has proved to be the Maginot Line in the defense of good sense against the panzer regiments of Women's Liberation. Being a citizen of the occupied territory behind it, I have become familiar — as which of us has not? — with one of the most disturbing manifestations of that movement's influence: the warping of language to suit the ideological line of the new feminism. My colleagues have become chairpersons and even "chairs." He/she's and Ms.'s abound. Every memo contains such terms, tacit sermons on or boosts for feminism. These ugly neologisms have long since spread to the media. The Pepsi Generation spawned the Pepsi People, who feel free. Not only have newspersons replaced newsmen, but TV football commentators have taken to referring to the "people" on the offensive line. One suspects unpublicized ukases from the network ex-

This paper is a revised version of a paper with the same title which originally appeared in Jane English, ed. *Sex Equality* (Englewood Cliffs, N.J.: Prentice-Hall, Inc., 1977): 216-219. Reprinted by permission of the publisher and the author.
*The present versions were prompted by the fact that the original short piece was pirated, reproduced, and widely distributed, without permission, by an irate feminist. Professor English was scrupulous about getting my consent, I should emphasize.
Further reflections on the issues discussed herein can be found in my "Sex, Language and the New Victorians," *The Nebraska Humanist* (Spring, 1980); "On Theory-Change and Meaning-Change," *Phil. Sci.* (Fall, 1978); and *Metaphysics and the Mind-Body Problem* (Oxford: Oxford University Press, 1979), pp. 152-156.

ecutives, a suspicion confirmed by my correspondence with the networks.

Like all bullies, the new feminists are attacking their easiest target — language. And make no mistake, language is under attack. Women's Lib has already shown itself willing to debase language, with its inaccurate talk of rape as a "political" crime (where were the caucuses and ultimata?), housewifery as "prostitution," and nearly everything as "oppression." This effort to mutilate English under the banner of "desexing" language is altogether pernicious. Efforts to legislate linguistic change to conform to a special world view have the net effect of making us unendurably self-conscious about our own language. Such a state of mind is profoundly unsupportable.

Language is the vehicle of thought and in an important sense we must be unconscious of our choice of words if we are to express our thoughts. When we become entangled with decisions about how to speak, we lose contact with the reality our speech is directed to. Surely the most uncomfortable moments of life are marked precisely by the need to think what to say: emotional scenes, awkward first dates, diplomatic negotiations with the boss. When things go smoothly we don't think about what words to use. We don't "choose our words" — they come unprompted.

Women's Lib has made everybody self-conscious about his use of language. Again, listen to your local commentator. There is a small but perceptible hesitation as he chooses his pronouns to describe the average consumer. He? She? He or she? He finally opts for "the average person" and avoids pronominal constructions as far as possible. Editorial decisions about pronouns become tedious, however, since they come at hundreds per day. He does not yet love Big Sister.

It might be hoped that this imposition will eventually collapse of its own onerousness. Nonetheless, as Justice Holmes remarked, the mode in which the inevitable comes to pass is effort, so part of the process of lifting the burden of self-consciousness must be the opposition of those who resent this very real and uncomfortable oppression. Perhaps women have the greater obligation in curbing the excesses of their *soi disant* sisters, since protestations like this one can always be dismissed as masculine insecurity. Yet acquiesence by men bending the knee to "progressive" women is more contemptible. If ingratiation is what they are after, a hen-pecked "Yes, dear" would have done nicely.

It will be replied that willfully altering language, however unpleasant the process, will expunge from it "sexist" prejudices. Does not "minuteman" create a presumption against women taking up arms? To the large claim that English is anti-woman a general scholium must be entered in rebuttal. *Pace* the speculations of some sociolinguists, the use of a language does not commit the user to any special theses or view of the world. Anything can be affirmed or denied in a natural language. Take "shrew," cited by feminists as a case of "linguistic sexism." That English does not commit us to the existence of shrews is shown by the fact that the existence of shrews may be denied in English. Anyone who wants to can say "There are no shrews." This would be *self-contradictory* if English were indeed sexually biassed. Now it may be that what the feminists are really aiming at is the straightforward elimination of words that express certain thoughts they find undesirable, such as the thought that some women are shrill and strident. But this is not making language "fair," It is the attempt to impose Newspeak, and the dangers of imposing Newspeak are patent.

(There is, incidentally, no real contradiction between denying that language affects thought and worrying about Newspeak. You can drive people crazy by punishing them for using words associated with perceived distinctions, and thereby punish them for making the distinctions themselves. What is shaping thought in Orwell's Oceania is not linguistic change, but the negative conditioning of speakers. But I will defer this general topic for another paper.)

Granted, English idioms change with social patterns. WW II gave us "Rosie the riveter." But we cannot even predict these changes, let alone try to dictate them. They occur at the same unconscious level as speech itself. It is certainly hard to imagine how the English scheme of pronominal reference could alter, centered as it is on "he." It fits the natural iambic rhythm of English as the feminine "person" does not. "He or she who hesitates is lost" and "Wonders are many, but the most wonderful of all are people themselves" fall flat.

I am not denying that language reveals something about ourselves, that features of language reflect reality and our perceptions. It is interesting to ponder the masculine and feminine nouns of languages which, unlike English, do have gender. Even more interesting are the inflected languages. In classical Greek the neuter coincides with the masculine roughly four times as often as it coincides with the feminine — and where it coincides with the feminine it coincides with the masculine as well. These presumably unintended features of language are the linguistic traces of ancient and perennial perceptions.

Consider, then, the title "Ms." Many people resist replacing the "Miss/Mrs." distinction by "Ms.," but can only cite as a reason the fact that "Ms." is a distasteful echo of caricatured Negro dialect. What function does the "Miss/Mrs." distinction actually serve? I suspect it is something like this. Evolution has selected bisexual intercourse as that reproductive method which best mixes fecundity with genetic variety. Under such a system one sex must be the aggressor, the other the acceptor. If neither aggressed nothing would happen. If both aggressed, either nothing *but* mating would go on, or, more likely, the similarity of mating behavior of the sexes would deprive members of one sex from pursuing members of the opposite sex rather than their own and the species would die out. In the human species Man is the aggressor and Woman the accepter. Hence a man has to know, when encountering a new female, if she is eligible for his overtures. A woman need know nothing similar of a new man, since she is not the one responsible for initiation. The Miss/Mrs. device signals the male immediately as to the potentials for his future relations with this new female. The possibility of sexual awareness always exists between man and woman, and Miss/Mrs. is one of the many ways of accomodating this. To deplore this fact and call men beasts — or pigs, in the current argot — is to deplore human sexuality itself. (This fact also creates unique complications for across-the-board on-the-job sexual integration.) Miss/Mrs. has come about through its evolutionary value and consilience with human nature.

The irate feminist might ask why no symmetrical device has evolved for women. The reason, I suspect, is that nature works as simply as possible. The male needs to know who is available when selecting a target, but the potential accepter's knowledge would simply be excess baggage until she is approached. Moreover, the mere act of approaching a female is the male's announcement of his availability. While male philandering is undeniably part of the human scene, social forms like natural ones evolve in line with the norm.

But thus concentrating on the signalling function of the Miss/Mrs. distinction would be to overlook the even more profound distinction it is used to mark. The most important fact of human existence is that women can have children and men cannot. The distinction at issue is the one which traditionally marks the juncture at which a female becomes an expected bearer of children. There just is no juncture in the life of a man who has achieved majority that is of comparable significance. What may rifle feminists about the Miss/Mrs. distinction is that it reflects the pervasive human belief that incomparably the most important aspect of a woman's existence is her capacity for motherhood. But it would surely be as appropriate (or inappropriate) to pity men their incapacity for true creation, their need to fall back on conquering empires and writing symphonies as compensation — to pity them the fact that nothing about them warrants a distinction comparable to Miss/Mrs.!

I imagine the feminist reply would be to deny outright the essential difference between male and female roles in sexual encounters and the significance of childbearing — to chalk this difference up to "social conditioning" (useless hypothesis for so ubiquitous a phenomenon) and ask why women should not have the sexual prerogatives of men. I am reluctant even to argue for my own claim, since to do so would imply that it is recondite or in some way less than completely self-evident. I can only appeal to each person's experience of trying to do things over the long haul in any way other than what Bill Cosby once called "the regular way." I fully expect to be told that many beliefs about "human nature" have fallen by the wayside, that blacks were once held to be subhuman, that Jews were thought to be of subnormal intelligence, etc. However, these past aberrations are all instances of xenophobia, easily explicable in terms of cultural differences. The differences between men and women I am stressing are so basic, so clear in animals (where culture is not an issue), that it is absurd to deny them. They are as essential as anything could possibly be to our natures. Of course, some views about the differences between men and women have proven false; upper-class Victorians thought that women should be confined during menstruation. But what have such cases to do with views that all experience confirms and are recognized by every culture? While it is *logically possible* that there are no innate differences between the mating instincts of men and women, it would be absurd to treat this possibility as the next thing to a fact. It is logically possible that we all live in Russia, and that our impression that we don't is the product of an elaborate conspiracy; but it would be absurd to take this hypothesis seriously and conclude that we might be living in Russia.

But I must confess a certain desire to see the feminist make the indicated reply, for it tips her real hand: not the desire to bring language into line with "equal treatment" but the desire to upset the whole sexual applecart. And the feminists are succeeding. They have managed to make us self-conscious about the language of sexuality, and with that threatens to come such self-consciousness about sex itself as to destroy spontaneity. And these are encroachments to resist.

Afterthought. Some irenicists have suggested that "Ms." *is* after all convenient for addressing females of unknown marital status, so why not use it? Well, first, the common stylistic practice of earlier days was to address such females as "Miss." But even waiving this, the unfortunate fact is that what would otherwise have been a useful and innocent device came into this world trailing clouds of ideology. As things are now, the "speech-act" force of using it is to place oneself squarely in the feminist camp. Had "Ms." been suggested as a stylistic simplification for form letters, fine. But it wasn't: it was explicitly introduced with the aim of counteracting the "sexist" idea that a woman's marital status is more important than a man's, and to speed the Great Day when women would be freed of the serfdom of sexual inequality. So anyone who uses it today, knowing how it was intended and knowing that everyone knows he knows how it was intended, is pledging allegiance to feminism. Sometimes there is no escaping provenance. A crossed hammer and sickle might be the most appropriate symbol for my local softball team (we're a bunch of farmers and pavement-smashers); nonetheless, since I know that everyone knows that I know who else has adopted the hammer and sickle, it would be at best quite disingenuous to say "Look, it's only something to put on our softball uniforms." So with "Ms." which would have been perfectly all right had it come along in a way other than it did.

L.M. Purdy

Against "Vs. Ms."

Feminists hold that English reflects the social inequality of women and that altering sexist language will help rectify this inequality. Michael Levin objects to altering English: "Language is the vehicle of thought, and in an important sense we must be unconscious of our choice of words if we are to express our thoughts. When we become entangled with decisions about how to speak we lose contact with the reality our speech is directed to." Furthermore, nothing will be gained by such changes, for " . . . the use of language does not commit the user to any special theses or view of the world." In support of this position he claims that anything can be affirmed or denied in a natural language: the mere existence of a derogatory sex-linked word (like "shrew") does not mean that shrews exist. If English were sexually biased, denying the existence of shrews would be self-contradictory. He also argues that the continued use of "Miss" and "Mrs." instead of "Ms." constitutes no sexual prejudice.

None of these claims is convincing: Levin's philosophy of language is unsophisticated and his position is undermined by his own examples. According to him, linguistic bias could occur only when the existence of a noun entails the existence of the corresponding object, and the object does not exist. But this condition is never met in English because words do not entail the existence of their objects.

Levin appears to be blind to other possible manifestations of linguistic bias. Take "shrew," for instance. Why should every

shrill and strident person be characterized as female? Shrill, strident males do exist, and the best epithet would therefore be a
sex-neutral one. As the matter now stands, we must call such individuals "male shrews." This would commonly be taken as a
double insult: it suggests both that the behavior is unpleasant,
and that it is unpleasant in a typically feminine way. Furthermore, the mere existence of sex-linked insults (like "shrew")
suggests that the sex in question is thought more likely to behave
in the indicated way—else why did the sexual connotation arise?
To the extent that language reflects such unfounded assumptions, it is biased.

Let us now consider Levin's rejection of "Ms." in favor of
the traditional "Miss/Mrs." distinction. He argues that the latter is preferable because it has an important signaling function
and because it used to mark a crucial point in women's lives.

Levin's argument for the first claim goes like this. First,
evolution has selected bisexual intercourse in humans. Secondly,
under such a system, one sex must be the aggressor, the other the
acceptor. Thirdly, among humans, man is the aggressor and
woman the acceptor. Fourthly, aggressors must know whether
new females they encounter are eligible for sexual overtures.
Fifthly, the use of "Miss" and "Mrs." informs the male immediately about the potential of any new relationship. Sixthly,
women do not need such information because they do not initiate sexual relationships.

The first thing that should be noticed about this argument is
that it embodies a world-view. Levin tries to evade this issue by
emphasizing that the distinction came about because of its
"evolutionary value and consilience with human nature." But
empirical claims state theses about the world, no matter what
their truth value or how they came to be true or false. He cannot
have it both ways. If language is neutral, then we can adopt
"Ms." without being commited to any theories about sex roles.
If language is not neutral, and to use "Ms." is to commit oneself
to a world view, then using "Miss/Mrs." also commits one to a
world view.

It only remains to be seen whether Levin's statements are true
(and hence represent a tenable view of the world) or not. The
first premise is unexceptionable. The second, however, is
dubious. Levin argues that if one sex is not an aggressor, neither
will aggress or both will do so. In the first case, "nothing would
happen." In the other, "nothing but mating would happen, or,

more probably, the similarity of the mating behavior of the sexes would deprive members of one sex of grounds for pursuing the opposite sex rather than their own, and the species would die out.''

We might ask why encounters must be characterized in terms of aggression. Perhaps this is the proper way to talk about encounters between rats or tigers, but men and women can and sometimes do behave in civilized ways, with expressions of interest replacing aggression.

Levin's individual arguments here are no more persuasive than his general position on human sexual aggression. I believe there is no fear that diffused responsibility for initiation of sexual encounters will diminish coupling. Most humans are sufficiently interested in sex to continue to seek out partners. If they find an attractive person, and the attraction is mutual and the circumstances propitious, sexual intercourse may occur. That ''nothing happens'' in the absence of these conditions is as it should be. The fears that ''nothing but mating would happen'' or that ''the similarity of the mating behavior of the sexes would deprive members of one sex of grounds for pursuing the opposite sex rather than their own'' are equally groundless. The first falsely implies that nobody ever thinks about anything but sex. The second denies that one of the chief satisfactions in sex is derived from pleasurable contact with complementary sex organs. Having such organs seems to me to constitute reason enough to pursue members of the opposite rather than the same sex. Hence the prospect of homosexuality extinguishing the species for this reason is remote.

Premise three is also dubious: it is well-known that women often chase men. The conjunction of premises four and six is no more plausible, for it sanctions a double standard of sexual morality: a man ought not to approach a married woman, but he may approach an unmarried one, whether he is married or not. That is why the ''Miss/Mrs.'' distinction is useful for women, but a similar one is unnecessary for men. This position is unjustifiable: extramarital sex is equally right or equally wrong for both sexes. To deny this is to hold that women's (but not men's) sexual desires should be tempered by ethical ideals such as faithfulness and commitment. This position is indefensible unless it can be shown that there is some essential difference between men's and women's sexual desires. For obvious reasons it is doubtful that there could be any such proof.

Premise five is plainly false. First, some married women keep thier maiden names with the prefix "Miss"; some divorced women and widows use "Mrs." But secondly, and more importantly, a woman's marital status does not determine her sexual morality. Like men, women devise their own rules: some unmarried women do not have sexual relations and some married ones engage in extramarital sex. A man's attractiveness probably affects the potential for a relationship at least as much as the marital status of the woman.

Not only is form of address an unreliable indicator of interest in a sexual relationship, but other indicators are far more reliable. Availability and interest can be (and are) broadcast by mannerisms, looks, dress, and conversation. Signals of this sort can be sent and received by both sexes; men are just as capable of determining whether a woman is interested as vice-versa. Neither sex needs a special form of address to show interest.

Thus Levin's argument for an important signaling function for "Miss" and "Mrs." contains both false statements and morally unacceptable ones. It therefore represents an untenable world view. Let us now consider his second argument for keeping the distinction. He writes: "The most important fact of human existence is that women can have children and men cannot. The distinction at issue is the one which traditionally marks the juncture at which a female becomes an expected bearer of children . . . What may rile feminists about the Miss/Mrs. distinction is that it reflects the pervasive human belief that incomparably the most important aspect of a woman's existence is her capacity for motherhood."

Many people (not all of whom could be described as feminists) would reject Levin's assertion that the "most important fact of human existence is that women can have children . . ." Among rival candidates are the abilities to reason abstractly, to make tools, or to alter the environment.

These are *human* capacities, and women are humans as well as females. True, one of the chief distinguishing biological features of female humans as females is their capacity to bear children. However, female humans are also human, and as such they share the distinguishing features of humanity with men. Thus a woman may enjoy childbearing, but she may also—if not stunted by a confining social role—enjoy writing philosophy papers, practising carpentry, or designing dams. To focus as exclusively as Levin does on women's purely biological possibilities at the expense of their intellectual and psychological ones is to imply that women have more in common with females of other species (like rats or cockroaches) than with men.

Levin tries to obscure this fact by glorifying childbearing and belittling men's pursuits as just "compensation" for the inability to have babies. This suggests that these pursuits are of little value, a claim which seems hypocritical in light of the rich intrinsic and/or extrinsic rewards available to successful men, rewards women would like to share. In any case, if Levin thinks men are in need of genuinely worthwhile activities, why does he not suggest that they participate equally in *raising* children—an endeavor far more challenging, long-lasting, and rewarding than baby-making?

Levin rightly foresees his opponents' denial that there are (or ought to be) rigid sex-linked behavior patterns governing encounters between men and women, and their denial of the overwhelming importance of childbearing. He replies: "I am reluctant to argue for my own claim, since to do so would imply that it is recondite or in some way less than completely self-evident."[1] His position is not recondite, but neither is it self-evidently true. If his assertions are empirical, then he lives in a different world than mine; if they are normative, they cannot be self-evident, for no moral claim is. His position needs support, whether he recognizes the fact or not.

Further debate about these important issues will have to wait another occasion, for my main concern here is language. Levin's discussion of "Ms." has, I think, amply proved my case: language is not neutral, and using or rejecting an innovation like "Ms." reflects and helps perpetuate fundamental assumptions about the world. If people continue to use "Miss" and "Mrs." for the reasons Levin supposes, then adopting "Ms." constitutes a stand against his position. This by itself would, in my opinion, justify its use. The alternatives frequently convey inaccurate information about a woman's marital status and sexual proclivities. But more important, they underline facts (or supposed facts) which ought not to be considered in most contexts. Marital status or sexual proclivities should be of no consequence when buying shoes or applying for a job: why should salespersons or potential colleagues be apprised of them? Not only might the information activate stereotyped notions, leading to unjustified discrimination, but it assumes a morally objectionable view of the nature and proper roles of women.

An additional advantage of "Ms." is that it makes it easier for women to keep their own names when they marry. One is then neither a "Miss" (for "Miss" is usually taken to imply that one is not married) nor a "Mrs." ("Mrs. Jones" implies that one is married to Mr. Jones). Keeping one's name is desirable because it helps make others aware of one as an independent individual who is not a mere appendage of one's husband. Such recognition is essential if women are to be thought of as equal members of society with the same rights and duties as men.

These considerations justify the use of "Ms." and also support the general claim that language does contribute to our conception of the world. Perhaps adopting neutral words will disrupt spontaneity for a time, but such disruption is a necessary evil if we are to eliminate the injustices embodied in our language. (The meaning of this passage is somewhat unclear; I take it that "claim" here refers to the denial of these denials.)

Alan Soble

Beyond The Miserable Vision of "Vs. Ms."

Michael Levin's essay[1] is devoted to arguing that "Ms." should not become entrenched in the English language. Four separate arguments are offered, which I call the (1) *male sexual aggression*, (2) *female childbearing*, (3) *ideological introduction*, and (4) *spontaneity* arguments. But Levin is equally concerned to reassert three claims which have come under criticism by feminists and other social and political philosophers, namely, that women are by nature sexually passive, that the most important property of women is their ability to bear children, and that women should be excluded from traditionally male professions and occupations. I propose to refute the four arguments against the use of "Ms." and to defend a feminist critique of two of Levin's three antiquated claims about women.[2]

I

Levin's *male sexual aggression* argument can be broken down into the following steps:

(A) Evolution has selected heterosexuality.
(B) In such a system, one sex must be sexually aggressive and the other must be sexually passive (the "accepter" sex).

* I wish to thank Professor Sandra Bartky for her extensive comments on the first draft of this paper. I am also grateful for the help and encouragement of Mary Vetterling-Braggin.

Step (B) is intended to follow from a *reductio* subargument which consists of two parts:

(B') If both sexes were sexually passive, no sexual intercourse would have occurred ("nothing would happen") and the species would have died out (which it hasn't).

(B'') If both sexes were sexually aggressive, then either (i) members of both sexes would have done nothing but engage in sexual activity and, consequently, the species would have died out, or (ii) "the similarity of mating behavior" (i.e., both sexes aggressive) "would deprive members of one sex of grounds for pursuing members of the opposite sex" and the resulting increase in "own sex"[3] pairings would have led to the species' dying out (which it hasn't).

Then Levin proceeds to assert:

(C) In humans, the male sex is the aggressive sex and the female sex is the passive (accepter) sex.

(D) Because males are the sexual aggressors, males have to know which of the females they encounter are eligible to participate in sexual activity.

(E) The linguistic convention "Miss/Mrs." has arisen to accommodate this need of males to know which females are eligible ("Miss" tells the male that she is eligible; "Mrs." tells him that she is ineligible; "Ms." tells him nothing.)

Therefore, Levin concludes, the linguistic convention "Miss/Mrs." serves a useful, adaptive evolutionary purpose, and is "consilient" with human nature — the distribution of innate sexual aggression and passivity.

Consider, first, claim (B''), part (i). If the members of a species did nothing but have sex all day, no one would be tending the garden or cleaning the bathroom (so much is analytically true), and the members of the species would surely die off — if not from starvation, at least from overexhaustion. But what reason is there to think that in a species in which both sexes were sexually aggressive, their being aggressive means that *all* the members would fritter away *all* their time on sex? Levin does say that it is more "likely" that a different mechanism would be responsible for a both-sexes-aggressive species dying out, in part (ii) of (B''). But, first, it does not follow from the fact that both males and females are sexually aggressive that their mating behavior would be "similar." This would be true only if mating behaviors were relatively unsubtle and the species had been genetically programmed to perform one specific set of mating movements (true for birds, perhaps, but not for humans). There is no reason to deny, that is, not only that there are in humans different gradations and colors of aggressive mating behavior, but also that both males and females could be sexually aggressive and yet have different aggressive movements. (For example, a male might express aggression by poking his erection against the buttocks of a female; a female might express her aggression by insistently presenting her hindquarters to the sight of a male.) Second, even if it were true that female and male sexually aggressive behaviors were so similar as to be perceptually indistinguishable, it would not follow that the members of the species would have *no* grounds for pursuing one sex or the other. There is a large number of "grounds" for pursuing one sex (the "opposite") rather than another ("one's own") which have nothing to do with aggression or passivity: odors, hair texture and distribution, gait and, more recently, clothing. The elimination of this single ground would not, therefore, result in an increase in "own sex" sexual activity.

Third, even if (1) male and female mating behaviors were indistinguishable and (2) the aggressiveness of the mating behavior were the only grounds for pursuit and/or selection of a sexual partner, it would still not follow that such a species would die out. This imaginary species would die out only if *all* the sexual activity occurring were "own sex" activity *and* the species did not possess a technology for reproducing its kind independently of physical intercourse. Granting both (1) and (2), we can safely say that 50% of the sexual contacts will be "opposite sex" and 50 % "own sex." But whether a species procreates and thereby survives depends not only on the percentage of heterosexual matings but also, and more acutely, on the efficacy of the heterosexual matings that do occur. If only 50% of all sexual activity were heterosexual, it seems reasonable to say (*ceteris paribus*) that would guarantee enough efficient reproductive acts.[4] And when we take into account the existence of reproductive technology, it of course becomes possible for an entire species to practice exclusively the delights of "own sex" sexual activity without the species dying out (not for that reason, anyway).

The argument for (B) based on (B') fares no better. It seems reasonable to deny that a person who is sexually passive or an accepter is one who never has an independent urge to engage in sex. Even the women (as characterized by Levin) who are the sexual accepters have some sexual desire that induces them to have sex. Therefore, even if both sexes were passive, there is reason to believe that enough efficient heterosexual matings would occur to preserve the species. Furthermore, even if sexual passivity did mean that one never had an inclination to have sexual relations, this would imply that only a species which also lacked an appropriate reproductive technology would die out.

There is yet another reason why (B') and (B'') do not support (B). Levin has committed a strange version of the fallacy of composition. If it were true that the survival of a species did depend on some of the members being only sexually aggressive and others being only sexually passive, it would not follow that all the members of one sex would have to be the aggressors and all the members of the other sex the accepters. Moreover, a species could very well survive if each individual were at some times aggressive and at other times passive. Levin elsewhere in his paper suggests that nature works in "simple" ways, and so he might say that nature would have arranged it that the members of one and only one *sex* were the aggressors. But a nature that divided the aggressive from the passive members along eye-color lines (for example) would be arranging things as simply as a nature that made the division correspond to anatomical sex. The required genetic mechanism would not be any more complicated or time- or energy-consuming. More importantly, it is sheer nonsense to speak of nature as "simple" or as "complex." These terms are meaningfully applicable only to human descriptions (hypotheses, theories) of nature. And the simplicity of a theory is a poor indicator of the truth of these human inventions, or even of their "likelihood."

The real howler, however, in Levin's argument is his claim (C): "In the human species Man is the aggressor and Woman the accepter." (How quaint his use of capitalization, as in "Woman, Thy Name is Frailty.") (C) is false. Levin writes that he is "reluctant even to argue for" (C), "since to do so would imply that it is recondite or in some way less than completely self-evident. I can only appeal to each person's experience of trying to do things over the long haul in any other than what Bill Cosby once called 'the regular way'." But the truth of (C) is not self-evident, and citing a stand-up comic provides no help. The difficulty of changing a mode of behavior is far from decent evidence that that mode of behavior is natural.

I want to consider three arguments offered on behalf of (C) by

Anthony Storr.[5] In one, he argues from the fact that spermatozoa actively swim to the passively awaiting ovum to the conclusion that there is a parallel differentiation in the sexual roles of males and females. To be nice, we could say that Storr, too, is "only" guilty of the fallacy of composition. More importantly, the sense in which male sexuality would be aggressive *if* the analogy were perfect, is only that it would be "motile." But, as any reasonably experienced person knows, women can be and are just as "motile" as any male, both in seeking out sexual relations and in muscular movement during the act of coitus. In his second argument, Storr relies on the necessity of male pursuit and penetration to support (C); the female counterpart behavior is to "yield" and "submit" to this penetration. But the fact that in coitus the male organ can penetrate and thrust in no way establishes (C). This is so not only because women can "ride" men in the superior position (in which case the male organ can become quite the passive spectator), but also because penis-vagina intercourse is hardly the be-all and end-all of male-female sexual relations.[6] Furthermore, the male pursuit mentioned by Storr does a great injustice to those women who actively pursue men.

Finally, Storr makes an appeal to the "mental life". "It is significant that there is a difference between the sexes in the type of phantasy which appeals to each. The idea of being seized and borne off by a ruthless male who will wreak his sexual will upon his helpless victim has a universal [sic!] appeal to the female sex." Perhaps Storr was the hapless victim of writing before journalistic sex studies became commonplace; at any rate, both the richness and variety of male and female sexual fantasies are astounding and well-documented (and these fantasies include some in which males are brutalized and humiliated by women). Most women have no difficulty entertaining erotic thoughts much more exciting and creative than this bland "Dominique" scenario. But even to the extent that women do report having fantasies involving their being raped or carried off by a valiant male on a horse, this fact in no way supports the claim that women are sexually passive. First, not all persons wish that their sexual fantasies be realized; as a result there is often a large gap between the content of a mental fantasy and a person's actual sexual behavior. Second, even if a woman does desire to be carried off by an aggressive knight, she could very well be aggressive in inducing him to do it. Finally, as soon as we enter the realm of the "mental life" we are fairly far from speaking about natural tendencies and properties. Those women who do have rape fantasies have them not because of anatomically- or physiologically-generated psychological sex-role differences, but because of psychosexual conditioning (a much more plausible explanation).

The big flaw in Levin's argument is that he never explicitly defines what it means to be sexually aggressive or passive. Nevertheless, there is an unstated but implied notion of "aggression" in his paper when he uses the words "overtures," "approach" and "target." An aggressive person is one who approaches another person for sex, or who makes overtures to a potential lover, the "target"; the aggressor is the pursuer, the one (like Alcibiades) who does the wooing, sends the flowers, and writes darling little poems. Levin does, however, seem to mean something else in addition to this. A sexually aggressive person is one who is always ready for sex, or who constantly has sex on the mind, or who would like to be having much more sex (as much as possible!) during the course of an average day — and who has the physical potency required for this performance. Levin seems to be saying that in humans, males are the ones who do the pursuing and women are the ones who passively react to these pursuits, *because* (and *only* because) males have a greater sexual desire than females, they have more natural interest in sex, and have more sexual energy than women. (This is the substance of the "male sexuality myth," according to which males have infinite desire and infinite capacity to satisfy that desire.) Now we can make sense out of Cosby's (and Levin's) *regular* way: the male, in this purportedly predominant pattern given to humans by their nature and difficult to contradict in practice, picks up the phone, calls the woman, makes a date, eventually comes by for her in his Corvette, takes her to dinner, fills her with wine, pays the check, and then makes his move under moonlight or on the sofa with Tony Bennett droning away in the background. During the rest of his time, the male is continually horny and is forever planning his attack against other "targets."

Is it true, then, that (only) human *males* are aggressive in this sense? Do human males naturally make the first move or initiate sexual activity? And do they naturally have a stronger sex drive than women? I think the answer to these three questions is quite clearly "No." In this sense of "aggressive," many women can be, are, and have been aggressive.[7] By this I mean not only that women initiate sexual activity by bringing up the subject verbally or by physically seducing others, but also that even when it is the male who proposes what it is they are to do (by making the first outward, explicit move), it is often the case that the woman has implicitly suggested, in a subtle aggressive way, that he should make such a proposal. That Levin overlooks the many ways in which women have always been sexually aggressive (see also my discussion of Storr, above) implies that he has become stuck in a world-view permeated more by ideology and wishful-thinking than by careful (even offhand) observation.

The little bit of truth in Levin's view is that at least one person must do some kind of initiating in order for a pair of persons to get together and have sexual relations. Put this way, claim (C) sounds like a Thomistic first-cause doctrine, and is trivially true. But all this means is that given any pair of persons, one of them must communicate the appropriate message, and this can be done either by making an explicit advance, or by hinting, or, more subtly and interestingly, by sending out various cues through body language, vocal intonation, and so forth. Once we understand that for humans the events that surround the commencement of sexual activity are highly sophisticated, we very quickly lose the stimulus for thinking in terms of "aggression" and "passivity" at all.

Actually, there are two ways of construing Levin's *male sexual aggression* argument. Levin is *urging* us not to abandon the old "Miss/Mrs." in favor of "Ms." We *should* retain the old convention and we *should not*, he seems to be saying, embrace the pretender. But on the first reading of the *male sexual aggression* argument what he "proves" is that to use "Ms." would be to fly in the face of a predetermined evolutionary course of human development; the use of "Ms.," that is, is not in the evolutionary cards, while evolution has dealt us the quite respectable hand of "Miss/Mrs." Now, at least from the time of J.S. Mill the evolutionary or naturalistic type of argument against or for anything has been met forcefully by the rejoinder that if a behavior is in fact natural or has been selected by evolutionary pressures, it is unnecessary to encourage it and futile to discourage it. Levin does write, quoting Holmes, that "the mode in which the inevitable comes to pass is effort." But if it is true, *pace* Levin, that effort is instrumentally important in encouraging or discouraging the use of "Ms.," then whether or not its use proliferates will depend on the competition between the two antithetical efforts. So we need to know: what *reason* does anyone have for exerting one effort or its contrary? And here Levin's *male sexual aggression* argument, in its first construal, is impotent to supply an answer, because it is supposed to record what has happened or will happen *after everything* (including, but not limited to, the influence of effort) has been taken into account.

The second reading of the argument does make it out to be an attempt to provide good *reasons* (rather than to state the relevant causal chains) for discouraging the use of "Ms." What Levin needs to do is to argue that we have a good reason for retaining the old convention because that convention serves a useful social function — and no mention need be made of "human nature" or innate male sexual aggression or evolutionary pressures. The old convention, then, is to be protected because it allows males to distinguish *in advance* those women who are eligible for sexual activity (those called "Miss") from those who are ineligible ("Mrs."). Now, if we are simply talking about ways in which people communicate to each other their sexual intentions, we can certainly dispense with "Miss/Mrs." These labels are much too crude and are cues that would be employed only by the sexually naive (or as a joke). The convention is hardly indispensable for that function and it is not very efficient in comparison with all the other ways in which people communicate their sexual intentions.

Levin might have more in mind than this. When he talks about "male philandering" he is referring to an ineligible male (a married man) approaching a woman (of unstated status, but at least not his wife) for sexual relations. This suggests that Levin sees "Miss/Mrs." as serving not merely a communicative function but also (or more importantly) a *moral* function. Those women called "Miss" are eligible for sexual relations with single men for moral reasons; for a single male to have sexual relations with a "Miss" would not violate the prohibition on adultery. Similarly, for a man to attempt to have sexual relations with a "Mrs." would be to violate that prohibition. But even if we grant some validity to a moral prohibition on adultery (a dubious proposition), surely the "Miss/Mrs." linguistic convention is neither indispensible nor particularly efficient in warding off potential prohibition-breakers. All the other communicative cues which say "no" are much more powerful than the appellation "Mrs." in declining clandestine relationships.

Levin might deny, despite his use of the suggestive term "philandering," that he intended the "Miss/Mrs." convention to mark a moral distinction. He does write "While male philandering is undeniably part of the human scene, social forms like natural ones evolve in line with the norm." By this he seems to mean either that (1) the prohibition of adultery is itself a product of evolutionary pressures, and therefore only a pseudo-moral prohibition, although still one to be taken seriously, or (2) evolutionary forces have selected successfully against the existence of persons who have a disposition to commit adultery. In the first case, "the norm" refers to the pseudo-moral prohibition; in the second case, it refers to the purported fact that the statistical behavioral pattern is most frequently (by a wide margin) nonadulterous, monogamous behavior. Levin's wording is so cryptic that I can't decide whether he means (1) or (2). At any rate, on either interpretation his claim fails for pretty much the same reason. Adultery is so common that the moral prohibition of it is not as firmly entrenched as we might expect it to be if it were in fact selected by evolutionary pressures. For the same reason, the statistical-frequency norm is no longer (if it ever was, regarding *both* men and women) on the side of monogamy and sexual fidelity. If nature has attempted to select for fidelity it sure has botched the job. But the two points to remember (the ones that show that Levin's reasoning in claims (D) and (E) is chimerical) are that (1) the "Miss/Mrs." convention marks a nonexistent distinction (hardly any women, or men, for that matter, are *a priori* ineligible), and (2) almost anyone who made it a practice to deliberately find out whether a woman was called "Miss" or "Mrs." before deciding whether or not to approach (*or* to answer an obvious overture from her) would be wasting a lot of valuable time and would be ignoring all the other cues that language and culture offer.[8]

II

I want to turn now to Levin's second argument against the use of "Ms.," the *female childbearing* argument. Levin claims that the old convention "Miss/Mrs." should be favored because it marks an "even more profound distinction" than that between eligibility and ineligibility for sexual relations. "The distinction at issue," writes Levin, "is the one which traditionally marks the juncture at which a female becomes an expected bearer of children.'' Levin never explains why the distinction requires a linguistic convention. Are we expected to reason that males need to know, in advance, which women are eligible to bear children? *That* would indeed be a silly justification of the convention. Just as people have many ways to communicate sexual interest or the lack of it, they also have numerous ways of finding out whether any particular person is willing and able to become a parent (either mother or father). "Miss/Mrs." is again, neither indispensible nor especially efficient for this purpose.

There is another argument suggested by Levin's claim that "the most important aspect of a woman's existence is her capacity for motherhood," to the effect that it makes sense to be able to commemorate this fact about women linguistically. The "good reason" for the convention, then, would be that language is a fitting, even flattering, way to celebrate what is important about people. In this case, to retain "Miss/Mrs." in order to praise linguistically the childbearing capacity of women would be like issuing a four-color engraved stamp in the honor of an American heroine (say, Anita Bryant). Now, I would not deny that language can be used fruitfully in this way, to enshrine in our vocabularly important properties of persons (it is very common in medicine; think about pasteurized milk). But what I do deny is the coherence of the claim that "the most important aspect of a woman's existence is her capacity for motherhood."

One difficulty I have is in understanding how one would go about deciding that one property rather than another was the most important property of an object. Suppose we were to notice, as Levin does, that all (normal) women have the potential to bear children while all (normal) men lack this capacity. That is, "women" names the class of all and only those persons who possess this property. But this is not a sufficient reason for deciding that the most important property of women is their ability to bear children. The class denoted by "women" contains members who share other properties in addition to their ability to bear children — and share them to the same extent. "Women," then, doesn't pick out merely one property but a number of internally-related properties. If so, then selecting one of these properties as *the* most important has no *logical* foundation (as opposed to some possible pragmatic foundation).[9] What is interesting is that Levin apparently overlooked two other properties of women which are equally strong candidates for the title "most important." Given his *male sexual aggression* argument, one might have expected Levin to repeat the locker-room wisdom that has it that "the most important aspect of a woman is her cunt" — meaning her capacity to service men sexually, rather than her capacity to bring life into the world via her vagina. On the other hand, given that Levin is convinced of the sexual passivity of women, it is no wonder that he overlooked another property, the one that Mary Jane Sherfey calls "satiation-in-insatiation" (women are sexually insatiable).[10]

Furthermore, even if we could designate one property possessed by all members of a set as the most important property, it would only be the most important property of the *set* and not necessarily, or even likely, the most important property of any *individual* member of that set. For example, take the set of all stamp collections. The most important property of the set, the property that is *shared* by all the members, is that each contains a sufficiently large number of stamps assembled according to some organizational principle. But the most important property of any particular stamp collection in that set may not be that it, *simpliciter*, contains stamps organized in conformity to some principle, but rather that it is *my* stamp collection, or that this one happens to include a very rare black-bordered German stamp, or that it has won a prize in a competition. Similarly, we might say that the most important property of the set of women is their shared capacity to bear children, without being committed to saying of any given woman that this is *her* most important property. In fact, it is consistent with the claim that the most important property of the set of women is their capacity to bear children, that it is true of absolutely *no* woman that her most important property is the capacity to bear children.

I think what this discussion brings out is the idea that "most important" is a relativistic or pragmatic concept, that we can only speak of "most important with-respect-to" something else. This idea receives support from the quite different attempt to equate "most important" with "unique" (rather than with "shared"). Surely my fingerprints are unique to me, but that does not mean that my fingerprints are, in *most* contexts, my most important property. In the context of a murder trial, my fingerprints could very well turn out to be my most important (and most unwelcome) property. Similarly, in the context of a traditional marriage a woman might consider her capacity to bear children to be her most important feature. But given the indefinite number of contexts women can find themselves in, how often will this be true of all women or of any woman? And *when* it is true, it is bound to be a social contingency.

Let us examine the "Miss/Mrs." convention itself, for we can learn an important lesson from Levin's treatment of it. Levin claims that convention marks *two* distinctions; thus we can draw up this table:

	Miss	*Mrs.*
(I)	—eligible for sexual relations	—not eligible for sexual relations
(II)	—not an expected bearer of children	—an expected bearer of children

The first thing that must be cleared up is the historical inaccuracy of Levin's claim that "Miss/Mrs." has *come about through* its evolutionary value and consilience with human nature. Originally (according to the *OED*) and up to, say, 1600, *both* "Miss" and "Mrs." were abbreviations for "mistress," which at the time referred to a kept woman, a concubine, a prostitute. It was only in the 1700's (to be rough) that "Miss" and "Mrs." took on their current meanings. This fact is interesting at least because the relative recency, from an evolutionary perspective, of the linguistic convention, and its more-or-less sudden adoption by English-speaking persons, argue against the convention's being "selected" by evolutionary pressures. It also indicates that the human species did quite well in terms of survival for an awfully long time without the "Miss/Mrs." convention as we know it today. In trying to explain why the convention arose when it did, we are better off saying that at that time various people believed (rightly or wrongly) that a social purpose was served by changing the meanings of "Miss" and "Mrs." (and so drastically), rather than saying that evolution got it into its head to allow those who continued to use the terms in their former meaning to die off without transmitting their linguistic habits to the young.

But there is something paradoxical about the convention as it stands today and as it is presented by Levin. A "Miss" is someone who is simultaneously[11] eligible for sexual relations but *not* yet at the age of being an expected bearer of children; similarly, a "Mrs." is someone who is *not* eligible for sex but who is expected to bear children. This air of paradox can be resolved easily, but doing so reveals something hidden below the surface of Levin's facile presentation of the convention. We, of course, can object to the "Miss/Mrs." convention because it apparently restricts women to only two categories (when, it is clear, there are many other categories of women beyond the crude ones of "Miss" and "Mrs."). But I would prefer to emphasize the fact that the "Miss/Mrs." convention restricts women to *one* (legitimate) category. The existence of two words conceals the underlying principle that dictates that women have only one status. This single category emerges from the process of stripping the "Miss/Mrs." distinction of its aroma of contradiction.

The paradox surrounding "Mrs." is resolved simply by pointing out that a "Mrs." is not eligible for sexual relations with any man other than her husband, and that she is expected to bear this man's children. It is not so much that she is ineligible *tout court*; she is just ineligible from the point of view of all men but one. Now, the paradox involved in asserting that a "Miss" is eligible for sexual relations but is not expected to bear children *could* be resolved by saying that a "Miss" is someone, therefore, who necessarily makes use of contraceptives to prevent pregnancy. But this does not truly represent the underlying principle (nor does it square with Levin's intention; see footnote 4). Rather, the underlying principle resolves the paradox by insisting that the woman who is eligible for sexual relations but not for pregnancy *make* herself eligible for pregnancy by marrying the man in question and, thereby, keep herself sexually eligible for *him*. The paradox of "Miss," then, is resolved by the transformation of the woman into a "Mrs." If so, "Miss" is a pseudo-category. If the internal contradiction involved in being a "Miss" can be resolved only by abandoning that status and assuming the other status, then "Miss" does not mark off a legitimate status at all. A "Miss" is merely not yet a "Mrs.," but is eligible to become one. To be a "Miss" is to be living in a no-woman's land, in limbo, awaiting the day when the title "Mrs." can finally be conferred.

It is thus ironic that Levin claims that the convention "Miss/Mrs." is useful because it marks a real and important distinction in a woman's life. On the contrary, the existence of the convention — because it is constituted by two separate words — actually sends up a smokescreen which barely conceals the fact that a woman has only one legitimate status. At least for this reason "Ms." is to be recommended; it calls a spade a spade.[12] But there is a more meaningful reason for "Ms." Although it does carry the implication that women are all of a kind, "Ms." does so with the advantage of refusing to enthrone in language the illusion of what it is that is at the heart of a woman's existence.

III

Of course, there are better, positive reasons for "Ms." which have to do with a woman's self-respect, the respect we express for her, and the reciprocal causal connections between the two. This consideration is one that Levin almost recognizes when he writes that "Ms." was "introduced with the aim of counteracting the 'sexist' idea that a woman's marital status is more important than a man's, and to speed the Great Day when women would be freed of the serfdom of sexual inequality." Levin prefers to describe in a derogatory way the quest for self-respect and the respect of others that has been a central theme in the various branches of the women's movement.[13] Thus his argument against the use of "Ms.": " . . . what would have otherwise been a useful and innocent device came into this world trailing clouds of ideology" and, therefore, anyone who now uses it "is pledging allegiance to feminism." This is what I call the *ideological introduction* argument. It fails miserably.

Remember that one of our tasks is to find good reasons either to encourage or to discourage the use of "Ms." If it is true that whenever "Ms." is used an ideological statement is being made or one is raising a feminist flag, this can in different circumstances either encourage *or* discourage the use of "Ms." For those who want to announce their feminism Levin has provided one reason why they should continue to use "Ms." and to influence others to follow suit. For those members of the other "panzer regiment" Levin's argument shows why they should refrain from pronouncing a certain monosyllable. So the dispute, "Ms." vs. no "Ms.," is a reflection of and parasitic on the more general dispute, feminism vs. anti-feminism. And, of course, the *ideological introduction* argument is irrelevant in settling the latter.

Anyway, it is false that to use "Ms." these days is to stand firmly behind "feminism." That might have been true ten years ago, but all sorts of people use "Ms." now without any or much thought as to what ideology they might be advancing. Only a paranoiac would worry about using "Ms." and being misunderstood as a feminist. A similar phenomenon occurred with "black." In the 1960s, to use "black" instead of "colored" or "Negro" was to indicate that one was thoroughly in favor of civil rights for blacks, and often much more than this — black nationalism. Nowadays one has to use "black" just to make sure that one is not thought square, and no one considers the use of "black" as branding the user a member of SNCC. To a certain extent this trend with "black" and "Ms." is a healthy reflection that social movements have had some good effects on our linguistic habits and our beliefs. Of course, it is also unhealthy to the extent that the words have been used too loosely and have been stripped of their emotive and persuasive meanings. What this means, simply, is that linguistic change cannot be the only or even a basic technique used by social movements to generate change. But this is not to deny that linguistic change can be a helpful part of a program of social change.

The fact that both "Ms." and "black" have been assimilated so effortlessly into English also speaks to Levin's *spontaneity* argument against "Ms." He writes: "Efforts to legislate linguistic change to conform to a special world view have the net effect of making us [sic] unendurably self-conscious about our own language . . . Language is the vehicle of thought and in an important sense we must be unconscious of our choice of words if we are to express our thoughts." I am not sympathetic with Levin's fear that linguistic change will undermine the smoothness of thought and communication with language. In addition to "Ms." and "black," there are important counter-examples in "he/she," "chairperson" (even "newsperson" and "policeperson"), and the use of "Dear Person" rather than "Dear Sir" in letters sent to an office whose current occupant is unknown. Certainly when one first attempts to use "he or she" or "she or he" or "his or her" while speaking, one feels awkward, takes more time than usual, and perhaps even stutters. Like magic, however, after delivering philosophy lectures ten or more times a week, one begins to use "he or she" nonconsciously. The habit takes a surprisingly short amount of time to establish, with a wonderful effect on students who see and hear in action a successful move to overcome one's own conditioning (think about carrying out the linguistic change during a course of lectures on free will). Thus we can agree with Levin that our choice of words should be spontaneous, and yet disagree that it is impossible or tedious to change one's linguistic habits. Old dogs can teach themselves new tricks.

The important question, of course, is whether there are good reasons for changing one's linguistic habits. Here Levin's *spontaneity* argument is irrelevant because it gets things backwards. Spontaneity in choice of words or in any other behavior is not necessarily good in itself, contrary to Levin's belief. Sometimes spontaneity is valuable: during the free association of Freudian analysis, while playing tennis, jazz improvisation, while speaking with friends and lovers, teaching. But sometimes spontaneity, not choosing one's words with extreme care and with deliberate, conscious censorship, is very bad: diplomatic relations, philosophy papers, asking for a raise, teaching. Therefore, if in fact the use of "Ms." (or "he or she") were to interfere with spontaneity, we would need to know whether this spontaneity could not be sacrificed or whether, instead, it was unnecessary or even a luxury. The point is that if the use of "Ms." is designed to serve a good purpose, then one hopes that its use could become spontaneous. The failure of the use of a word to become spontaneous does not automatically refute the advice that the word be used more often.[14]

Levin's presentation of the *spontaneity* argument is confused. Immediately before his statement of the argument he gives examples of what he considers to be proposals for linguistic change, but which are not that at all. As an example of the "mutilation" of English proposed by "the new feminists" who threaten the spontaneity of language, he cites the "talk of . . . housewifery as prostitution." Levin intends this to be an example not only of a proposal for linguistic change, but also of an attempted "desexing" of language. But the claim that housewifery is prostitution (made as early as 1930 by Kingsley Davis and even earlier by Havelock Ellis, hardly feminists) is neither of these; it is, rather, a redescription of a phenomenon based upon what is claimed to be a more penetrating analysis of housewifery than one which is usually offered by social scientists. Not one feminist claims that we ought to speak of Mr. Smith's *Hausfrau* literally as a prostitute; the answer to the question "What does Mr. Smith's wife do for a living or with her time?" is still "She's a housewife," not "She's a whore." The analysis wants to show that in some respects being a housewife is like being a prostitute. (Similarly, not one feminist claims that what is accomplished by seeing the ways in which a housewife is like a prostitute is what is accomplished by desexing English by, for example, advocating "he or she" — or "tey" —

instead of "he.") The redescription of a housewife as a prostitute is close to what poets do with metaphor, and sometimes that procedure opens our eyes, yields a beautiful perception, or is intellectually rewarding. It is not a procedure that we could easily do without in the development of thought and language and of society itself. Ironically, more than once in his paper Levin does precisely that which he takes the feminists to task for doing. For example, in his sentence "One suspects unpublicized ukases from the network executives . . . " Levin (unwittingly?) uses "ukase" in what is known as a *transferred* meaning (see the *OED*). A ukase, in its original and strict sense, is a decree or edict issued by a Russian emperor (of which there are no more). To use the term "ukase" in describing the memos sent by Fred Silverman to the Not Ready For Prime Time Players is to commit a metaphor, is to *re*describe a common practice in a new way in order to bring out previously unrecognized features of the practice. (Such attempts at redescription, of course, may be felicitous or infelicitous. And sometimes they are meant only to induce laughter.) Despite the fact that Levin himself uses metaphor, it is quite understandable why he would fault the feminists for doing so. The conservative impulse behind the objection to "Ms." and in support of the traditional "Miss/Mrs." convention is the same impulse that shies away from any change, be it social or linguistic. Except, of course, change that reestablishes the wisdom of earlier times.

NOTES

1. Michael Levin, "Vs. Ms.," in Jane English (ed.), *Sex Equality* (Englewood Cliffs, N.J.: Prentice-Hall, 1977) pp. 216-219. Revised and reprinted in this volume, pp. 217-222.

2. I will not bother to do what has been done well enough by this time, to defend the claim that considerations of justice, equality and freedom require that women be fully integrated into traditionally male professions and occupations. At the end of his paper Levin admits that the type of argument he advances in "Vs. Ms." had been applied earlier in order to treat blacks and Jews unfairly. But he argues that those earlier arguments were mistaken and influenced by "xenophobia," and he implies that his present position is free of such defects. My suggestion — although this is not meant as a philosophical objection to his views — is that we might suspect that some "gynophobia" is causally related to analogous views about the "proper" place of women in society.

3. In his original paper Levin had said that *homosexuality* would wipe the species out; in the revised version he says that "own sex" sexual activity would do the job. This change suggests that Levin is aware that a behavioristic (minimal) description (as opposed, perhaps, to a mentalistic or dispositional analysis, like Freud's) may not be adequate in characterizing "homosexuality." What is curious is that when revising his paper Levin would pay attention to this relatively minor tangle and yet ignore all the gross defects in his arguments against "Ms."

4. Levin, mysteriously, assumes that all sexuality is reproductive or that the essential function of sexuality is reproduction. This mistake infects his whole paper, but it especially undermines the evolutionary argument being considered at this stage. Nonreproductive sexuality (including homosexuality as well as any sexuality primarily intended by the participants to yield pleasure rather than babies) can indeed serve evolutionary purposes. See Alex Comfort, *Nature and Human Nature* (London: Weidenfield and Nicholson, 1966), p. 30.

5. Anthony Storr, *Human Aggression* (New York: Atheneum, 1968). Passages quoted appear in Alison Jagger and Paula Struhl (eds.), *Feminist Frameworks* (New York: McGraw-Hill, 1978), pp. 278-279.

6. "Furthermore, even during coitus the passive role . . . of the vagina may coincide with a very active ego attitude. . . . Similarly, the male's active thrusting pleasure in coitus may coincide with a passive ego attitude." Gad Horowitz, *Repression* (Toronto: University of Toronto Press, 1977), p. 93.

7. Sociological research (as far back as Kinsey) has shown that the sexual activity and the extent of passivity of women, as well as the type of heterosexual lovemaking they enjoy the most, are strongly

influenced by socioeconomic variables. The evidence in favor of class distinctions is powerful enough to repudiate simplistic accounts of the natural passivity of women.

8. Consider the following facts. (1) Some men may prefer not to approach a "Miss" for sexual relations because a "Miss" is likely to be too young and inexperienced, while a "Mrs." is almost guaranteed to have *some*. (2) Some men may prefer to approach a "Mrs." because these men get a thrill from adultery; or because these men are themselves married and can only rationalize sex with a married woman. (3) Some men may prefer to approach a "Ms." for sexual relations because they believe that a "Ms." is necessarily liberated and therefore more of a challenge; or because these men think that such women deserve especially nasty treatment. (4) Some men may prefer not to approach a "Ms." for sexual relations because a "Ms." is, in their world-view, a man-hater and would only begrudgingly try to provide sexual pleasure for her partner. (I'm sure the list can be extended. It ought to include, also, statements about the real sexual preferences of women who do go under the labels of "Miss," "Mrs." and "Ms.").

9. The problem is similar to the Goodman paradox. Levin apparently resolves our present problem in a way analogous to resolving the Goodman paradox by appealing to the "entrenched" predicate when he writes that the idea that the most important property of a woman is her capacity to bear children is "a pervasive human belief." But I doubt that we are ever required to count the pervasiveness of a belief as evidence of its truth or coherence.

10. Mary Jane Sherfey, *The Nature and Evolution of Female Sexuality* (New York: Vintage Books, 1973), p. 112. For Sherfey's account of the physiological basis of the aggressive, demanding sexuality of women, see also pp. 51-52, 96, 103-104, 108, 113-114, 122, 132 and 138. I would like to suggest that it is the male's unconscious recognition of female sexuality as described by Sherfey (capacity for multiple orgasms) that gives rise to the conscious (and opposite) doctrine which I have called the "male sexuality myth" (that it is the male, and not the female, who has infinite desire and infinite capacity to satisfy that desire).

11. It is unclear whether Levin intends "Miss" to apply to, say, ten- to twelve-year-old girls. Surely they are not expected bearers of children, but neither are they eligible for sexual relations. Sandra Bartky pointed out to me that Levin's presentation of the "Miss/Mrs." convention not only ignores class distinctions but is also racist. Marriage, for many blacks and/or poor women in our society (and others), is hardly the juncture at which they become expected bearers of children. Levin's white middle-class perspective is evident not only here but also in his talk of "male philandering."

12. "All women are the same" is true in the same sense that "All workers are the same" is true. It is a central bourgeois *principle* that labor be homogenized. By analogy, then, bourgeois principle has it that "Ms." is the correct title for women. It is only bourgeois *apologetics* or *ideology* (which serves the purpose of covering up bourgeois principle) that has it that women are to be classified as either "Miss" or "Mrs." For an explanation of this distinction, see Derek Allen, "Is Marxism a Philosophy?", *Journal of Philosophy 71*, No. 17 (1974): 601-612.

13. Levin too often writes of "the feminists" and "the new feminists" as if the Women's Movement were monolithic. Nothing could be further from the truth. For a discussion of the various forms of feminism, and their philosophical disagreements, see *Feminist Frameworks* (fn. 5).

14. Levin is not so much worried about the loss of spontaneity in language as he is with the loss of spontaneity in sexual relations. My points about spontaneity in linguistic behavior remain the same with respect to sexual behavior. First: one can change stereotypical sexual behavior so that a new pattern becomes as spontaneous as the old, abandoned pattern. In particular, it is not impossible to repudiate Cosby's regular way and to embark upon new, less offensive and nonsexist ways of getting together with other people for sexual relations. Second: spontaneity is not in itself valuable, nor does it necessarily outweigh other values. Surely some restraint on sexual spontaneity is required in many domains. We do not want the rapist justifying his attack on the grounds that he was acting spontaneously; indeed, the "spontaneity" of the obsessive-compulsive child-molester is definitely a defect rather than a virtue. But to say this is not to deny that when two (or more) persons agree to go to bed together their pleasure will be enhanced, in most cases, to the extent that they enjoy each other's bodies spontaneously. Levin would be foolish to argue (although he does imply this) that the change from "Miss/Mrs." to "Ms." (and other linguistic reforms) would destroy spontaneity in that domain.

Part IV

Sexist vs. Racist Language Use

Introduction

A. ANALOGIES BETWEEN THE USE OF SEXIST AND THE USE OF RACIST WORDS AND SENTENCES

By now, the reader has probably noticed that many of the authors have advanced the view that the use of sexist language (insofar as this includes certain words and sentences) and the use of racist language are alike in morally relevant respects. ROBERT BAKER (PART III B), for example, argues that the user of racist language has a morally objectionable denigrating *conception* of blacks[1] just as the user of sexist language has a morally objectionable denigrating conception of women. ROBIN LAKOFF (PART II) suggests that the use of racist language is connected to inferior *social roles* of blacks in much the same way as the use of sexist language is connected to inferior social roles of women. And although she herself does not explicitly advance the view, SARA SHUTE's (PART I) type of reasoning might be used to support the thesis that the use of racist language is itself a morally objectionable activity for the same reasons the use of sexist language is, i.e., that it has a negative *effect* on certain persons.

In the introduction to PART II, however, yet a fourth kind of analogy was hinted at. There, it was pointed out that if the language we use reflects the way we think (as Baker, Moulton, and Ross suggest) and if it is also true that the way we think causes us to *behave* in certain ways, then the use of both sexist and racist language can have serious implications for women and minority group members.

This latter argument has a good deal of initial plausibility. For we expect the person who has racist and sexist thoughts to engage in certain behavior as a result of his or her way of thinking. That is, we expect that person to overlook women and minority group members when he or she is in the position of providing jobs or job promotions, to resist social contact with women and minority group members, and so on.

But not all are willing to accept this analogy. LAURENCE THOMAS, for example, argues that even if a male has a sexist conception of women, it is natural for that male to behave in ways beneficial to women. On the other hand, if a white person has a racist conception of blacks, it is not natural for that person to behave in ways beneficial to blacks. It is natural, he says, for a sexist male to protect women and to provide women with the comforts of life. In fact, it is tied to his very notion of his own self-esteem to do so. The racist thinker, on the other hand, suffers no loss of self-esteem in failing to act as a benefactor of blacks. It is for this reason, Thomas concludes, that sexist behavior lends itself to a "morally unobjectionable description" whereas racist behavior does not.

In order to reject, on the basis of Thomas' line of reasoning, the original analogy we began with, we must be convinced that more often than not, the sexist thinker behaves toward women in ways clearly morally acceptable, whereas more often than not, the racist thinker behaves toward blacks in ways that are clearly morally objectionable. Thomas seems to think that this thesis is true on the grounds that behaving in ways *beneficial* to women is *required of* (which is what he means by "natural to") the sexist thinker, whereas behaving in ways beneficial to blacks is not required of the racist thinker.

Both B.C. POSTOW and SARA ANN KETCHUM reply that a) the "beneficial" behaviors toward women that Thomas has in mind are not morally acceptable ones and b) selection of "beneficial" behaviors is not actually required of the sexist thinker. Postow argues that even if it is "natural" for the sexist thinker to behave in ways beneficial to women (and she thinks that this thesis is itself suspect), it is far from clear that protecting and providing for women is morally unobjectionable. "For one thing," she says, "protecting and providing for women against their will would presumably be objectionable.'' And even if the protection and comforts of life received by women from (male) sexist thinkers were done so in accordance with their will, a case could be made for the view that women are still harmed by this behavior. She says, ''Even if it is not morally objectionable for individuals to behave according to sexist roles in certain situations, the social *arrangement* where men and women behave according to these roles is not obviously unobjectionable because it shapes people to the roles, limits their freedom, etc.''

SARA ANN KETCHUM makes the stronger claim that the sexist thinker's behavior (as opposed to the social arrangement whereby men and women behave in certain ways) is itself always morally objectionable. The sexist husband, she says, provides for and protects his wife for the same reason a factory owner (feudal lord, slave owner, etc.) provides for and protects his workers (peasants, slaves, etc.). In all these cases, those in power are providing protection and the necessities of life to those under their control not because they view the latter as persons, but rather because they view them as property which has to be maintained. To provide for and to protect someone for this reason, Ketchum concludes, is clearly morally objectionable.

In order to accept this reply, one must be able to accept a Marxian analysis of the nature of the relationship between those in power and those controlled. Presumably, Thomas would wish to deny the validity of this analysis in the case of the sexist husband (although he may wish to accept it in the other cases cited by Ketchum). That is, Thomas may want to advance an argument to the effect that the sexist husband, unlike the slave owner, factory owner, or feudal lord, provides for and protects his wife because he considers her a complete (although inferior) person whom he loves and not because he considers her his property. The resolution of this debate, in short, rests on the acceptance or rejection of the definition of a ''sexist'' husband as one who has a conception of his wife as property to be maintained. Ketchum clearly wants to accept this definition whereas Thomas would probably want to deny that there is a necessary connection between sexist thinking and'viewing women as property, although he does not explicitly do so in his article.

But as Ketchum goes on to point out, even if all behaviors ''beneficial'' to women in some sense of that term were morally acceptable, many clearly unbeneficial and morally unacceptable behaviors toward women are also consistent with sexist thinking: physical mutilation (such as footbinding), physical intimidation (rape), training from childhood into physical, emotional and intellectual weakness, etc. On her view, there is no necessity to the sexist thinker's selecting the "beneficial" behaviors; in fact, she says it is *unlikely* that he will do so. And if selection of beneficial behaviors toward women is merely an option that a sexist thinker has,[2] yet other grounds must be advanced to show that the sexist thinker in facts selects benevolent (and morally acceptable) behaviors more often than the unbenevolent (and morally unacceptable) ones, whereas the racist thinker does not.

B. IMPACT OF SEXIST AND RACIST STATEMENTS ON THEORIES OF TRUTH

Up to this point, most of the authors included have concerned themselves with sexist 'language' only insofar as it is a matter of words or sentences. A further controversy appears to arise in considering claims or statements and theories of truth. PATRICK GRIM proposes that examples such as

1) Broads (niggers) will benefit from improvements in medicine. pose a particular problem. If we hold that (1) represents a statement which is either true or false, says Grim, we are thereby "committed" to the claim that

2) It is either true that broads (niggers) will benefit from improvements in medicine or false that broads (niggers) will benefit from improvements in medicine.

But commitment to (2) is commitment to an overtly sexist (racist) claim. On ethical grounds, he concludes that we must avoid any theory which classifies examples such as (1) as either true or false, and substitute for it one which holds that such examples are neither true nor false.

One possible objection to the above argument is this: commitment to a theory which holds that (1) is either true or false does not commit us to (2); what it commits us to is the *truth* of (2). And it is, after all, the assertion of (2) which would be morally reprehensible, not its truth; provided we never assert such a statement, there is no particular moral difficulty in holding that (2) represents a statement which is in fact true.

Grim finds this objection less than satisfactory. The objection, he says, requires us to commit ourselves to the truth of 'unassertables.' But a theory which requires the unassertability of true statements is in conflict with a standard ideal of rational discourse, which involves a willingness to assert the truth. And yet, the objector has a quite plausible response to Grim's reply: any ideal of rational discourse which would in this sense commit us to the assertion of sexist (racist) statements, even if they are true, is itself suspect and in need of modification. If Grim is right, this ideal would commit us to a willingness to assert all kinds of offensive (but true) remarks, not all of which are sexist or racist:

> Those lousy politicians will either win the election or they will not win the election
> That fat pig will either die from stuffing its face or it will not.

and so on.

A.J. STENNER offers the following objection to Grim's argument. We can maintain the theory of truth which Grim rejects, he says, by paraphrasing (1) into

3) Women (blacks) will benefit from improvements in medicine. [I believe that it is appropriate to speak of women (blacks) as broads (niggers).]

where brackets "serve to indicate what is suggested but not stated by the original. Bracketed material then is not construed as expressing part of the truth-conditions of the original."[5] On this analysis, the original theory is maintained by assigning a contingent truth-value to (3), and it is only what is suggested by statements such as (1) that is morally objectionable.

But Grim may well wish to reply that there is something odd about Stenner's notion of statements suggesting anything at all, particularly when they are not actually asserted. That is, although it is clear what it means to say that a *person* suggests something when he or she asserts a statement or uses a sentence, it is not clear how a sentence or statement can itself "suggest" anything at all. Moreover, it might be replied that (3) is a debatable paraphrase of (1) in the case of an individual who asserts (1) and then adds, "and by (1) I *mean* that women (blacks) are broads (niggers), not just that I believe them to be."

However, a variation on Stenner's argument would avoid these objections. Suppose that (1) were paraphrased into

3′) Women (blacks) will benefit from improvements in medicine. [Either women (blacks) are broads (niggers) or I believe that women (blacks) are broads (niggers).]

where brackets serve to indicate what is suggested but not stated by a person who asserts (1). On this analysis, we can assign a contingent truth value to (3′) and hold that it is only what is suggested by a person who asserts (1) [i.e. a false claim or that person holds a false belief] that is morally objectionable.

KRISTE TAYLOR agrees with Grim in arguing that examples such as (1) lack truth values. But she argues that (1) lacks a truth value not on ethical grounds, but rather because it involves a failure of reference. Therefore, she claims, the utterance of (1) could not count as the making of a claim or statement. On her view, examples such as (1) are similar to

4) Green ideas sleep furiously.

and

5) The present king of France is bald.

in that 'broads,' 'green ideas,' and 'the present king of France' are expressions that do not refer and hence cannot be used as subject terms of predication.

A critic of this position may wish to argue that utterances such as (1), (4), and (5) *can* be used in order to make statements with truth values even when there is a failure of reference to objects that exist. On this view, provided that the terms 'broad,' 'nigger,' 'green ideas,' and 'the present king of France' are meaningful ones, they can be used as subject expressions in statements with truth values. Acceptance or rejection of the Taylor position thus rests on acceptance or rejection of the view that only those utterances the subject terms of which have existing referents can have truth values.

NOTES

1. Blacks will be taken as the paradigm of minority group members in what follows. This is not to deny that there are minority group members other than blacks or that racist behaviors can be engaged in toward persons other than blacks.
2. It might be argued that the racist thinker also has such options. He or she could, for example, hire a black person as a "token," which might be "beneficial" to the black in some sense of that term (although it is not a morally acceptable behavior).

Part IV (A)

Analogies Between The Use Of Sexist And Racist Words And Sentences

Laurence Thomas

Sexism and Racism: Some Conceptual Differences

How should we understand the difference between sexism and racism? Is the difference merely that we have women as victims of the former and blacks (or some other minority group) as victims of the latter? Or, are there differences of a deeper sort?

Consider: If a black were to report to his colleagues (all of whom are white) that he had just been called a "nigger," one could be reasonably certain that, since he is black, his colleagues would convey considerable sympathy toward him for having

This paper is reprinted from *Ethics*, Vol. 90, No. 2 (Chicago: University of Chicago Press, Jan., 1980): 239-250 by permission of the author and publisher.
*I was first prompted to think about the topic of this paper in the fall of 1976 when I received an invitation from Stanley M. Browne, on behalf of Talladega College (Alabama), to give a talk on it. Versions of this paper have since been read at Georgia State University, Tuskegee Institute, Union College, Western Michigan University, and the American Philosophical Association Meetings (Pacific Division). Lawrence Alexander saved me from a number of slips and stylistic infelicities. Lyla H. O'Driscoll and Alison M. Jagger forced me to be more careful than I would have been in my remarks about the sexual identity of men. Section III of this paper was extensively revised in the light of the very forthright criticisms of my APA commentator, Robert C. Williams. Among others who have been kind enough to offer extensive comments are: C. Freeland, D. Jamieson, J. Narveson, H. McGary, J. Nickel, and A. Soble. A special word of thanks goes to Sandra Bartky and Connie Price for their encouragement in writing this paper from the very start. The completion of later drafts of this paper was facilitated by my having an A. W. Mellon Faculty Fellowship at Harvard University for the 1978-79 academic year.

been subjected to such extreme verbal abuse. But if a woman were to report to her colleagues (all of whom are male) that she had just been called a "chick," "fox," or even a "dumb broad," I suspect that her colleagues—and it is the reaction of her male colleagues which should concern us—would not be likely to suppose that she had been subjected to equally extreme verbal abuse;[1] and, therefore, they would be less inclined to view her as deserving of or in need of sympathy, let alone considerable sympathy. I believe that the different reactions that we would get here are indicative of some fundamental differences between sexism and racism. In this essay, I shall argue that the following are two such differences: (*a*) Sexism, unlike racism, readily lends itself to a morally unobjectionable description. (*b*) The positive self-concept of men has been more centrally tied to their being sexists than has been the positive self-concept of whites to their being racists. An unfortunate consequence of *a* and *b*, I am afraid, is that racist attitudes are relatively easier to give up than sexist ones. This perhaps is what one would expect given the different reactions that we would get from the two parallel situations which I have just described. Before getting underway, though, I want to make a few preliminary remarks.

1. Sexism and racism are obviously very large topics to try to cover in a single essay. My discussion, therefore, will be extremely one sided in that I shall be concerned with the attitude of the sexist and the racist qua perpetrator only, and not qua victim. This, of course, is not to say that a person cannot be on both sides of the fence.[2] Thus, I shall make no attempt, except in passing, to give an account of the self-concept which a victim of either sexism or racism has. It seems to be a fact that women are less likely to see themselves as victims of sexism than blacks (say) are to see themselves as victims of racism.[3] I believe that what I shall have to say on these two topics will be compatible with this fact.

2. Undoubtedly, there are different conceptions of sexism and racism, just as there are different conceptions of justice.[4] However, my aim is not to defend a particular conception of either social phenomenon; instead, I shall offer only a skeletal account of both which others, no doubt, will flesh out in different ways.

3. I mean only to be explaining the difference between sexism and racism. I do not in any way suppose that either can be morally justified. Moreover, I shall not be concerned with

whether one is more morally objectionable than the other. For both are sufficiently objectionable, on moral grounds, that everyone should be equally concerned to perpetuate neither.

4. Finally, although I hardly think that blacks constitute the only ethnic group which has been the victim of racism, I am going to limit the discussion to blacks nonetheless. For not only will this make the discussion more manageable; I am, for the most part, concerned with racism (and sexism) in the United States; and it is fair to say that, because of both their physical features and numbers, blacks have been the primary target of racism in the United States.

I

Obviously enough, if *a* and *b* are true, then sexism and racism must differ in the way in which each views its victims. The following social phenomenon sheds some light on the matter. In response to the demands of liberated women, men are forming groups in order to come to grips with their conception of themselves as men, that is, in order to understand what the male role comes to.[5] However, whereas the struggle against sexism has sent men back to the drawing board, as it were, in order to redefine their maleness, the struggle against racism has not resulted in a similar reaction on the part of whites. Whites have not found themselves at a loss to understand themselves qua white persons. The point here is not that the lives of whites have gone unaffected in this regard. Rather, it is that, although men often perceive the women's movement as an affront to their masculinity, the black movement has not been perceived in a similar vein by whites. Whites have not taken being less of a racist to mean being less of a white in the way that men have taken being less of a sexist to mean being less of a man (see Section III). Why is this? The answer which readily recommends itself is that the conception which men have of women is much more central to the conception which men have of themselves than is the case for whites with respect to blacks. I shall refer to this view as the racial sexual identity (RSI) thesis. Lest there be any misunderstanding, I should note that it no more follows from the truth of this thesis that sexism exists than it does that racism does not.

The truth of the RSI thesis is, I believe, well supported by the following considerations: (1) Since the beginning of humanity, women and men have had to interact for the purpose of procreation in order for the human species to survive. (2) There are male and female members of every race; hence, no race is dependent upon the members of any other race for its survival. (3) Any male and female member of any race can have offspring. (4) Whereas one can be racially mixed, one's gender is an all-or-nothing matter. A person is either male or female, taking the sexual organs to be the determining factor.[6] (5) The races are not regarded as biological complementaries of one another, but the two sexes are. Thus, it suffices that there exists some race or the other which is different from a person's own race in order for it to be possible for that person to have racial identity; such identity does not require the existence of a particular race. Our sexual identity, however, is clearly predicated upon the existence of a particular sex, namely the opposite one. I shall assume that the RSI thesis is well supported by these five considerations. The thesis will be central to the account which I shall give of the way in which sexism and racism each conceives of its object: women and blacks, respectively.

Now, I should note that sexism and racism are commonly taken to be quite similar. This is because both racist and sexist attitudes rest upon the view that, respectively, there are innate differences between whites and blacks, on the one hand, and men and women, on the other, which in each case make it natural for the latter to be subordinate to the former.[7] For instance, blacks and women have been stereotyped as being both intellectually and emotionally inferior to whites and men, respectively. But closer inspection reveals that even this similarity is not without a fundamental difference. For whereas the woman's lack turns out to make her naturally suited for the home and raising children and, therefore, natural for her to be around, the conclusion that it is natural for blacks to be around is not forthcoming. Indeed, it has been said by both blacks and whites alike that things would be better if all blacks were back in Africa.[8] So we encounter a difference between sexism and racism even in the respect in which they are thought to be most similar. It takes only a moment of reflection to see that this difference can be explained by reference to the considerations offered in support of the RSI thesis. There is no biological role for blacks to play in the reproduction of white offspring, however much whites may find it desirable to have blacks around for other reasons. It is in this light that the remarks of this paragraph must be understood.

Taking my cue from the preceding discussion, the way in

which sexism and racism each conceives of its object can be put as follows: Sexism entails the view that although (*a*) women are inferior to men in some sense, (*b*) biological considerations dictate that women ought to be around in order to insure the survival of the human species. Moreover, in view of *a* and *b*, (*c*) it is appropriate for women to cater to the wants and needs of men; indeed, women are understood as complementing men. Racism entails the view that (*a*) blacks are in some sense inferior to whites and that, in view of this, (*b*) it is appropriate for blacks to cater to the wants and needs of whites, but not the view that (*c*) biological considerations dictate that blacks ought to be around whites and, therefore, that blacks complement whites. It goes without saying that I am merely stating what I take to be the core of a sexist conception of women and a racist conception of blacks; in no way do I mean to be endorsing either.

Some explanatory remarks are in order. What I mean by the claim that women complement men is aptly expressed by the saying "Behind every man there is a good woman." Women are supposed to possess or excel at those virtues which make them naturally suited for being supportive of, and bringing out the best in men.[9] For instance, women are supposed to possess a greater capacity than men for being understanding, encouraging, and sympathetic. (The first capacity, which has to do with patience and tolerance, is not to be confused with the capacity to understand, which has to do with intellectual ability.) Thus, it is thought to be to a man's benefit to associate himself with the right woman, since the right woman, so the view goes, will be a man's constant source of support and encouragement thereby enabling him to excel at what he does. Women, then, are thought to play a central role in the self-development of men and, thus, in men having a positive conception of themselves. Nothing of the sort is thought to be true of blacks vis-à-vis whites. There are no time-honored sayings to the effect that "behind every white there is a good black." It has not been thought that by associating with the right black whites will enhance their chances of excelling at whatever they do, of being their best as whites.[10]

We now have before us a skeletal account of the way in which sexism and racism construe women and blacks, respectively. As I have remarked, others may wish to flesh out these accounts in different ways. In any event, we are in the position to make good the claim that the following are two of the fundamental differences between sexism and racism: (*a*) Sexism, unlike racism, readily lends itself to a morally unobjectionable description. (*b*) The positive self-concept of men has been more centrally tied to their being sexists than has been the positive self-concept of whites to their being racists. In the order mentioned, I turn to these two claims in the sections which follow.

II

I shall proceed in this section by arguing first that sexism readily lends itself to a morally unobjectionable description and then for the claim that racism does not.

A major aspect of the traditional male role is what I shall call the benefactor role. It is the role of men to protect women and to provide them with the comforts of life. That men should be the benefactors of women (in the sense described) is, it should be observed, a natural outcome of a sexist conception of women. For it will be recalled that, according to that conception, women play a central role in the self-development of men. And, of course, any person has good reasons to protect and provide for that which plays a central role in her or his self-development. But it goes without saying that this aspect of the traditional male role hardly seems morally objectionable.[11] For we do not normally suppose that a person does that which is morally wrong in benefiting someone. And on the face of it, surely, providing a person with the comforts of life would hardly seem to be a morally objectionable thing to do. After all, are they not desired by nearly everyone? At first blush, then, the traditional male role seems quite immune to moral criticism, which explains why the charge of sexism often seems to be lacking in moral force. Indeed, it is not uncommon to hear a man boast of being a sexist—even nowadays!

Now, of course, an arrangement where men benefit women is not morally objectionable—in and of itself, that is. 'What is morally objectionable, though, are the presuppositions behind it, one of the most important of them being that this sort of arrangement is ordained by nature.[12] From this presupposition, a number of things are thought to follow, such as men should earn more money than women (period) and the work which women do around the home is not as important as the work which men do on the job. These matters could be pursued at length, but I shall not do so here. For my concern has been to show that sexism readily lends itself to a morally unobjectionable description. And to show that it is a natural outcome of a sexist conception of women that men should be the benefactors of women (in the sense described) is to show this much.

Let us now look at racism. The first thing we should observe is that a racist conception of blacks does not naturally give rise to the view that whites should be the benefactors of blacks. This should come as no surprise, for it will be remembered (a) that both blacks and whites alike have thought that things would be better off if all blacks were back in Africa and (b) that blacks have not been thought to play a central role in the self-development of whites. For blacks were thought to be too inferior for that. Whites, then, have never conceived of it as their role qua whites to be the benefactor of blacks. And, as history shows,[13] the benefit of blacks has hardly been the concern of racist arrangements. For the most part, the benefit of blacks was incidental to (an unintended side effect of) such arrangements or, in any case, up to the whim of those responsible for such arrangements. These facts, alone, make it very difficult for racism to be viewed in a morally unobjectionable light.

Now it might be objected that racism can be so viewed if we suppose that whites held blacks to be inferior in their moral status to whites.[14] But not so. For one thing, the case of women shows that persons can have what I have called the benefactor role even with respect to living things presumed to be of inferior moral status. After all, it is impossible to understand the doctrine of coverture (e.g.) without supposing that according to it women are inferior in their moral status to men.[15] For another, the cruel treatment of living things of inferior moral status is morally wrong in any event, as the case of animals shows. Racism, though, has often called for the cruel treatment of blacks, whose moral status has most certainly not been thought to be inferior to the moral status of animals. So the objection fails.

A satisfactory case, I believe, has been made for the claim that sexism, unlike racism, readily admits of a morally unobjectionable description.

III

The task of this section is to show that the positive self-concept of men has been more centrally tied to their being sexists than has been the positive self-concept of whites to their being racists.

I shall first say a few words about what a person's positive self-concept comes to.

There are various aspects of a person's positive self-concept. However, the one which is germane to our discussion is what is called self-esteem.[16] It is the attitude which we have towards ourselves regarding our ability to interact effectively with our social environment, to achieve the goals which we set for ourselves. Respectively, our self-esteem is positive or negative if we have a reasonably favorable or unfavorable attitude towards ourselves in this regard. No person without deep psychological problems desires to have a negative conception of her- or himself. Thus, those activities which we believe will enhance our self-esteem have a natural attraction for us. So we are disinclined to give up those activities the successful pursuit of which enhances our self-esteem unless we have reason to believe that we can maintain our self-esteem by engaging in other activities. Obviously enough, the range of our abilities is very relevant here. The wider it is the more options there are that are open to us.

But now it is our values which determine the sorts of activities whose successful pursuit will enhance our self-esteem. Hence, having an excellent voice for classical music will do little to enhance our self-esteem if we have no interest in such music. On the other hand, if being able to sing classical music well is very important to us, then our self-esteem will suffer a severe blow if we are told by someone whose opinion we highly respect that this is an end which is beyond our reach. In large measure the social institutions among which we live determine the sorts of values which we come to have. And those values which have been instilled in us since childhood by our familial, educational, and religious institutions may have such a tenacious hold upon us that we find ourselves unable to give them up even when the ends which they call for prove to be beyond our reach. These few remarks about self-esteem, as sketchy as they are, should give us enough of a handle on the concept to permit us to proceed with the task of showing that the positive self-concept (self-esteem) of sexists is more centrally tied to the fact that they are sexists than is the positive self-concept (self-esteem) of racists to the fact that they are racists. (Throughout the remainder of this essay, I shall use the term 'self-esteem' instead of 'self-concept.')

If the RSI thesis is sound, then our sexual identity is clearly central to the conception which we have of ourselves. As things stand, though, while our gender is clearly relevant to our sexual identity, it is far from being the sole determiner of it.[17] Our beliefs about the sorts of roles we should play have a most powerful influence in this regard. There is, we might say, as much a social sense of the terms 'woman' and 'man' as there is a biological one. A person is a woman or man in the biological sense merely in virtue of having the appropriate biological properties. But to be a woman or man in the social sense not only must one have the appropriate biological properties; one must also have the appropriate aspirations and social behavior. The traditional female and male roles define a social sense of the terms 'woman' and 'man.' Hence, a woman's self-esteem can turn upon the fact that she measures up to the traditional female role; a man's self-esteem can turn upon the fact that he measures up to the traditional male role.

Now we have seen that, according to the traditional male role, men have what I have called the benefactor role with respect to women: they are supposed to protect women and provide them with the comforts of life. That men should have this role with respect to women is, without a doubt, one of the most deeply entrenched views of our society. A "real" man is one who "wears the pants around the house." He is the bread-winner. Indeed, the benefactor role is not an optional feature of the traditional male role—something which a man may take or leave as it pleases him. For it will be remembered that it is supposedly ordained by nature that men should have the benefactor role with respect to women. Unless there is some excuse, such as that of being a priest, it follows, according to the traditional male role, that men ought to be the benefactors of women. Thus, men believe that it is appropriate for their conception of themselves to turn upon how well they live up to the benefactor role. And, in the cases of those men who do so reasonably well, their self-esteem is enhanced precisely because their success in this regard constitutes an affirmation of their ability to be men in the social sense of the term. In view of the considerations advanced in this and the preceding paragraph, there is no getting around the fact that the positive self-esteem of men has been centrally tied to their being sexists.

We do not encounter an analogous situation between the black and white races. One very important reason why this is so is that there is only a biological sense of the races, and, so, the black and white races. Thus, racial identity for whites, and any other race, is something which has been more or less entirely settled by biological considerations. To be a full-fledged white person one has never had to own black slaves or even to hate blacks. This latter point is well illustrated by the case of the nigger lover. To be sure, many whites looked rather disparagingly upon the nigger lover. But this is not because whites considered her or him to be a white person *manqué*. The nigger lover was not a mulatto! A mulatto can no more be a nigger lover than a male a tomboy or a female a sissy. As for the first point, suffice it to say that American slaveowners were hardly of the opinion that European whites were less than full-fledged whites on account of the fact that black slavery was not a very prominent feature of European white societies.

Of course, I do not mean to deny the obvious fact that whites have perceived there to be fundamental differences among themselves, as, for example, class differences.[18] Nor do I mean to deny that whites have thought certain forms of conduct to be inappropriate for them, as, for example, the conduct of a nigger lover. What I do mean to deny, however, is that the racial identity of whites turned upon any of these differences. And if I am right about this, then it follows with impeccable logic that the racial identity of whites has not turned upon their being racists.

Now, to be sure, there have been many whites whose self-esteem has been enhanced by the fact that they were racists. At one point in his life George Wallace was certainly such an individual. It is significant to note, though, that the word 'racist' is not the name of an institutional role, as are, say, the words 'teacher,' 'governor,' and 'spouse.'[19] Moreover, the definitions of such roles do not make any reference to the sorts of activities which, under some description or the other, are properly characterized as racist. No one, for instance, supposes that a person cannot be a teacher, governor, or spouse unless she or he is a racist,[20] though, to be sure, many may think that only racists should occupy such roles. If, therefore, it is true that for any institutional role K a person S can perform K without being a racist, under some description or the other, then it has to be equally true that if S were a racist, then S could cease to be one without S's self-esteem being jeopardized with respect to the performance of K. When this consideration is coupled with the fact that the racial identity of whites has not turned upon their being racists, what follows most straightforwardly is that the self-esteem of whites has not been centrally tied to their being racists.

Now the word 'sexist' is not the name of an institutional role either. However, there is at least one institutional role, namely that of being a spouse (traditionally understood), which by definition makes reference to the sorts of activities which are sexist under at least some description. For the attitudes which the traditional male spouse has towards women (his wife, in particular) are, needless to say, dictated by the traditional male role, as what I have called the benefactor role should make clear. And as we have seen, in their endeavors to measure up to the benefactor role, the self-esteem of men has been centrally tied to their being sexists.

I should conclude this section by noting that nothing I have said implies that the self-esteem of slavemasters did not, or could not have turned upon their owning slaves. For their slaves were their property; and one's self-esteem can turn upon how much property one owns, whether that property is land, cattle, houses, or black slaves. Thus, it would be a mistake to suppose that the fact that the self-esteem of slave owners turned upon their owning slaves militates against the arguments of this section. For being a slave holder was not, surely, a defining characteristic of either a racist or a white person during the times of slavery; and so, a fortiori, it has not been since the passing of slavery.

IV

Throughout this essay, I have assumed that the traditional male role can be described in a morally objectionable way. I do not now want to argue the case. Rather, I would like for the reader to engage in a brief thought experiment with me. Suppose that men were the victims of sexism and that

> [everything a man) wore, said, or did had to justified by reference to female approval; if he were compelled to regard himself, day in day out, not as a member of society, but merely . . . as a virile member of society. If the centre of his dress-consciousness were the codpiece, his education directed to making him a spirited lover and meek paterfamilias; his interests held to be natural only in so far as they were sexual. If from school and lecture-room, press and pulpit, he heard the persistent outpouring of a shrill and scolding voice, bidding him remember his biological function. If he were vexed by continual advice how to add a rough male touch to his typing, how to be learned without losing his masculine appeal, how to combine chemical research with education, how to play bridge without incurring the suspicion of impotence. If, instead of allowing with a smile that "women prefer cavemen," he felt the unrelenting pressure of a whole social structure forcing him to order all his goings in conformity with that pronouncement.[21]

I have no doubt that most men would find a world thus described quite objectionable—and on moral grounds. If so, then there is indeed a morally objectionable way of describing the traditional male role in this world.

The differences between sexism and racism go much deeper than, as is commonly supposed, the fact that women are victims of the former and blacks of the latter. If I have argued soundly in this essay, then we have seen that sexism and racism are not two ways of referring to the same social monster, but two rather different ones.

V

My objective in this essay has been to show that there are at least two fundamental differences between sexism and racism: (*a*) Sexism, unlike racism, readily lends itself to a morally unobjectionable description. (*b*) The positive self-concept of men has been more centrally tied to their being sexists than has been the positive self-concept of whites to their being racists. As I said at the outset of this essay, it is, I believe, a consequence of the truth of *a* and *b* that racist attitudes are relatively easier to give up than sexist ones. I shall not attempt a defense of this claim at this point. Let it suffice to say, first of all, that persons must see that something is morally objectionable before they take themselves to have a moral reason for giving it up. We have seen that sexism presents a greater difficulty than racism in this regard. Secondly, it is a fact that people are disinclined to alter their behavior if they have reason to believe that in doing so they would jeopardize their self-esteem.[22] And we have seen that sexism presents a greater difficulty than racism in this regard as well.

In this essay, I have argued that there are some fundamental differences between sexism and racism. I have not denied that there are any similarities between the two; nor have I meant to do so.

NOTES

1. A sexual parallel here would have to be denigrating, but not vulgar. Thus, words such as 'bitch' and 'cunt' do not parallel the racial epithet 'nigger.' Indeed, in certain contexts, the word 'nigger' is not even denigrating: a black woman may call a black man with whom she is in love her "sweet nigger." Of the three expressions men tioned in the text, I suspect that "dumb broad," suggested to me by A. Soble, is the closest parallel to "nigger," though it still miss- es the mark.

2. Marabel Morgan, it would seem, is a woman who is on both sides of the fence. The "total woman" classes organized by her are based on the view that for a married woman "love is *unconditional* acceptance of him [her husband] and his feelings" (emphasis added). [See *The Total Woman* (New York: Pocket Books, 1975), p. 161.]

3. See Eugene D. Genovese, *Roll, Jordon, Roll: The World Slaves Made* (New York: Pantheon Books, 1974).

4. On the difference between the concept and a conception of justice, see John Rawls, *A Theory of Justice* (Cambridge, Mass.: Harvard University Press, 1971), pp. 5-11.

5. Cf. David Gelman, *et. al.,* "How Men Are Changing," *Newsweek* (January 16, 1978), and Peter Knobler, "Is It More Difficult to Be a Man Today?" *The New York Times,* (May 27, 1978), p. 19. Also, there is Gene Marine, *A Male Guide to Women's Liberation* (New York: Avon Books, 1972), and many other books of this genre.

6. Among persons and other higher animals, there can only be what is called pseudohermaphroditism, i.e., genetic abnormalities or hormonal imbalances. (See *The Encyclopedia Americana,* International Ed., s.v. "hermaphrodite").

7. In connection with sexism, two of the most sophisticated writers whom I have come across are Mary Wollstonecraft, *A Vindication of the Rights of Women* (first published in 1792) and Dorothy L. Sayers, *Unpopular Opinions* (New York: Harcourt Brace and Co., 1947).

8. Among blacks who have held this view, Marcus Garvey comes foremost to mind. See Edmund David Cronon, *Black Moses: The Story of Marcus Garvey and the Universal Negro Improvement Association* (Madison: The University of Wisconsin Press, 1969).

9. Cf. Marable Morgan. Wollsteoncraft speaks of men having the pleasure of commanding flattering sycophants. See p. 13 of the edition of *A Vindication of the Rights of Women* edited by Carol H. Post (New York: W.W. Norton and Company, Inc., 1975). Wollstonecraft's point is developed in a contemporary vein by L. Blum, M. Homiak, J. Housman, and N. Scheman, "Altruism and Women's Oppression," *Philosophical Forum,* 5 (1973): 196-221.

10. During the times of slavery American whites did not think that European whites needed to find themselves the right black in order to better themselves.

11. In order to keep down the length of this essay, I have deliberately not said anything about the traditional male role in connection with sex. The sexual exploitation of women is surely one of the worst aspects of the traditional male role. In the work compiled by the Sex Information and Educational Council of the United States, *Sexuality and Man* (New York: Charles Scribner's Sons, 1970), we find the following remarks: "Four major premarital sexual standards exist today: Abstinence, the formal standard of forbidding intercourse to both sexes; the Double Standard, the Western world's oldest standard, which allows males to have greater access to coitus than females; Permissiveness with Affection . . .; and Permissiveness without affection . . ." (p. 40). And this is to say nothing of the humiliation to which women have been subjected in connection with rape. It was once common practice for men to sexually abuse the women they captured. And, even today, many rapes go unreported because of the humiliation to which the victims are subjected. See Gerda Lerna, *The Female Experience: An American Documentary* (Indianapolis: The Bobbs-Merrill Company, Inc., 1977), pp. 433ff. It goes without saying that I have also left aside the traditional female role in connection with sex and childbearing. For an excellent discussion in connection with the former, see Christopher Lasch, "The Flight From Feeling: Sociopsychology of Sexual Conflict," *Marxist Perspectives,* 1 (1978):74-95 This essay was brought to my attention by Eugene Rivers.

12. I am indebted to Linda Patrik (Union College) for much of the way that I have put this paragraph.

13. See Genovese, *Roll, Jordon, Roll.*

14. In my "Rawlsian Self-Respect and the Black Consciousness Movement," *Philosophical Forum,* 9 (1978):303-14, I have distinguished between having full, partial, and no moral status. A thing has no moral status (e.g., stones) if there are no rights which it can have and there are no duties which it can have or which can be owed to it. A thing has only partial moral status (e.g., animals) if there are duties which can be owed to it, but there are no duties which it can have. A thing has full moral status (e.g., persons) if there are rights and duties which it can have. As for whether or not animals can have rights, suffice it to say that they cannot, unlike persons, have rights against one another. A dog does not violate any rights of the squirrel which it catches and kills or hurts.

15. The doctrine reads thus: "By marriage the husband and the wife are one person in law; that is, the very being or legal existence of the woman is suspended during the marriage, or at least incorporated and consolidated into that of the husband; under whose

wing, protection, and cover, she performs everything. See William Blackstone, *Commentaries on the Laws of England,* reprinted ed. (London: Dawsons of Pall Mall, 1966), p. 430.

16. See, among others, Stanley Coopersmith, *The Antecedents of Self-Esteem* (San Francisco: W. H. Freeman and Company, 1967); L. Edward Well and Gerald Marwell, *Self-Esteem: Its Conceptualization and Measurement* (Beverly Hills: Sage Publications, 1976); and Robert W. White, "Ego and Reality in Psychoanalytic Theory," *Psychological Issues,* 3, monograph 11 (1963). I have tried to show the importance of distinguishing between self-esteem and self-respect, which I have defined in terms of having the conviction that one has and is deserving of full moral status. See my "Morality and Our Self-Concept," *Journal of Value Inquiry,* 12 (1978): 258-68.

17. In a non-sexist society, perhaps the difference between gender identity and sexual identity would collapse. See Richard Wasserstrom, "Racism, Sexism, and Preferential Treatment: An Approach to the Topics," *U.C.L.A. Law Review,* 24 (1977): 581-622. For some illuminating discussions concerning the roles of women, see the collection of articles in Jo Freeman, ed., *Woman: A Feminist Perspective* (Palo Alto: Mayfield Publishing Company, 1975); and Michele Garskof, ed., *Roles Women Play* (Belmont: Brooks/Cole Publishing Co., 1971).

18. See, for example, Patricia Hollis, ed., *Class and Conflict in Nineteenth Century England 1815-1850* (London: Routledge & Kegan Paul, Ltd., 1973).

19. In the use of the word 'institutional,' I follow John Rawls, "Two Concept of Rules," *The Philosophical Review,* 64 (1955): 3-32.

20. Indeed, it would seem that this is true even of the role of slave-master. Aristotle thought it natural that there should be slaves. I do not see, though, that he thought it natural that the slaves should be black. (See Bk. I of his *Politics*).

21. Dorothy L. Sayers, *op. cit.,* pp. 143-145. A later paragraph reads as follows: "If, after a few centuries of this kind of treatment, the male was a little self-conscious, a little on the defensive, I should not blame him. If he traded a little upon his sex, I could forgive him. If he presented the world with a major social problem, I would scarcely be surprised. It would be more surprising if he retained any rag of sanity and selfrespect."

22. The fact that a person's self-esteem may be enhanced by the successful pursuit of morally unacceptable ends is often proffered as an explanation as to why those for whom street crime is a way of life do not accept the more traditional moral values. See, for instance, Charles Silberman, *Criminal Violence, Criminal Justice* (New York: Random House, 1978), chs. 2 and 3.

B. C. Postow

Thomas On Sexism

In "Sexism and Racism: Some Conceptual Differences,"
Thomas's point of departure is the contrast between the way
that racist and sexist epithets are perceived by those who are not
members of the classes of victims of racism and sexism: Racist
epithets are more likely than sexist ones to be regarded as extremely abusive. His article is an essay in explicating the
significance of this contrast. Now most feminists would take the
significance of the contrast to be that more people are sensitive
to the oppressiveness of racism than are sensitive to the oppressiveness of sexism. Antifeminists, on the other hand, would
take it to be entirely appropriate that sexist epithets are not
regarded as extremely abusive; they would say that the epithets
are not extremely abusive because they do not typically express
morally repugnant attitudes or lead to morally repugnant non-
linguistic behavior or arrangements. Although Thomas would
presumably reject this latter position,[1] several of his claims give
the appearance of supporting it. In particular, he claims that "it
is a natural outcome of a sexist conception of women that men
should be the benefactors of women" and that this arrangement
is not morally objectionable in and of itself. If these things were

This paper is reprinted from *Ethics*, Vol. 90, No. 2 (Chicago: University of
Chicago Press, Jan., 1980): 251-56 by permission of the publisher and author. I
am grateful for helpful comments by Mary Vetterling-Braggin. This paper was
written while I was a summer fellow at the Center for Advanced Study in the
Behavioral Sciences in Stanford, California.

true, they would count against the feminist presumption that language which expresses sexist conceptions is a good indication (if not actually a cause) of objectionable behavior and arrangements. If a natural outcome of a sexist conception of women is morally unobjectionable and even beneficial to women, it would be appropriate that epithets which express this sexist conception not be regarded as abusive to women in the way that epithets which express a racist conception of blacks are regarded as abusive to blacks. Only a detailed examination of Thomas's article will determine whether his position actually is compatible with the view that sexist language is a good indication of extremely objectionable nonlinguistic behavior and arrangements.

Thomas makes the following major claims: (*a*) "Sexism, unlike racism, readily lends itself to a morally *un*objectionable description." (*b*) "The positive self-concept of men has been more centrally tied to their being sexists than has been the positive self-concept of whites to their being racists." (*c*) "An unfortunate consequence of *a* and *b* . . . is that racist attitudes are relatively easier to give up than sexist ones."[2] (*d*) Sexism and racism are two rather different social monsters, not merely two aspects of the same monster. In discussing these claims, I shall confine my comments mainly to a clarification and evaluation of Thomas's reasoning concerning sexism, touching on the relation between sexism and racism only in my discussion of *d*.

Both claim *a* and Thomas's arguments for it are in some need of untangling. He says that he is not trying to defend any particular conception of sexism, but only to offer a skeletal account. Still, it seems fair to say that Thomas uses "sexism" to encompass at least certain attitudes, beliefs, behaviors, and social arrangements. And sexism as a social phenomenon certainly does include all these elements. Thus claim *a* seems to mean that sexist attitudes, beliefs, behaviors and social arrangements readily lend themselves to a morally unobjectionable description. (A "morally unobjectionable description," I take it, is a description that does not indicate that that which it describes is morally objectionable.) Now if only some of the elements of sexism readily lent themselves to a morally unobjectionable description while other elements did not, it would not seem accurate to say that *sexism* readily lends itself to a morally unobjectionable description. But Thomas reasons otherwise. He thinks he establishes that certain sexist *behavior* readily lends itself to a morally unobjectionable description, but points out that the *beliefs* presupposed by this behavior are (clearly?) morally objectionable (sec. II). In view of these supposed facts, Thomas concludes that sexism readily lends itself to a morally unobjectionable description. Obviously, we need an analysis of the notion of something "readily lending itself" to a morally unobjectionable description.

Now every act, arrangement, etc. "lends itself" to a morally unobjectionable description in the sense that a morally unobjectionable description can be found for it. An act of cold-blooded murder, for example, may be truly describable as an act of gratifying a whim—a morally unobjectionable description. But an act of murder would not *readily* lend itself to that morally unobjectionable description because that description obviously omits some morally relevant features of the act. Something "readily lends itself" to a given description, then, only if the description does not obviously omit some morally relevant features of the thing described. What is obvious to one person may not be obvious to another so whether something readily lends itself to a certain description will vary with the judger. But we shall assume a modicum of good faith on the part of the judger.

Let us now look at Thomas's description of sexist behavior and arrangements and consider whether it is a description to which sexism readily lends itself. Later we shall consider whether it is a morally unobjectionable description. Thomas describes sexism as an arrangement where men live up to the ideal that "it is the role of men to protect women and to provide them with the comforts of life." One would have to be astonishingly ignorant of a large number of feminist arguments and insights which are current today not to think that this description obviously omits some morally important features of sexism. Thus sexism would not "readily lend itself" to this description in the judgment of anyone who was not ignorant of fairly current feminist arguments and insights. But let us assume such ignorance, and ask whether sexism might readily lend itself to Thomas's description in this case. Thomas thinks that it does because it is "a natural outcome of the sexist conception of women" "that men should be the benefactors of women (in the sense described)." His grounds are these: "It will be recalled that, according to that conception, women play a central role in the self-development of men. And, of course, any person has good reasons to protect and provide for that which plays a central role in her or his self-development." I find these grounds unconvincing. The reasons which one has to protect and provide for that which plays a central role in one's self-development are also reasons to do whatever is necessary to guarantee that the person who serves one's self-development will function properly in her facilitating role and not usurp one's own role as the person whose self-development is in question. This is especially true for men who have the sexist conception of women, according to which "women are inferior to men in some sense" and "it is appropriate for women to cater to the wants and needs of men."[3] In view of these considerations (which could easily be multiplied), it does not seem that most people could, in good faith, take the description to which Thomas says sexism readily lends itself as capturing the morally relevant features of sexism; most people would judge that Thomas's description obviously omits some morally important features of sexism. If this is so, however, Thomas is unjustified in claiming that sexism readily lends itself to this description.

Aside from the question of whether sexism readily lends itself to this description, it seems far from clear that the description is morally unobjectionable. For one thing, protecting and providing for women against their wills would presumably be objectionable, yet sexism makes no distinction between proper behavior towards women who want sexist roles and those who do not. Furthermore, there is good reason to think that even if they do not realize it, women are harmed by economic dependence on their husbands.[4] Even if it is not morally objectionable for individuals to behave according to sexist roles in certain situations, the social *arrangement* where men and women behave according to these roles is not obviously unobjectionable, because it shapes people to the roles and limits their freedom. In fact, the arrangement of sexist roles seems to be an unjust arrangement, denying equal access to positions of unequal power and distributing power in a way which benefits one group at the expense of the other. In view of the fact that the most appealing description of sexism which Thomas could come up with is not obviously unobjectionable, and of the previously established fact that it is not a description to which sexism readily lends itself, I conclude that we cannot accept Thomas's claim that sexism "readily lends itself to a morally unobjectionable description."

Thomas' claim *b* is hard to evaluate because it makes a comparative statement—namely, that the positive self-concept of men has been *more* centrally tied to their being sexists than has the positive self-concept of whites to their being racists. To simplify the task of evaluation and because my main focus is on sexism, I shall limit my attention to a claim which is informally implicit in *b*, and which we may call *b'*, namely, that the positive self-concept of men has been very centrally tied to their being sexists. I do not want to dispute this claim, but I do want to clarify it and to point out weaknesses in Thomas's argument. His argument for *b* and *b'* is divided between sections I and III of his article. In section I he argues for the thesis (RSI thesis) that the conception which men have of women is much more central to the conception which men have of themselves than is the case for whites with respect to blacks. Following my previous practice, I shall take it that implicit in the RSI thesis is what we may call the RSI' thesis: that the conception which men have of women is very central to the conception which they have of themselves. The use that Thomas makes of the RSI and RSI' theses in section III is surprising. One would expect him to argue from RSI' to the conclusion that it significantly enhances the self-concept of men to regard women as inferior. Instead, the use which Thomas makes of the RSI and RSI' theses is this: "If the RSI thesis is sound, then our sexual identity is clearly central to the conception which we have of ourselves." I am quite willing to grant the consequent of that statement; I take it to be less controversial than the antecedent. The rest of Thomas's argument for *b'* goes roughly as follows: It enhances a person's self-concept to perform well a role which is defined as essential to one's sexual identity. The role of benefactor to women (in the sense described) is defined by sexism as essential to masculine sexual identity. Men have performed this role well. Therefore, the positive self-concept of men has been very centrally tied to their being sexists.

Now I grant that there is a three-way relationship among a man's acceptance of the sexist definition of the role essential for masculine sexual identity, his performance of that role, and his self esteem. Given that he performs the role well, it supports his positive self-concept to retain his sexist beliefs. And given that he retains his sexist beliefs, it is essential to his positive self-concept that he perform the sexist role well. But it is misleading to express these facts by saying simply that his positive self-concept is very centrally "tied" to his being a sexist, for this way of putting it obscures the following important points: (1) Successful fulfillment of a sexist male role is essential for a man's positive self-concept only on the assumption that the man has sexist beliefs (or is so overwhelmingly surrounded by sexists that he cannot reject their demands); and (2) Insofar as the male role as defined by sexist ideology is a humanly desirable role, successful fulfillment of this role can enhance the self-concept of nonsexists as well as sexists. If certain elements of the role are valuable, then it should enhance the self-concept of nonsexists to exemplify these elements. When these points are obscured, it is easy to have an unduly pessimistic view of the prospects of inducing men to give up sexism. It seems to me that such an unduly pessimistic view is expressed in what I have called Thomas's claim c.

Claim c, you will recall, is that it is "an unfortunate consequence of a and b . . . that racist attitudes are relatively easier to give up than sexist ones." Implicit in this, I think, is the simpler claim c' that sexist attitudes are very hard to give up. Now I agree with this, but I think the picture is not as bleak as Thomas's remarks would lead us to believe. For although it is true that men who derive very important enhancement of their self-concept from fulfilling a sexist-defined masculine role have a strong motive to retain sexist beliefs and attitudes, it is also true, in view of points (1) and (2) above, that a man can reasonably expect to maintain a positive self-concept while abandoning sexist beliefs and objectionable sexist behavior. Thus it is not unreasonable to think that men who are not afflicted with an undue amount of bad faith will be able, with social support, to reject sexism.

We turn now to claim d, namely, that sexism and racism are two rather different social monsters. This claim can be taken in two different ways. Taken in one way, d simply denies that the only difference between racism and sexism is the identity of the victim (and oppressor) classes. Taken this way, the claim is obviously true if sexism and racism differ in any one of a number of other ways: the "proper role" assigned to the victim class, the rationalizations for this role, the degree to which oppressors and oppressed recognize themselves as such, and soon. I do not know of anyone who would seriously dispute d interpreted in this way. Another way to take d is much more interesting theoretically because, unlike the first interpretation, it yields a claim which has been vigorously denied by feminists of various schools. On this second interpretation, d denies that thère is one fundamental source of oppression which explains both racism and sexism. Both radical feminists and Marxist feminists have held that there is such a single fundamental explanation.[5] It is not clear that Thomas meant d in the second way. He does say, "The differences between racism and sexism go much deeper than . . . that women are victims of the former and blacks of the latter" (sec. IV). But "much deeper" may mean either that racism and sexism have fundamentally different explanations, or simply that there are other important or numerous differences between racism and sexism besides the identity of the victim class. At any rate, the question of interest seems to be whether Thomas has in fact provided grounds for thinking that the fundamental causes of racism and sexism differ. In my opinion his arguments for claim b constitute some tentative steps towards providing evidence for d interpreted in this second way, but they would have to be supplemented by an argument to the effect that the psychological motives for being sexist and racist are fundamental causes of sexism and racism.

In conclusion, let us return to Thomas's and our point of departure. It seems that he has given us a hint as to why sexist epithets are less likely than racist ones to be regarded by nonmembers of the victim class as extremely abusive—namely, that it is more threatening to the nonoppressed group to acknowledge that they are abusive, because it may be more threatening to recognize that sexism is morally objectionable. Thomas's remarks in support of his claim a may appear to lend support to the stronger view that sexist epithets *are* less abusive than racist epithets, but this is due to a confusion in his use of the complex and slippery notion of a phenomenon readily lending itself to a morally unobjectionable description. Once this is untangled, we see that Thomas's article has done nothing to undermine the presumption that sexist conceptions and the language which expresses and reinforces them support a highly objectionable complex of behaviors, arrangements, expectations and beliefs.

NOTES

1. In his introductory section he says that both sexism and racism are seriously objectionable. Although he declines to say which is more objectionable, he gives the impression that he thinks they are at least roughly comparable in objectionableness.
2. Thomas assigns letters only to *a* and *b*. I have added the designations *c* and *d* to the other claims for ease in reference.
3. These are from Thomas's own characterization of sexism in sec. 1.
4. See B. C. Postow, "Economic Dependence and Self-Respect," *The Philosophical Forum,* forthcoming.
5. Shulamith Firestone, for example, holds in *The Dialectic of Sex* (New York: Bantam Books, 1971) that sexism is the most basic form of oppression and that the explanation of this and all other oppression lies in the basic biopsychological dynamics of the family structure. Mary Daly in *Beyond God the Father* (Boston: Beacon Press, 1973) holds that inauthentic being is at the root of all oppression and that a realization of true being is possible only through confronting and combatting sexism. Marxist feminists, of course, claim to find the fundamental cause of all oppression in economics.   See Margaret Benston, "The Political Economy of Women's Liberation," *Monthly Review,* 21, no. 4 (Sept. 1969): 13-27; reprinted in Alison M. Jaggar and Paula Rothenberg Struhl (eds.) *Feminist Frameworks* (New York: McGraw Hill, 1978), pp. 188-196.

Impact Of Sexist And Racist Statements On Theories Of Truth

Sara Ann Ketchum

Moral Redescription and Political Self-Deception

Laurence Thomas's comparison between racism and sexism suffers from two general weaknesses: First, his dismissal of racist parallels to sexist conceptions results in portraying the white racist as someone who does not benefit much from racism. Second, he approaches the problem of sexist and racist *attitudes* as if they could be entirely abstracted from sexist and racist social/political/economic structures. He proposes to offer an explanation of why "racist attitudes are relatively easier to give up than sexist ones."[1] However, he does not even mention the possibility that the greater difficulty in giving up sexism might be explained in terms of some greater benefit to the dominant in terms of power or wealth.[2]

Thomas's account of the relevant differences between racism and sexism is stated in the following terms:

> (a) Sexism, unlike racism, readily lends itself to a morally unobjectionable description. (b) The positive self-concept of men has been more centrally tied to their being sexists than has been the postive self-conception of whites to their being racists.[3]

Thomas's argument for (b) rests on (a) and his argument for (a) appears to rest on little more than an assumption that the sexist self-deception of the male is somehow innately more plausible than the racist self-deception of the white.

Thomas's attempt to provide an explanation of the greater relative tenacity of sexist attitudes as compared to racist attitudes fails to the degree that the characteristics he singles out as explanatory are shared by both systems; indeed they may be characteristics which are shared by all inegalitarian systems of distribution of power and resources.

I. PROTECTION, BENEVOLENCE AND GENEROSITY

The weakest part of Thomas's paper is his claim, in section II, that "sexism readily lends itself to a morally unobjectionable description . . . racism does not."[4] His argument for the first claim is based on the observation that sexist males regard themselves as the benefactors of women and that this way of thinking of themselves is part of the conceptual scheme of sexism. I will argue that Thomas exaggerates whatever contrast there is by abstracting from and ignoring history, and by viewing sexism from the point of view of the oppressor and racism from the point of view of the oppressed.

At first glance, Thomas's original statement of his thesis appears as trivially false. Any state of affairs can be truly (although not completely) described in morally unobjectionable terms. All that is necessary is to leave out of the description those characteristics of the situation which make it morally objectionable; that is usually a fairly simple matter, as evidenced by centuries of ideological description. Some of the most imaginative of these efforts occur during wartime: concentration camps become "refugee centers" or "relocation centers"; massacres may be described as "pacification programs," and so on. Thomas fails to note the racist description of slavery which is parallel to the sexist description of marriage that he offers: "American slavery was an economic system whereby rich whites provided food and housing for propertyless blacks." Here we have a true description of the historical situation which describes slavery as morally unobjectionable and which portrays white slave owners as benefactors of black slaves in basically the same way and through the same mechanism that Thomas claims sexism portrays men as benefactors of women.[5]

Thomas offers a more detailed explanation of the contrast he proposes: 1) It is part of the sexist conception of the "role of men to protect women and to provide them with the comforts of life."[6] 2) "history shows that the benefit of blacks has hardly been the concern of racist arrangements."[7] Far from showing a contrast between racism and sexism, these statements illustrate the familiar and expected contrast between ideology and practice, between the self-justification of the oppressor and the practical experience of the oppressed. Males, as beneficiaries of an unjust system, have no historical monopoly on congratulatory self-deception. Most ruling or dominant groups (aristocrats, capitalists, legislators, monarchs, whites, males, and so on) have thought that the world was better off because they were ruling or dominant; and most absolutist systems have been defended as being, in the long run, beneficial to the ruled. Thomas is here either underestimating the capacity of whites for self-deception or perhaps engaging in a bit of self-deception himself (in assuming, without argument, that unlike aristocrats who think peasants are better off being subservient to aristocrats and whites who think that blacks are better off being subservient to whites, males who think that women are better off being subservient to men are not self-deceptive).

If the dominant controls the resources, it will necessarily be the case that they provide (in an amoral sense of 'provide') whatever necessities and "comforts of life" the dominated receive; this is true, for example, of feudalism, capitalism, the patriarchal family, and slavery. The feudal lord provides for the peasant by letting the peasant use his (the lord's) land; the factory owner provides for the worker by paying wages out of which the worker derives what he needs; the father/husband provides for his wife and children by allowing them, at his discretion, to live under his roof and to eat food bought with his paycheck; the slave-owner houses and feeds his slaves. Note that in all these cases, if we shift our focus of value from ownership to labor (as the socialist does in the case of capitalism), the relations become reversed: the peasants provide for the feudal lord by producing food for him to eat, clothes to wear, and so on; the workers provide for the factory owner by producing the products which he sells in order to buy the comforts and necessities of life for himself; the wife provides for the husband/father by maintaining his physical environment and by producing the food that he eats; the slave provides for the slave-owner in any or all of these ways. However, those who believe that the relevant system of distribution of power is justified—that the resources are, *morally* speaking, the property of the aristocrat, the husband/father, the factory owner, the slave-owner—will regard the first set of descriptions as the morally appropriate ones. Thus, they would conclude that the person who controls the resources (aristocrat, factory owner, husband/father, slave-owner) is, morally speaking, generous to the other (peasant, worker, wife, slave).

When we come to the second "benefit" which Thomas claims to be part of the conception of the role of the male towards the female—that is, protection—we arrive at a distinction between the present manifestation of sexism and the present manifestation of racism. However, the contrast is not one between sexism as such and racism as such—as Thomas appears to be suggesting. In fact, the notion of protection points to a similarity between present sexism and past racism, thus serving to underscore the similarities between the two systems of supermacy.

Racists *now* tend *not* to think of themselves as protectors of blacks. This change appears to be related to the transition from being slaves, through a quasi-serf status (sharecroppers) to "free" (although discriminated against) labor in a market economy. The white racist's protectiveness, like the male sexist's protectiveness, is tied to possessiveness, to the degree to which the relation between superior and inferior is conceived of either literally or metaphorically as a property relation. It was, and is, "I protect *my* slaves," "We protect *our* Negroes," "I protect *my* wife," "We protect *our* women." When the black ceases to be the property of the white, the sense of protectiveness vanishes and a different justification of white-supremacy takes its place. Now that blacks are "those people" rather than "our colored," the white racist has no property in the black person to protect; just so, the sexist feels no need to protect women who are "those women" rather than "our women." (The Ku Klux Klan, for example, "protects" not women as such, but white women, "*our* women.")

This ambiguity of the concept of protection mars Thomas's argument for the claim that the benefactor role of men follows from the sexist conception of women:

> That men should be the benefactors of women (in the sense described) it is, it should be observed, a natural outcome of a sexist conception of women. For it will be recalled that according to that conception, women play a central role in the self-development of

men. And of course, any person has good reasons to protect and provide for that which plays a central role in her or his self-development.[8]

If x's are central to the self-esteem and self-development of y's because x's are beings that y's can feel superior to (that is, if the relation is the standard self-esteem producing supremacist relation as occurs in racism, sexism, anti-Semitism, etc.), then, far from its being in y's self-interest to protect x's *as autonomous persons*, it is in y's interest to make x's as inferior as possible in order to enhance the comparison. The most obvious and best-known example of this is Chinese footbinding.[9] Crippling women works as a means of enhancing men's self-esteem because it is easier to feel superior to someone who is visibly inferior in an empirical sense than it is to feel superior to someone who is healthy and capable. The principle is the same whether we are talking about explicit physical mutilation (footbinding, genital mutilation, etc.) physical intimidation, or training from childhood into physical, emotional, and intellectual weakness; by producing in the dominated a set of inferiorities (that is, inabilities and weaknesses), the dominators gain both a justification of their power and a boost to their self-esteem.

It takes little reflection to see that protection of property rights in other persons is not only not the same as, but is often inconsistent with, protection of that person *as a person*. But it is only protection of the person as a person that is, morally speaking, a benefit to that person. Racist protection of blacks was never inconsistent with beating or lynching blacks or with the rape of black women by white men. Sexist protection has never been inconsistent with rape, beating, mutilation or killing of women, as long as the violence was committed either by the appropriate male (husband, father, lover, pimp, and so on) or against a woman who does not have the appropriate relation to some male. The protection is not directly a protection of the black or woman, but of the white's or male's right to exclusive use. Thus, sexist protection of women is no more benevolent than racist protection of blacks and, objectively speaking, should require no less an effort of self-deception on the part of the white male who wants to think of himself as the benefactor of blacks and women.

Not only does Thomas abstract from and ignore history but his comparison of racism and sexism is not within parallel structures. Blacks and women, and particularly black women, serve on the job market as cheap reserve labor; that is, they are paid less than white men (in the case of black women, less than half) and are the first to be fired in a slow-down or recession. White male employers who use blacks and women as reserve labor do not show any signs of regarding their actions towards women workers as any more benevolent than their actions towards black workers. The ideology of protection and provision belongs more appropriately to the other side of the double exploitation of women, that is, to sexual and reproductive exploitation and to the institution of the family.[10]

When blacks were slaves, they were in an extended sense members of the family and, therefore, subject to "protection." This sense of protectiveness is associated with paternalistic systems—for example, slavery, feudalism, and the family—rather than with market systems. Paternalistic institutions exact feeling as well as labor from the dominated and carry a tradition of *noblesse oblige*, of the obligation of the superior *qua* superior. Justifications use the father-child relation as a model of benevolent dominance performed for the sake of the dominated. The superiority of the dominant—the liege lord, the white, the male—gives them the *obligation* to rule, and makes it reasonable to expect gratitude and loyalty from the dominated. Feudalism and the family make feeling an explicit legal/contractual obligation: the serf, in the ceremony of vassalage, swears fealty; the wife, in the ceremony of marriage, promises to love and obey.[11] The racist ideology of the "White Man's Burden" is part of this tradition because it presents the domination of blacks by whites as an expression of the generosity of whites in being willing to care for, protect, and guide the childlike inferior races. It is this history that Thomas is ignoring when he claims that whites "have never conceived of it as their role qua whites to be the benefactor of blacks."[12]

In conclusion, Thomas fails to show that sexism is easily described in morally unobjectionable terms while racism is not. Instead of demonstrating a difference between racism and sexism, his account of sexism illustrates the general proposition (which applies to both racism and sexism) that any situation *can* be described in terms which do not convey to the hearers that which is morally objectionable about the situation. Such a description may rely on the manipulation of language (for example, "We protect our blacks/women" as the acceptable version of "We protect our property rights to our blacks/women"), on leaving out morally relevant details ("We provide the necessities of life for our slaves/workers/wives," leaving out "what we get in return is labor, sexual access, power"), and on the bias of the hearer's conceptual scheme.

The self-deception of the dominant of the sort that Thomas mentions can be regarded as an effect, as a constitutive element, or as a means of perpetuating the social/political structure of sexism or racism. It is easier to maintain one's dominant position if one can convince oneself and others that the dominance is beneficial to the dominated and distracting from both the benefits to the dominators and the harm to the dominated. How easy we find such self-deception depends on our language as well as our conceptual scheme.

II. DOMINANCE, VIOLENCE, AND SELF—ESTEEM

The simple and obvious similarity between the self-esteem producing properties of sexism and racism is this: for white racists, blacks are always people one can feel superior to, no matter what they do; one can always say, "At least, I'm better than they are. At least, I'm not one of *them*." For the sexist male, there is always one kind of person he can look down on and feel superior to, one category of person he can feel proud distinguishing himself from, namely women.

Thomas chooses to concentrate instead on the benefactor role as a self-esteem enhancing (for men) feature of sexism. That his description of the sexist conception of the male role as essentially a benefactor role is misleading, if not false, is illustrated by the following examples:

Dick prides himself in never getting "caught" by a woman and in never having to pay for sex or for housework. He persuades women with whom he has sexual affairs to do housework, typing, and other personal chores for him; he does not perform personal chores for them, nor does he provide them with money. Women who are not willing to engage in either activity with him can at least be raped.

Harry has a close non-sexual friendship with Sally. When Sally is in difficulties, he supports her, both financially and emotionally, helps her to get a new job, and so on.

Tom is the stereotypical henpecked husband and then some. He turns his paycheck over to his wife and then does all the housework.

According to the traditional sexist conception of the male role, Dick is clearly a "real man" (although perhaps not an upstanding pillar of the church) while Harry and Tom are equally clearly not. If they were relying on the sexist conceptual scheme for self-esteem, Tom and Harry would find that their roles as non-dominating benefactors of women would count against them rather than for them—they would be sissies or fools rather than real men or good samaritans. Dick, on the other hand, would find his role of dominating non-benefactor to be a useful source of pride as a "real man." Thomas even suggests that it is domination rather than benefit that defines the male role when he says, "A 'real man' is one who wears the pants around the house."[13]

The example of Dick shows why Thomas is wrong in asserting that "the benefactor role is *not* an optional feature of the traditional male role."[14] Most of the criteria of masculinity (in modern society at least), unlike the criteria of femininity, are unrelated to sexual and reproductive function. On the sexist conceptual scheme, while the nature of *woman* is necessarily fulfilled by a reproductive role (and, hence at least in part, related to men), the nature of *man* consigns him to a role in the "real" world, i.e., the world of men from which women are excluded. Thus, apart from the necessary demonstrations of heterosexuality, a man can demonstrate his masculinity entirely in all male (or virtually all male) arenas—the football field, the battleground, the boardroom, and so on.

Even if a man does feel compelled by sexism to take on the husband role (which appears to be what Thomas is describing as "the benefactor role"), he still has various self-esteem enhancing options available. He could, as Thomas describes, take pride in providing for and protecting his wife. On the other hand, he could take explicit pride in domination through, for example, having her so terrorized by repeated beatings that she is completely submissive and obedient. Whichever option he takes, he is still taking pride in being a "real man."

If benevolence were either an essential or an important part of the sexist male role, we would expect not only that Tom and Harry, rather than Dick, would be the "real men," but also that violence against women would be contrary to the male role. Quite the opposite: the rapist, the wife-beater, the wife-killer, the womanslaughterer may be called many things by a sexist society, but *never* in virtue of *those* acts a sissy, unmasculine or effeminate, never "less of a man." Moreover, the male role as assaulter of woman is presupposed by the male role as protector of woman. What he is protecting her *from* is assaults by other men.[15]

The sexist conception of the male role can include both benevolence and violence towards women because the benevolence that counts (for example, in the description Thomas gives) is a benefit of dependence; that is, "providing for" and "protecting" women is "real man"-making when it is an expression of or productive of the woman's economic dependence on the man. As such the near interchangability of "providing for" women and violence against women is easily explained. Both count towards being a sexist "real man" to the degree that they are expressions of domination over women; defensive violence or nondominating benefit do not count.

But, if the essential self-esteem producing element of sexism is domination, we no longer have a sharp contrast with racism. The poor white can reassure himself and his fellows of his racial superiority (his whiteness) by the use of violence against blacks. Such violence or threat of violence against blacks performs the service of separation—"I am not one of them"—and reassures the poor white that he is still a member of the dominant race.

Thomas's description of the sexist conceptual scheme as more readily lending itself to benevolent description than does racism is pernicious in that it helps foster the myth that sexism is an unusually gentle, kind, and nonviolent oppression—that the violence perpetrated against women by men is private and personal (either individual crime or a mere "family spat") while the violence perpetrated against blacks by whites is political and worthy of our attention. Anyone who admits that it is more dangerous for a woman to go out at night than for a man to do so, is conceding that violence against women is a part of our culture—not gentle and not private.

In at least one respect, violence against women is a more intimate and essential element of the sexist conceptual scheme than violence against blacks is of the racist conceptual scheme. Racists have indeed thought of blacks as suffering less than whites from the same injuries, but they have not regarded blacks as *enjoying* pain. Whereas, women have been portrayed both as enjoyers of pain—as being, by nature, seekers of pain—in the Freudian tradition, and as being condemned by God to a life of pain, in the Judeo-Christian tradition. This perversity in the sexist conceptual scheme makes the violence against women both invisible (as it appears to be to Thomas) and in some cases, particularly brutal.

Thomas may be right in claiming that male self-esteem has been more closely tied to sexism than white self-esteem has been to racism. However, his claim that this is because sexism, unlike racism, readily lends itself to a morally unobjectionable description commits him to distorted portrayals of both racist and sexist conceptual schemes. Contrary to his account, both political systems are sophisticated enough to include a wide set of innocuous sounding descriptions of dominance relations as part of the conceptual schemes which help perpetuate such relations. Sexism, being the older of the two, has embedded such descriptions more deeply into our conceptual schemes and into our language, making them more difficult to detect or to give up.

NOTES

1. Laurence Thomas, "Sexism and Racism: Some Conceptual Differences," p. 267 in this volume.
2. This is not necessarily to suggest any greater oppression of individuals. In the distribution of limited positions and resources, the increased chances of members of the nondiscriminated against group are, other things being equal, greater the larger the group being discriminated against; women are a majority of the population, blacks are a minority (white males are also a minority—a fact often obscured by the "value-free" move of substituting 'minority group' for 'oppressed group').
3. Thomas, *op. cit.,* p. 257 in this volume.
4. *Ibid.,* p. 261 in this volume.
5. The comparison between marriage and slavery goes back at least to John Stuart Mill; see Ch. 2 of "The Subjection of Women" in John Stuart Mill and Harriet Taylor Mill, *Essays on Sex Equality,* edited by Alice Rossi (Chicago: University of Chicago Press, 1970). See also Sara Ann Ketchum, "Liberalism and Marriage Law" in *Feminism and Philosophy,* edited by Mary Vetterling-Braggin, Frederick A. Elliston and Jane English (Totowa, N. J.: Littlefield, Adams and Co., 1977), pp. 268-270.
6. Thomas, *op. cit.,* p. 261 in this volume.
7. *Ibid.,* p. 262 in this volume.
8. *Ibid.,* p. 261 in this volume.
9. See Andrea Dworkin, "Gynocide: Chinese Footbinding," Ch. 6 of *Woman Hating* (New York: E. P. Dutton and Co., 1974) and Mary Daly, "The Sado-Ritual Syndrome: the Re-enactment of Goddess Murder," the Second Passage of *Gyn/Ecology* (Boston: Deacon Press, 1978). Thomas clearly states his preference for the pre-second wave theories of Wollstonecraft and Sayers (in footnote 7), but does not explain why he finds their analyses more "sophisticated" than the political theory that has been written in the last twenty years.
10. See Lorenne Clark, "The Rights of Women: The Theory and Practice of Male Supremacy" and Lynda Lange, "Reproduction in Democratic Theory," both in *Contemporary Issues in Political Philosophy* (New York: Neal Watson Academic Publications, 1976).
11. For an analysis of marriage as a quasi-feudal institution, see my "Liberalism and Marriage Law," *op. cit.,* pp. 264-5.
12. Thomas, *op. cit.,* p. 262 in this volume.
13. *Ibid.,* p. 264 in this volume.
14. *Ibid.*
15. See Susan Rae Peterson, "Coercion and Rape: The State as a Male Protection Racket" in *Feminism and Philosophy, op. cit.,* pp. 360-71.

Patrick Grim

A Note On The Ethics
Of Theories Of Truth

I have argued elsewhere that all sexist statements are either false
or carry (informal) implications which are false.[1] Such a position allows for the possibility of literally true sexist statements,
though in the same breath it insists that they will have false (informal) implications of some kind. Consider, for example, the
sexist statement 'Broads will benefit from improvements in
medicine.' This is a prime example of a type of statement for
which it is tempting to claim literal truth, however quick we
might be to point out other things wrong with it.

    In what follows I want to propose an argument for a
somewhat stronger position; an argument to the effect that we
should think of this type of sexist statement, and a similar type
of racist statement, as *neither* true nor false.[2] The argument is
also of interest, I think, because it is clearly of an unorthodox
form: it urges a particular choice between rival theories of truth
on *ethical* grounds.[3] Despite this unorthodoxy the argument is
at least a plausible one, and at present I know of no fatal flaws.
Nonetheless I offer it as an intriguing proposal worthy of further
consideration rather than as a final proof.

I

Consider two importantly different things someone might say:

1. Blacks will benefit from improvements in medicine.
2. Niggers will benefit from improvements in medicine.

In standard contexts, at least, the first is not a racist claim. But in standard contexts (2) clearly is a racist claim, and it is clear that it is so because of the term 'niggers.'[4] Not every claim in which the term 'niggers' appears need be a racist claim, of course; in ' 'Nigger' is a racial epithet' the term is mentioned rather than used, and the claim as a whole is not itself racist. Though somewhat more debatable, there may also be special cases in which the use of the term is not racist; 'All us niggers have to stick together,' uttered by the right speaker in the right context, might escape such a charge. Nonetheless claims in which the term "nigger" is used as it is used in (2) in standard contexts are paradigmatically racist claims, and are so because of the use of the term "nigger."

Consider also a quite similar pair of claims:

3. Women will benefit from improvements in medicine.
4. Broads will benefit from improvements in medicine.

Here 'broads' does all the dirty work with respect to sexism that 'niggers' did with regard to racism. In standard contexts (4), unlike (3), is a sexist claim, and is so because of the use of the term 'broads.' 'Broads,' like 'niggers,' might be mentioned rather than used (as both are mentioned rather than used in this sentence), and there may be special contexts analogous to those mentioned above in which even the use of 'broads' escapes a charge of sexism. Nonetheless, claims in which 'broads' is used as it is used in (4) in standard contexts are paradigmatically sexist claims just as claims in which 'nigger' is used as it is used in (2) in standard contexts are paradigmatically racist claims. The reasons why (2) is racist and (4) is sexist, moreover, are nearly identical. 'Broads' is to sexism what 'niggers' is to racism.

Since 'niggers' is a term of this sort, each of the following claims is as racist as is (2) above:

>   5. It is true that niggers will benefit from improvements in medicine.
>   6. It is false that niggers will benefit from improvements in medicine.

Similarly, because of the use of the term 'broads,' each of these claims is as sexist as is (4):

>   7. It is true that broads will benefit from improvements in medicine.
>   8. It is false that broads will benefit from improvements in medicine.

The lesson here is simply that the use of 'niggers' makes a claim racist and the use of 'broads' makes a claim sexist no matter how deeply each is buried in syntax. A racist or sexist claim employing 'niggers' or 'broads' gives us a similarly racist or sexist claim if we tack on either 'it is true that . . .' or 'it is false that . . .,' simply because 'niggers' or 'broads' is still used in the same way.

All of this might appear to be a purely ethical matter, or at best a matter of the ethical use of language. What I hope to argue, however, is that it also has intriguing ramifications for theories of truth.

Consider again two of the examples presented above:

>   2. Niggers will benefit from improvements in medicine.
>   4. Broads will benefit from improvements in medicine.

Is (2) something which is either true or false, or something which is neither true nor false? Is (4) something which is either true or false, or something which is neither true nor false? An answer to these questions seems important for at least certain types of theories of truth. It would be nice to have a theory which told us whether particular claims we propose or particular things people say can be true or false (on the model of 'The cat is on the mat') or not (on the model of 'Green ideas sleep furiously' and perhaps 'Smith has left off beating his wife' in certain circumstances). Theories which involve either treatment for (2) and (4) above, however, face certain difficulties and may be forced to certain auxiliary claims in order to avoid those difficulties.

Let us suppose, to begin with, that we choose a theory of truth which leads us to claim that (2) and (4) are either true or false. Here ethical difficulties arise. It would appear that if we are committed to the claim that (2) is either true of false we are thereby committed to the claim that:

> 9. Either it is true that niggers will benefit from improvements in medicine or it is false that niggers will benefit from improvements in medicine.

Similarly, it would appear that if our chosen theory commits us to the claim that (4) is either true or false we are thereby committed to the claim that:

> 10. Either it is true that broads will benefit from improvements in medicine or it is false that broads will benefit from improvements in medicine.

But (9), like (5) and (6), is a racist claim. (10), like (7) and (8), is a sexist claim. Thus a theory which committed us to the claim that (2) is either true or false would commit us to a racist claim, and a theory which committed us to the claim that (4) is either true or false would commit us to a sexist claim. If either racist or sexist claims are to be avoided, it would appear that a theory of truth which committed us to such claims should also be avoided.

If this argument is legitimate, there are reasons - ethical reasons - to avoid a theory which maintains that (2) and (4) are either true or false. But consider also a possible objection. The argument at issue, at least as presented above, relies heavily on 'commitment' to (9) and (10). But if this 'commitment' amounts merely to commitment to the truth of (9) and (10), the argument may not present the ethical difficulty it pretends to. Let us agree that we ought not make sexist or racist claims. Let us further agree that if we hold a theory of truth concerning (2) and (4) which entails (9) and (10), we must hold on pain of contradiction that at least some sexist and racist claims - (9) and (1), for example - are true. But is there really a conflict here? We would violate the ethical injunction against making sexist and racist claims were we to *make* such claims, were we to propose or assert (9) or (10). But whatever our theory forces us to, it does not force us to propose or assert (9) or (10) or to actually make such claims. No theory, for that matter, forces anyone to *assert* anything. If the ethical principle at issue regarding sexist and racist claims merely prohibits certain *assertions*, we can hold whatever theory we wish and avoid apparent ethical difficulties by the simple expedient of maintaining a close and guarded silence.[5]

It must be admitted, in response to this objection, that the 'commitment' at issue in the argument above is not a matter of being forced to actually *make* sexist or racist claims. But this admission need not mean that whatever other form of commitment holds-including a 'conditional'. commitment of a certain sort—is safely brushed aside. Were we to hold an 'either true or false' theory regarding (2) and (4), and were we to actually make all claims that theory entails, we *would* end up making racist and sexist claims. Were we, on the basis of our theory, to answer directly and forthrightly certain questions put to us, we would similarly end up making sexist and racist claims. This is, of course, only a 'conditional' commitment to making sexist and racist claims. We might always avoid actually making such claims by refusing to answer direct questions directly and by churlishly avoiding certain topics of intellectual conversation; by hiding our theoretical candle under a performatory bushel. Our chosen theory would carry 'unassertables' as theorems, though it would not actually force us to assert them. Conditional commitment need not involve actually making sexist and racist claims, and entailed 'unassertables' are not necessarily asserted. Nonetheless, I think, there are reasons to avoid a theory which saddles us with either. [6]

One mark against 'unassertables,' and against a theory which carries them, is the fact that they conflict with a standard ideal of rational discourse. The ideal, or paradigm, or stereotype[7] of rational discourse is one in which holding a theory involves a willingness to assert and defend a set of claims and their entailments. This is, admittedly, *only* an ideal (there are problems regarding infinite sets of entailments, for one thing), but even our ordinary attempts at rational discourse would be quite different were this not the ideal. A theory which entails 'unassertables' is clearly at odds with such an ideal, since the ideal demands a willingness to assert and defend entailments which, if 'unassertable,' we are not willing to assert or defend. The conditional commitments of such a theory do not become harmless by being 'merely' conditional, since our ideal of rational discourse is conditional in much the same sense.

Is conditional commitment to racist and sexist claims, or the entailment of 'unassertables,' then sufficient reason to discard a theory with these features? Certainly these are not as powerful a disqualification with regard to our choice of theories as is, for example, blatant inconsistency. If our choice is exclusively between a patently inconsistent theory and one which entails 'unassertables,' we should clearly choose the latter; and we should also, I might add, seriously reconsider the supposed 'unassertability' of relevant entailments. Nonetheless, I would propose, a theory which does not carry 'unassertables' is *ceteris paribus* to be preferred over a theory which does. 'Unassertables' are, after all, something of an intellectual embarrassment, and a rival theory which avoids them is to that extent to be preferred.

II

Is there, in the case at hand, a rival theory which avoids such difficulties? Let us try the alternative; a theory of truth which leads us to claim that (2) and (4) are neither true nor false. Is this an escape? It might be thought that if we are committed to the claim that (2) is neither true nor false we are thereby committed, in the same sense as above, to the claim that:

> 11.   It is neither true that niggers will benefit from improvements in medicine nor false that niggers will benefit from improvements in medicine.

It might similarly be thought that if we choose to claim that (4) is neither true nor false we are thereby committed to:

> 12.   It is neither true that broads will benefit from improvements in medicine nor false that broads will benefit from improvements in medicine.

Since (11) is as racist as (5) and (6) and since (12) is as sexist as (7) and (8) we would once again have a theory of truth which commits us to sexist and racist claims.

As it stands, either type of theory of truth we choose would appear to get us into trouble. But there is a fairly traditional way out for a 'neither true nor false' theory, traditional in spirit of practice if not in codified theory. It has long been held that

'Green ideas sleep furiously' is neither true nor false. But no one has proposed that such a position commits one to (13):

13. It is neither true nor false that green ideas sleep furiously.

(13) is of course as much a piece of gibberish as the original phrase it includes, and any theory which forced (13) on us would force gibberish on us. Thus we might propose that claiming that 'S' is neither true nor false need not involve committing oneself to the claim that it is neither true nor false that S. Though for importantly different reasons (racism and sexism are not as innocuous as mere gibberish), we might similarly propose that (2) and (4) are neither true nor false, but resist the idea that that forces us to adopt the racist (11) or the sexist (12). By distinguishing carefully between 'S is neither true nor false' and 'It is neither true nor false that S' in such a way we may arrive at a theory of truth which allows us to claim that (2) and (4) are without truth-values without thereby committing ourselves, even conditionally, to racist or sexist claims.

A similar way out might be proposed for the first theory considered. We might, that is, insist that (2) is true or false, but that that does not commit us to (9), and that (4) is true or false, but that that does not commit us to (10). We might more generally propose that 'S is true' does not commit the speaker to 'It is true that S,' that 'S is false' does not commit the speaker to 'It is false that S,' and that 'S is either true or false' does not commit the speaker to 'It is true that S or false that S'. This is not, I think, nearly as plausible a move with respect to an 'either true or false' theory as it is with respect to a 'neither true nor false' theory. Initial implausibility aside, such subtle (not to say moot) distinctions between 'S is true' and 'It is true that S' have been far from standard features of theories of truth. Were we to adopt such a theory, we would have to reject familiar principles of 'disquotation' tracing back to Tarski.[8]

III

It thus appears that we have three options in choosing a theory of truth to handle cases such as (2) and (4) as well as a range of similar racist and sexist claims. We may choose a theory which maintains that (2) and (4) are neither true nor false, and are to be treated in some respects as 'Green ideas sleep furiously' has traditionally been treated. This, I think, is the happiest choice.

Or we may choose a quite radical (and perhaps radically troublesome) theory which maintains that (2) and (4) are either true or false but that 'S is true' somehow does not commit one to 'It is true that S'. Or, finally, we may choose a theory which entails 'unassertables' and carries a conditional commitment to racist and sexist claims. The moral of the story is that there are important ethical matters concerning English usage, and that to ignore them even in considering theories of truth is to run an ethical risk.[9]

NOTES

1. See my "Sexism and Semantics" in *Feminism and Philosophy,* M. Vetterling-Braggin, Jane English, and Frederick Elliston, eds. (Totowa, N.J.: Littlefield, Adams and Co., 1977). The possibility of literally true sexist statements is at least allowed for in "Sexist Speech: Two Basic Questions," also in this volume.

2. The argument presented here concerning examples (2) and (4), if adequate, will also hold for any sexist or racist claim S which meets the minimal condition that 'It is true or false that S' is also a sexist or racist claim. Lurking in the background may be a more general position that sexist and racist claims should never be considered true; that all such claims should be considered either false or neither true nor false. But the argument presented here is not alone sufficient for that more general position.

3. Though of course there might be other arguments, more orthodox in form, for the same conclusion. The strongest, perhaps, would be an argument which also explained why particular sexist claims are neither true nor false, which the argument presented here does not.

4. It should be clear here and throughout that I am using the terms 'claim' and 'statement' as well as the phrase 'something someone might say' in a broad ordinary sense. In this common sense of 'claim', as opposed to a sense corresponding to the philosophical term 'proposition,' there are ambiguous and even meaningless claims as well as true or false claims. The use of a 'propositional' sense of 'claim' here would cause difficulties, since in the end I argue that (10) and (2) are neither true nor false, whereas to refer to them as 'propositions' or the like (commonly *defined* as either true or false) would in effect preclude this possibility. In arguing that (1) and (2) should be considered neither true nor false I am in effect arguing that they should not be considered 'claims' in this more restricted 'propositional' sense.

5. I am obliged to Mary Vetterling-Braggin for suggesting this objection.

6. For a similar attack on a different position, see B. C. Postow, "Dishonest Relativism," *Analysis* 39.1 (January 1979). Postow is also concerned with some kind of 'commitment' - admittedly quite difficult to characterize - on the basis of which she condemns a particular relativist view as 'dishonest.' A similar charge of 'dishonesty' might be levelled against the theory at issue here.

7. The term 'stereotype' is Hilary Putnam's, though he does not (as I do) propose a stereotype for rational discourse. See "The Meaning of 'Meaning'," in *Mind, Language, and Reality: Philosophical Papers,* Vol. 2 (Cambridge: Cambridge University Press, 1975). I think it quite possible that this 'stereotype' of rational discourse is as closely tied to the meaning of 'rational discourse' as is the stereotypical tiger to the meaning of 'tiger.' But whether the tie in either case is as close as Putnam maintains is a matter I will not address here.

8. 'Disquotation' is Hilary Putnam's term as well. I speak of principles of 'disquotation' tracing back to Tarski, rather than referring simply to Tarski's principle (or a 'Tarskian principle'), because of doubts as to how little or how much Tarski's originally really commits us to. See Hilary Putnam, *Meaning And The Moral Sciences* (New York: Routledge and Kegan Paul, 1978).

9. I am grateful for the amiable harassment I have received from Richard Rudner, Alfred Stenner, and Kriste Taylor, and am obliged to Kriste Taylor for helpful comments on an earlier draft. This paper was originally written under the auspices of a Mellon Faculty Fellowship administered by Washington University.

A.J. Stenner

A Note On Logical Truth And Non-Sexist Semantics

In his paper, "A Note on the Ethics of Theories of Truth," Patrick Grim argues for a quasi-Strawsonian position in regard to the semantic analyses of sentences with a sexist or racist flavor. The conclusion he draws is that such sentences lack a truth-value. I wish to address the same issue but will not speak directly to the argument in Grim's paper. Rather, I shall attempt to show that other more or less "standard" analyses are still viable options for persons who take both their ethics and their semantics with more than a grain of salt. Although I happen to prefer one of the modes of analysis over the others and have reasons for my preference I shall not argue in detail or *in extenso* on behalf of my preferences. My plan rather is to show that a resolution of the "paradox" posed by Grim's paper can be obtained without biting the Strawsonian bullet.

Certain sexist sentences in English appear to pose a problem for semantics. They are sentences which appear offensive for what are obvious reasons; yet we call them false at the risk of rejecting relatively well-accepted semantic principles. What I shall attempt to do in this note is to show that there is a fairly straightforward method for resolving such difficulties, a method which does not require that a theory of truth be put at sword's point with a viable ethical theory.

Consider

> (1)   Any stupid broad who gets what she deserves gets what she deserves.

and

> (2)   When a woman driver sticks her arm out the window she is going to turn right or she isn't.

On the surface it appears that we cannot challenge the truth of such sentences. Each is an instance of a logically valid schema, (1) being an instance of "Any F which is a G is a G" and (2) being an instance of something like "Any F is either a G or a non-G." On these grounds it hardly seems plausible to claim that a person who has uttered either (1) or (2) has failed to tell the truth. On the other hand (1) is clearly sexist and (2) is a "standard" put-down.

The problem is not new. It has always been possible to speak the truth in a way that will mislead. (1) is a case of a more general malady which afflicts discourse employing words having emotive significance. There are analogues in politics as elsewhere:

> Any stupid Republican (or Democrat) who gets what he deserves gets what he deserves.
> Whenever a politician makes a promise either he will keep it or he won't.

and in race relations:

> Any stupid R who gets what he deserves gets what he deserves.

In this example we simply let "R" be replaced by "nigger," "honkey," "gook," "wop," "kike," etc.)[1]

In each of the above cases we have what appears to be a logical truth; consequently, one would suppose that its truth is beyond challenge. Yet something seems to have gone wrong. Although we frequently find the truth to be offensive, it is the *truth* which is offensive and not its mode of presentation. In the present case it is not the truth which is offensive (How can a logical truth be offensive?) but its mode of expression or some of the expressions occuring within it.

When truth is offensive for the right reasons, we may suppose, it forces us to face some unpleasant fact about ourselves or our world. It forces us to a decision: either change views about the world or continue to hold false beliefs. Sometimes we may choose the second horn and simply refuse to face the truth. But our resistance to (1) and (2) is not like this. For again, it seems not to be the truth of (1) or the truth of (2) that bothers us. If we replace the expression 'stupid broad' in (1) with 'woman' and replace the feminine pronouns in (2) with less emotively charged expressions the results are non-sexist rephrasals of the originals.

All of this is so obvious that it hardly seems worth repeating. But none of the above remarks solves the initial problem. If someone utters (1) has he said something true? On principles of Tarski's semantics (1) is true if and only if any stupid broad who gets what she deserves gets what she deserves. But this fact hardly seems like an advance. It appears to require a sexist formulation of the T-principle which is supposed to state the truth conditions for (1). Can we eliminate the offense from the T-principle by a suitable modification? Suppose we simply rewrite the T-principle so that the right-hand biconjunct of that principle lacks the offensive expressions. It would then read:

(A)   (1) is true if and only if any woman who gets what she deserves gets what she deserves.

But this will not solve our problem. Consider:

(3)   Any woman who gets what she deserves gets what she deserves.

The T-principle for (3) is

(B)   (3) is true if and only if any woman who gets what she deserves gets what she deserves.

But from (A) and (B) we can obtain

(C)   (1) is true if and only if (3) is true and hence (1) and (3) are semantically equivalent. I think, therefore there is little likelihood of solving our problem by trying to rewrite the semantic principles for (1) and (3). It seems to me that what is needed is a more careful analysis of the original sentence. We seem to be faced with a problem not unlike the one which confronted Russell in his attempt to analyze 'The present King of France is bald.' I shan't repeat what by now is well-known history except to remark that Russell's success depended on a rephrasal of the original to make its "logical structure" clear. For (1) I propose a similar approach. It seems to me that a person who utters (1) may be claiming not only that trival truth that any woman who gets what she deserves gets what she deserves; he may also be claiming that it is appropriate to speak of women as stupid broads. So my first attempt at analysis of (1) is

>　(1a)　Any woman who gets what she deserves gets what she deserves; moreover it is appropriate to speak of women as stupid broads.

On this analysis the first conjunction of (1a) is unobjectionable. It is a logical truth and contains no offensive expression. The second claim, however, is not logically true but is contingent and presumably false. Consequently it turns out, contrary to what we might have expected at the outset, that (1), on this mode of analysis is false, since its analysans is false.[2]

　Consider, however the following objections. An utterer of (1) is not claiming that it is appropriate to speak of women as stupid broads; he is merely claiming to believe that it is appropriate to speak of women as stupid broads. Here the difference to be marked is that between 'p' and 'I believe that p' or between asserting 'p' and asserting that I believe that p. If this is correct as a principle of analysis of (1), then (1) is to be analyzed as:

>　(1b)　Any woman who gets what she deserves gets what she deserves; moreover, I believe it is appropriate to speak of women as stupid broads.

On this analysis, assuming that the second conjunct of (1b) is true of anyone who utters (1), both conjuncts of (1b) are true and hence (1) turns out true after all. Our original problem appears not to have been solved. But it seems to me that there is nothing incompatible between the two types of analysis. On the method which yields (1b) logical truths (at least those whose appearance is that of logical truths) still come out true, but only because the contingent second conjunct of the analysans is likewise true. The problem of choosing between (1a) and (1b) is the more general problem of deciding what (1) asserts. It is a problem for which unfortunately I can provide no conclusive or general answer.

　An analysis that doesn't require a choice between (1a) and (1b) is the following:

(1c)   Any woman who gets what she deserves
gets what she deserves; moreover it is appropriate to speak of women as stupid
broads and I believe that it is appropriate
to speak of women as stupid broads.

There are some who may object that the third element of (1c) is
otiose inasmuch as it is implied by the second conjunct (in G.E.
Moore's sense of 'implies'). But this objection concerns only the
elegance of the result, not its semantical adequacy. On this account (1c) is still false.

In some cases it may be necessary to replace the indexical 'I'
by a proper name or a definite description in order to indicate
the speaker in question. But this is a more general difficulty and
need not cast doubt on the adequacy of the proposed analysis.

One possible objection to the present mode of analysis is this:
granted that anyone who utters (1) strongly suggests that he
believes it is perfectly appropriate to speak of women as stupid
broads, there is nevertheless a difference between what one
asserts to be the case and what one merely suggests is the case.
One can suggest what is the case by one's vocabulary or tone of
voice or a look. But as far as truth claims are concerned we are
concerned only with what a person asserts and not what he suggests. So a person uttering (1) is only suggesting, but not claiming, that it is appropriate to speak of women in the offensive
way under discussion. A much simpler case in which we can
distinguish between what an utterance asserts and what it suggests is:

(3)   She was widowed and impoverished at
thirty and left with four small children;
but she managed to complete her education and to help each of her children
through college.

The word 'but' in the above sentence does double duty: it not
only serves as a truth-functional operator, (a sign of conjunction) but also suggests that given the truth of the first conjunct
one would not expect the second conjunct to be true. Suppose,
however, we attempt to build this suggestion into the analysis as
in

(3a)   (She was widowed and impoverished at
       thirty and left with four small children).
       (She managed to complete her own edu-
       cation and to help each of her children
       through college). (Given the former, one
       wouldn't have expected the latter).

On this analysis (3) is construed as a conjunction with three conjuncts, the last of which states what is suggested by the use of
'but' rather than 'and' in this context. The inadequacy of this
analysis, however, is clearly brought home by considering the
case where the first two conjuncts of (3) are true and the third
false. On this analysis (3a) is false (containing as it does one false
conjunct) while (3) is clearly true (although the use of 'but' in
these circumstances may appear peculiar to anyone who finds
nothing unusual about the joint assertion of the two conjuncts
of (3). The example appears to be a paradigm of the principle
that an analysis ought not contain what is suggested by an utterance but only what is clearly stated or asserted. I know of no
easy method to distinguish between what a statement asserts and
what it suggests. But one rough and ready principle suggests
itself: If the truth conditions of the analysans are different from
those of the analysandum, the analysis is flawed.[3]

On the basis of these observations, let us try to analyse (1)
along somewhat different lines. We can paraphrase (1) as

(1d)   Any woman who gets what she deserves
       gets what she deserves. [I believe it is ap-
       propriate to speak of women as stupid
       broads.]

where the brackets serve to indicate what is suggested but not
stated by the original. Bracketed material then is not construed
as expressing part of the truth-conditions of the original. On this
analysis (1) comes out true after all. While I have no knock-
down argument in support of (1d), it does seem to me preferable
to the others on the grounds of simplicity. It also seems to me to
afford us with a perfectly appropriate response to (1):

What you claim is trivially true, but nevertheless what you suggest I find highly offensive.

Sentence (2), however, poses a different type of problem. In (2)
there appears no objectionable phrase which can be eliminated
by paraphrase. It is clearly of the form of a logical truth but it

lacks any emotive expression whose use constitutes the basis for the objectionable character of the sentence. I want to argue, however, that (2) poses no problem for semantics. What is clear is that almost any sentence can be used to cast aspersions on something or other, provided that it is given the appropriate tone of voice or the accents are placed upon the correct syllables. Logical truths as well as any other sentences lend themselves to this type of behavior. In the case of (2) the antecedent describes an event of a kind which is, under normal circumstances, intended as a signal to the effect that the person employing the signal is about to take a certain course of action. What makes (2) "sexist" lies in the fact that the consequent of the conditional, since it is a logical truth (or logically valid), is true independently of the truth value of the antecedent. So this particular logical truth can be used to suggest that a woman's signal from an automobile is absolutely irrelevant to her subsequent course of action. One may suppose therefore that the mode of analysis which yielded (1b) from (1) would yield the following:

(2a)   When a woman driver sticks her arm out the window she is going to turn right or she isn't; furthermore a woman's signal from an automobile is absolutely irrelevant to her subsequent course of action, and I believe that a woman's signal from an automobile is absolutely irrelevant to her subsequent course of action.

and that mode of analysis which yielded (1d) would yield

(2b)   When a woman driver sticks her arm out the window she is going to turn right or she isn't. [I believe a woman's signal from an automobile is absolutely irrelevant to her subsequent course of action.]

as a paraphrase of (2).

At present, however, I'm inclined to suppose that (2a) is a case of overkill and that (2) itself is adequate as it stands. I am not, on the other hand, prepared to be dogmatic on the matter, and anyone who finds it offensive to include some utterance of (2) in the class of logical truths has (2a) or (2b) available as an analysis.

NOTES

1. Up to this point in the discussion I have been trading heavily on some examples and comments provided by Patrick Grim. From this point on in the paper, I must assume full responsibility.

2. It is not the case that a person uttering (1a) has failed to say something true. The first conjunct of the analysans is clearly true. But those who utter conjunctions one of whose conjuncts is clearly false clearly utter a false sentence. So we confront what appears to be a paradoxical claim: one can say something true while uttering a false statement. But once we understand the source of the puzzle the air of paradox vanishes. The fact that we can say something true while uttering a false statement was suggested to me while reflecting on some of the comments in the latter part of Keith Donnellan's essay, "Reference and Definite Descriptions." In Jay Rosenberg and Chas. Travis, *Readings in the Philosophy of Language,* pp. 195-211, originally published in *Phil. Review,* 1966, vol. LXXV, No. 3.

3. I am indebted to Robert B. Barrett both for the analysis of 'but' on which the above example is based and for calling my attention forcefully to the need for distinguishing between what a statement asserts and what it suggests.

Kriste Taylor

Reference and Truth: The Case of Sexist and Racist Utterances

Individuals use their language in multifarious ways and succeed in doing a variety of things in the course of so doing. They can succeed in making claims about how things are in the world, express their likes and dislikes, get married, make promises, insult, degrade, and offend others as well as exhibit their own attitudes, be they kind, benevolent and understanding, fascist, sexist, or racist. In what follows I want to focus attention primarily on the use of language which is sometimes characterized as the claim-making, statement-making, and/or assertive use of language. When an individual succeeds in making a statement, claim or assertion, we can go on to talk about whether that individual, in making a particular claim, statement or assertion, also succeeded in insulting, offending, or degrading anyone. But we can also go on to talk about the truth or falsity of what was stated, claimed, or asserted irrespective of whether or not that individual succeeded in insulting, offending, or degrading anyone.

In 'A Note On The Ethics Of Theories Of Truth'[1] Patrick Grim at least implicitly argues that in certain cases the attribution of *any* truth value is in part, or should be in part, dependent on whether or not a particular 'claim' is sexist or racist. He argues that in order for us not to be 'committed' to sexist or racist 'claims,' we perhaps ought to 'opt' for a 'theory of truth' which would not assign a truth value to certain sorts of racist and sexist 'claims.'[2]

While perhaps put forward with the best of intentions, I find Grim's position bizarre, if not philosophically untenable. We simply do not decide on the truth or falsity of a claim, or whether or not a claim will even have a truth value, on the basis of ethical commitments or judgements. If we did, our entire notion of 'truth' would change drastically. To argue on ethical grounds that we *ought* to do so seems to me suspiciously like arguing on ethical grounds that we have a moral obligation to fly in the face of certain unpleasant facts with the justification that we need not accept certain truths nor be 'committed' to them if we find them morally objectionable. I am not even sure it makes sense to say that we ever *could* have a moral obligation not to acknowledge the truth. Rather than argue against Grim's position however, in the following I shall present an alternative rationale for why it is that the utterance of certain sorts of sexist and racist sentences do not constitute the making of a claim, assertion, or statement or the saying of something that admits of a truth value. In so doing I hope to shed some light on the relationship between certain sorts of sexist and racist expressions and the making of claims, assertions, or statements, as well as to somewhat legitimize the intent at least, of certain aspects of Grim's position.

I

(1) Women and blacks are inferior to white males.
(2) Women and blacks ought to be shot.
(3) Niggers and broads ought to be shot.
(4) The niggers and broads in this town will benefit from improvements in medicine.

All the sentences above are syntactically well-formed and take the form of subject-predicate declaratives. Although there is some disagreement among philosophers as to what sorts of things 'truth' and 'falsity' are predicable of (statements, claims, propositions, assertions, etc.), it is generally accepted that sentences themselves are not the sorts of things that can be true or false.[3] Rather, sentences can be used in order to make statements, assertions, claims, etc., that are either true or false, but the sentence uttered is not itself a claim. For example, the sentence 'The cat is on the mat' might be used in order to make a true or false claim about some particular cat, but it is the particular utterance of the sentence which results in the making of a true or false claim.[4]

However, the mere utterance of a declarative sentence at a particular time need not result in a claim or statement being made. For in the course of making a claim one must succeed in referring to some individual(s) and succeed in predicating something of the individual(s) referred to. When individuals utter sentences in order to make claims some expressions are used in order to refer to the subject and some expressions are used in order to attribute something to the subject. Hence, one succeeds in making a claim or statement by uttering a particular sentence in order to make a claim only if:

(a) The expression used in the sentence in order to refer to a subject denotes or picks-out a subject.

(b) The expression used in the sentence in order to attribute something to the subject *does* attribute something to the subject.

Accordingly, if one succeeds in making a claim, what one has said is either true or false. The claim will be true just in case the subject denoted has the properties or attributes predicated of it and will be false just in case the subject referred to does not have the properties or attributes predicated of it. In the following I want to limit my analysis to the first of the above conditions, which I shall call (following Strawson[5]) the referential or the referring use of an expression in uttering a sentence in order to make a claim or assertion.

When one succeeds in making a claim one succeeds in saying something that is either true or false. One can succeed in uttering a sentence in order to make a claim, but not succeed in making a claim, hence not succeed in saying something that has a truth value. I want now to talk about the relationship between making a claim and using an expression in a sentence in the referential way in attempting to make a claim. Consider the following two sentences:

(5) Green ideas sleep furiously.

(6) The present king of France is bald.

In ascertaining whether either sentence could be used by a speaker in order to succeed in making a claim or statement, the referring expressions, 'green ideas' and 'the present king of France' must denote something or someone. Since there are no green ideas and since there is no present king of France, neither the utterance of (5) nor (6) by a speaker could count as the making of a claim.

Strictly speaking, although an individual could have used these expressions in order to refer to something or someone (supposing the speaker believed ideas were colored and that d'Estaing was a king) the speaker could not *succeed in referring* to something or someone by the use of these expressions. If I use the expression 'my dog' in order to refer to my cat, I do not succeed in making a claim about my cat when I utter the sentence, 'My dog is gentle' even if by pointing to my cat or by some other means of ostensive behavior I succeed in getting a listener to make out or understand who in fact I *intended* to refer to or what claim I *intended* to make, but didn't.[6] Since neither the utterance of (5) nor the utterance of (6) could count as the making of a claim, if one did in fact utter these sentences in order to make a claim, the attempt would miscarry and nothing would have been said that was either true or false.

Although neither sentence (5) nor (6) could be uttered by a speaker now in order to successfully make a claim, there is an important difference between the two sentences. The utterance of sentence (5) will never and could never have counted as the making of a claim while an utterance of (6) could have (say, in 1775) counted as the making of a claim. Hence, if the utterance of a particular sentence like (5) or (6) does not count as the making of a claim it is not, as Grim seems to suggest, because the sentence itself is 'a piece of gibberish' to which we do not want to be 'committed.'[7] Sentence (6) is a meaningful sentence and there is nothing 'gibberishy' about it. It is because an individual cannot succeed in referring to any individual by using the expression 'the present king of France' that an utterance of (6) could not count as the making of a claim or of saying something either true or false. Likewise, it is because one could not succeed in referring to anything by the use of the expression, 'green ideas' that (5), even if uttered, could not count as the making of a claim by any individual.

Now, let us turn our attention to sentences 1-4. Most individuals would claim that there is 'something' sexist and racist about each of them.[8] Since I am concerned here with the referential use of expressions I want to limit my attention to sentences similiar to 4. If (1) and (2) are somehow racist and sexist, it is not because of the use of the referring expressions 'women and blacks.' Indeed, we might say that any utterances of (1) and (2) are indicative of certain beliefs a speaker must have in order to put forward such a claim (that is, if the sentences were uttered in order to make a claim). However, if sentence (4) could be used in order to make a claim, it would be sexist and racist *just* because of the fact that *a particular referring expression* was used by a speaker in attempting to make a claim or statement. It is the *use* of the referring expression 'niggers and broads' that makes any utterrance of (4) somehow sexist and racist. Sentence (3) falls into both categories since its utterance by a speaker would be indicative of certain racist and sexist beliefs held by the speaker in attempting to make such a claim and would also be a case in which a particular racist and sexist expression was used in order to refer to some individuals in the course of making a claim. Since an utterance of (4) is only racist or sexist because of the use of a particular referring expression, I shall limit my analysis to sentences falling within this category.

II

(7)   Martha, Mary, Myrtle and Tom, Dick,
      and Harry will benefit from improve-
      ments in medicine.

(8)   The blacks and women in this town will
      benefit from improvements in medicine.

(4)   The niggers and broads in this town will
      benefit from improvements in medicine.

Let us imagine a speaker who lives in a town in which there are only three blacks: Tom, Dick, and Harry; and three women: Martha, Mary, and Myrtle. Could this speaker utter the sentences (7) and (8) and succeed in making a claim? Obviously, the speaker could. The speaker could use either the expression 'Martha, Mary, and Myrtle and Tom, Dick, and Harry' or the expression 'The blacks and women in this town' in order to refer to certain individuals, and succeed in so doing. Furthermore, we could say that the speaker could succeed in making the same claim by either uttering (7) or (8) since the same individuals are being referred to and the same thing is being said of those individuals.

It might be objected that if certain things are true about the utterance of one sentence used in making a claim that are not true of another sentence used in making a claim, that the *same* claim could not be being made by the utterance of the two sentences. But this simply is not true. In the course of making a claim I can, by certain inflections in my voice or by using one rather than another referring expression, succeed in being sarcastic, belligerent, insulting, etc. But if I have also succeeded in making a claim, the truth conditions and the truth value of what I have said are not in any way affected by the manner in which what was said, was said. The truth value of a particular claim that has been made is determined merely by whether or not the individual one has referred to by the use of an expression (no matter what expression was used in order to refer to the individual) has the attributes or properties predicated of it. The utterance of one sentence will count as the making of the same claim as the utterance of another sentence just in case the same individual has been referred to and the same thing has been said of that individual referred to. If what is said is true about the individual, then what is said is true about that individual irrespective of how that individual was successfully referred to. Neither the claim nor the truth value of the claim change just because of the use of certain other co-referential expressions or because of the manner or tone in which the sentence was uttered.

The question now is whether or not our hypothetical speaker could utter sentence (4) — 'The niggers and broads in this town will benefit from improvements in medicine' — and succeed in making a claim, and if so, could it be the same claim as would be made by the utterance of (7) and (8)? More specifically, we want to know if a speaker, using the expression 'the niggers and broads in this town' in order to refer to certain individuals can succeed in so doing. If so, then the utterance of (4) could count as the making of a claim in certain situations. As with the expressions 'green ideas' and 'the present king of France,' we have to determine whether or not there are individuals denoted by the expression, 'the niggers and broads in this town' and if so, whether Martha, Mary, Myrtle and Tom, Dick, and Harry are the individuals denoted.

Suppose that we say, 'No. There are no niggers or broads, so of course there are none in town and so of course, Martha, Mary, Myrtle and Tom, Dick, and Harry are not denoted by the expression 'the niggers and broads in this town.' Someone might object: 'But you think there are blacks and women in town and that Martha, Mary, Myrtle and Tom, Dick and Harry are the only blacks and women in town. And, by 'niggers' I mean blacks and by 'broads' I mean women...so it is not the case that you don't believe there are niggers and blacks in this town.' This individual would in effect be claiming that an utterance of (4) would or could count as the same claim as an utterance of (7) and (8). We know that when this individual says 'niggers and broads' he *means* to refer to or *intends* to refer to the blacks and women in town. But just as in the example of one intending to refer to their cat by the use of the expression 'my dog,' we can go on to ask whether or not one *succeeds* in referring to blacks and women and cats by the use of the expressions, 'nigger,' 'broad,' and 'dog.'

In 'On Referring,' Strawson suggests that there is 'a set of rules or [linguistic] conventions' which determine whether an expression can be used in such a way as to allow reference to be made.[9] I think that Strawson is correct, but unfortunately the notion of 'rules and conventions' is somewhat nebulous. Consider first the matter of rules. Can we say that a speaker is not following a particular rule when he uses the expression 'niggers and broads' in order to refer to blacks and women and for *this* reason does not succeed in referring to blacks and women? If so, we should be able to say *what* rule was violated or was not followed, but what rule might this be? I know of no such rule that states that one cannot succeed in referring to an individual in a derogatory, insulting, or denigrating fashion. If there were such a rule I would not be able to make a claim about my neighbor by uttering the following sentence: 'The racist, sexist, and stupid man next door to me is finally going to move out.' This, is counter-intuitive, at the least. Though it may be unfortunate, some people surely are racist, sexist, and stupid; and if the man next door to me is, then I can refer to him with the expression 'the racist, sexist, and stupid man next door.' It is no help to say that there is a rule which prohibits certain sorts of expressions from securing reference when there is no formulation of the rule and/or no way to determine if the use of an expression does or does not violate the rule.

We can be more successful with 'linguistic convention' since we to some extent can 'look to see' if certain forms of reference are 'customary' or agreed upon, or accepted practices amongst the speakers of a language. It is in the area of 'linguistic convention' that the ethical intent behind Grim's position can perhaps be legitimized. For the speakers of a language can *shape* linguistic convention *by practice*. If the speakers of a language, for pragmatic or ethical reasons decide not to use or regard the use of certain expressions as securing reference, then the customs and accepted practices — the very 'conventions for the use of referring expressions' — can change.[10]

It is important however, to distinguish between ontological commitments and linguistic conventions. There is a vast difference between these two questions:

(a)   Are there such things as niggers and broads?

(b)   Does the referential use of the expression 'niggers and broads' ever secure reference to individuals?

To answer (a) we might first 'look to see' what sorts of things there are in the world, but to answer (b) we would 'look to see' whether or not it was 'customary' or 'agreed practice' to refer to blacks and women as 'niggers and broads.' However, I suggest that in order to be in the position of being able to 'look and see' whether or not there were any niggers and broads in the world one would have to know what sorts of things niggers and broads were. But to say that niggers and broads are blacks and women is to already *presuppose an affirmative answer to (b)* — that is, that the expression 'niggers' can be used to successfully refer to blacks and the expression 'broads' can be used successfully to refer to women!

So, what in the end, are we to say about the sentence,

(4)   The niggers and broads in this town will benefit from the improvements in medicine.

I propose that an utterance of this sentence could not count as the making of a claim,[11] and hence does not have a truth value. One could not succeed in making a claim by the use of this sentence because one could not secure reference to any individuals by the use of the expression 'niggers and broads.' One could not secure reference to any individuals by the use of this expression because there is a linguistic convention — an agreed upon practice — that prohibits successful reference by the use of this expression. In effect, there are no niggers or broads.

One might object: 'But wait a minute. It is indeed customary for a number of people to regard the use of the expressions 'nigger' and 'broad' as securing reference.' It is here perhaps that Grim's notion of an ethical obligation regarding our attitudes toward certain expressions may be legitimized. For even if it were true that a certain group of speakers regarded it as an accepted practice to refer women as 'broads' and blacks as 'niggers,' other speakers of the language might have a moral obligation to work at changing the 'customs' and practices of the other speakers.[12]

III

Given the preceding account, if sentences like (4), that is, grammatical English sentences of subject-predicate form with racist or sexist expressions in referential position, cannot be used in order to make any claim or statement, it is because reference is not secured, rather than as Grim suggests, because we do or should 'opt' for a 'theory of truth' that does not assign a truth value to these 'claims' on ethical grounds. I have suggested that there may be however, ethical considerations involved in whether or not *reference is secured* and I find this alternative more defensible than Grim's. It does not demand that we have any moral obligation to 'opt' for a particular 'theory or truth' and it does not demand that we, in principle at least, list all the claims individuals could make and then decide on ethical or other grounds which were to receive truth values.

⸱ Although my analysis does provide a good reason for thinking that sexist and racist individuals cannot succeed in making claims or statements by the utterance of certain sorts of sentences, there is a sense in which it is of small consolation. Even if they do not succeed in making certain sorts of claims, more often than not racist and sexist individuals do succeed in making their point and in getting listeners to understand what it is they intend or mean by uttering the words they do. Hence unfortunately, they can still succeed in using their language in order to successfully offend, insult, and degrade others as well as to exhibit and display their own sexist and racist attitudes and ⸱ beliefs.

NOTES

1. See pages 290-298 in this volume.
2. Grim maintains that he uses the notion 'claim' in a "broad ordinary sense." (See Grim's Note 4). Since the assignment of a truth value is so important in his argument I would have liked to have seen a more clear account as to what in fact, truth and falsity are predicated of. As it stands, it is sometimes unclear whether or not one is ethically 'committed' to sentences just because they are grammatically well-formed or to statements or claims made by the use of certain sentences. Since there is some equivocation as to what has a truth value, there is a problem in determining just what one's 'commitments' amount to.
3. If they were, one would not be able to explain why two different utterances of the same sentence at a different time or by a different person could count as being one time true, one time false, and also why two people can utter different sentences and can properly be said to have 'said the same thing.'
4. Hereafter I shall talk of true and false *claims* but since nothing hinges on my preference for claims, one may regard it as a shorthand for 'claims, statements, propositions, or assertions.'
5. P.F. Strawson, 'On Referring,' reprinted in *Readings in the Philosophy of Language*, by Jay F. Rosenberg and Charles Travis, eds. (New Jersey: Prentice-Hall, Inc., 1971).
6. I regard the making of a claim as a speech act, so that succeeding in getting one's intentions across or in getting a listener to 'see' what it is one has in mind, is not necessarily to succeed in the speech act of referring and making a claim.
7. Grim does not analyze an example such as (6) but he does use (5) as an example of a claim which will lack a truth value, or *should* lack a truth value just because we do not want to be 'committed' to gibberish (p. 7). In his examples of sexist and racist 'claims' he wants to deny them a truth value on ethical grounds instead. I don't know what grounds he would come up with in order to deny (6) a truth value, but the point is that in my account, a truth value will be denied an utterance of a sentence used in order to make a claim only when no one claim has actually been made. That is, either reference was not secured or nothing was in fact predicated of the individual(s) referred to. This is a major difference between Grim's account and my own as I claim that the problem is one of reference while Grim maintains it is one concerning the 'commitments' forced on one by certain 'theories of truth.'

8. Actually I do not think sentences or statements or claims are the sorts of things that *can* be sexist or racist. Just as it is only people who can refer, be belligerent, mean, unkind, and nasty — not words themselves — I think only people are the sorts of things that can be sexist or racist although they can use words in order to refer, hurt, offend, abuse, and exhibit their racist and sexist attitudes. This is not an important point in this paper and often I have spoken as if claims or sentences were 'somehow' racist and sexist.

9. Strawson, 'On Referring,' *op. cit.*, pp. 188-189.

10. I do not mean to imply that this is true of all referential words or expressions. Certain proper names can always be used in order to successfully refer and unique descriptions that denote individuals will denote those individuals as long as the individuals denoted satisfy the unique description. I have in mind terms or expressions used in order to refer to 'sorts' or 'kinds' of individuals. It might be claimed that at one time individuals could have used the term 'gold' in order to refer successfully to what we now refer to as gold as well as what we now refer to as fool's gold. I suggest that many word changes such as this one are conventional and inspired by pragmatic or other interests rather than as some suggest [See Hilary Putnam in 'Meaning and Reference,' *Journal of Philosophy* LXX (November 8, 1973): 699-711] discovery of the real underlying nature of gold.

11. At least not at the present time.

12. It is unclear as to the extent in which individuals can be said to *share* the same language while having incompatible linguistic conventions. I would suggest that it is a matter of degree.

Further References

Ackerman, Louise M. " 'Lady' As a Synonym for 'Woman.' " *American Speech* 37:4 (December 1962): 284-5.

Anshen, Frank. "Sex and Obscenity at Stony Brook." Unpublished. Stony Brook, L.I., N.Y.: State University of New York, Linguistics Program, 1979.

Baker, Robert and Frederick A. Elliston, eds. *Philosophy and Sex.* Buffalo, N. Y.: Prometheus Books, 1975.

Barnhart, Joe and Mary Ann Barnhart. "Sexism and Racism as Sociocultural Systems." Unpublished. Denton, Texas: North Texas State University, Department of Philosophy, 1979.

Baron, Naomi. "A Reanalysis of English Grammatical Gender." *Lingua* 27 (August 1971): 113-40.

Barron, Nancy. "Sex-Typed Language: The Production of Grammatical Cases." *Acta Sociologica* 14:2 (1971): 24-42.

Beardsley, Elizabeth. "Referential Genderization." *Philosophical Forum* 5 (1973-4): 285-93.

————————. "Traits and Genderization." In *Feminism and Philosophy*, edited by Mary Vetterling-Braggin, Frederick A. Elliston, and Jane English. Totowa, N.J.: Littlefield, Adams and Co., 1977.

Beauvior, Simone de. *The Second Sex.* Translated by H. M. Parshley. New York: Knopf, 1953. Introduction.

Bodine, A. "Androcentrism in Prescriptive Grammar: Singular 'They,' Sex-Indefinite 'He,' and 'He or She.' " *Language in Society* 4 (1975): 129-46.

Bosmajian, Haig A. "The Language of Sexism." *Etc.* 29:3 (September 1972): 305-13.

Burr, Elizabeth; Dunn, Susan; and Farquhar, Norma. *Guidelines for Equal Treatment of the Sexes in Social Studies Textbooks.* Westside Women's Committee, P.O. Box 24 D 20, Los Angeles, California 90024.

Caputi, Jane. "The Glamour of Grammar." *Chrysalis: A Magazine of Women's Culture* 4: 35-43.

Chamberlain, Alexander F. "Women's Languages." *American Anthropologist* 14 (1912): 579-81.

Conklin, Nancy F. "Toward a Feminist Analysis of Linguistic Behavior." *University of Michigan Papers in Women's Studies* 1:1 (February 1974): 51-73.

Converse, Charles C. "That Desired Impersonal Pronoun." *The Writer* 3 (1889): 247-8.

Daly, Mary. *Gyn/Ecology: The Metaethics of Radical Feminism.* Boston: Beacon Press, 1978, particularly the Preface and footnote 32 on p. 428.

Dubois, B.L. and I. Crouch. "The Question of Tag Questions in Women's Speech: They Don't Really Use More of Them, Do They?" *Language in Society* 4 (1975): 129-46.

_____, eds. *The Sociology of Languages of American Women.* San Antonio, Texas: Trinity University Press, 1976.

Ellis, Albert and Albert Abarbanel, eds. "Language and Sex." In *The Encyclopedia of Sexual Behavior*, Vol. 2, pp. 585-98.

Ervin-Tripp, S. "The Connotations of Gender." *Word* 18 (1962): 249-61.

Fairlie, Henry. "On the Humanity of Women." *The Public Interest* 23 (1971): 16-32.

Faust, Jean. "Words That Oppress." In *Women Speaking.* Reprint available from KNOW, Inc., P.O. Box 10197, Pittsburgh, Pa. 15232.

Feminist Writers Workshop. *An Intelligent Woman's Guide to Dirty Words: Women in Patriarchal Society.* Chicago: YWCA, Loop Center, 1973.

Frazer, Sir James George. "A Suggestion As To the Origin of Gender in Language." *Fortnightly* 73 (January 1900): 79-90.

Furfey, Paul Hanley. "Men's and Women's Language." *American Catholic Sociological Review* (1944): 218-23.

Garry, Ann. "Pornography, Sex Roles and Morality." *Social Theory and Practise*, vol. 4, no. 4 (Spring, 1978): 395-421.

Gary, Sandra. "What Are We Talking About?" *Ms.* (December 1972): 72-73.

George, Mary Lee. "Alternatives to Sexist Language." In *Sexism in Education.* Available from Emma Willard Task Force on Education, University Station, Box 14229, Minneapolis, Minn. 55414.

Green, Laura. "Dictionaries Think Just Like Male Chauvinist Pigs." *Chicago Sun-Times* (May 22, 1973): Section 2, p. 3.

Grim, Patrick. "Sexism and Semantics." In *Feminism and Philosophy* ed. by Mary Vetterling-Braggin, Frederick A. Elliston, and Jane English, Totowa, N.J.: Littlefield, Adams and Co., 1977.

Graham, Alma. "The Making of a Nonsexist Dictionary." *Ms.* (December 1973): 12-14.

Hall, Robert A., Jr. "Sex Reference and Grammatical Gender in English." *American Speech* 26:3 (October 1951): 170-72.

Hancock, Cecily Raysor. " 'Lady' and 'Woman.' " *American Speech* 38 (October 1963): 234-5.

Hayakawa, S.I. "Semantics and Sexuality." *Etc.* 25 (June 1968): 135-53.

Hole, Judith and Ellen Levine. "The Politics of Language." In *Rebirth of Feminism*, New York: Quadrangle Books, 1971.

Hook, D. "Sexism in English Pronouns and Forms of Address." *General Linguistics* 14:2 (1974): 86-96.

Howard, Pamela. "Watch Your Language, Men." *More: A Journalism Review* 2 (February, 1972): 3-4.

Jaggar, Alison M. and Paula Rothenberg Struhl, eds. *Feminist Frameworks*. New York: McGraw-Hill, 1978.

Jesperson, Otto. "Sex and Gender." In *The Philosophy of Grammar*. New York: W.W. Norton, 1924.

_____. "The Woman." In *Language: Its Nature, Development and Origins*. London: Allen and Unwin, 1922.

Kanfer, Stefan. "Sispeak: A Misguided Attempt to Change Herstory." *Time* (October 23, 1972): 79.

Kelly, Edward Hanford. "A 'Bitch' by Any Other Name Is Less Poetic." *Word Study* 45:1 (October, 1969): 1-4.

Key, Mary Ritchie. *Male/Female Language*. Metuchen, N.J.: Scarecrow Press, 1975.

Komisar, Lucy. "The Image of Woman in Advertising." In *Woman in Sexist Society: Studies in Power and Powerlessness*, edited by Vivian Gornick and Barbara Moran. New York: Basic Books, 1971.

Kramerae, Cheris. "Women's Speech: Separate but Unequal?" *Quarterly Journal of Speech* 60:1 (February 1974): 14-22.

_____, ed. "The Voices and Words of Women and Men," vol. 3., no. 2 of *Women's Studies International Quarterly*. New York: Pergamon Press, forthcoming.

Lakoff, Robin. "You Are What You Say." *Ms.* (July 1974): 65-7.

Langenfelt, Gosta. "*She* and *Her* Instead of *It* and *Its*." *Anglia* 70:1 (1951): 90-101.

Lawrence, Barbara. "Four-Letter Words *Can* Hurt You." In *Philosophy and Sex*, edited by Robert Baker and Frederick Elliston. Buffalo, N.Y.: Prometheus Books, 1975.

Lennert, Midge and Norma Wilson. *A Woman's New World Dictionary*. Available from 51% Publications, Box 371, Lomita, Calif. 90717.

McConnell-Ginet, Sally. "Women's Minds and Lives: Making Linguistic Connections." Unpublished. Ithaca, N.Y.: Cornell University, Department of Linguistics and Women's Studies, 1979.

_____. "Prototypes, Pronouns and Persons." In *Boas Sapir and Whorf Revisited*, edited by M. Mathiot. The Hague: Mouton, forthcoming.

_____. "Our Father Tongue: Essays in Linguistic Politics." *Diacritics* (Winter 1975): 44-50.

_____. "Linguistics in the Feminist Context." Delivered at the Modern Language Association's Women and Language Forum, 1978. Available from the author at Ithaca, N.Y.: Cornell University, Department of Linguistics and Women's Studies.

_____. "Address Forms in Sexual Politics." In *Women's Language and Style*, edited by D. Butturff. Akron, Ohio: University of Akron Press, 1979.

McConnell-Ginet, Sally, Ruth Barker and Nelly Furman, eds. *Language in Women's Lives: Literature, Culture and Society*, forthcoming.

Meredith, Mamie. " 'Doctoresses,' 'Authoresses,' and Others." *American Speech* 26:3 (October 1953): 231-2.

Miller, Casey and Kate Swift. "De-sexing the English Language." *Ms.*, preview issue (Spring 1972).

_____. *Words and Women*. Garden City, New York: Anchor Press/Doubleday, 1976.

_____. *The Handbook of Nonsexist Writing*. New York: Lippincott and Crowell, forthcoming.

Millet, Kate. "Instances of Sexual Politics." In *Sexual Politics*. Garden City, New York: Doubleday, 1970.

Moe, Albert F. " 'Lady' and 'Woman': The Terms' Use in the 1880's." *American Speech* 38:4 (December 1963): 295.

Moore, S. "Grammatical and Natural Gender in Middle English." *Proceedings of the Modern Language Association* 36 (1921): 79-103.

Morgan, Robin. "Know Your Enemy: A Sampling of Sexist Quotes." In *Sisterhood Is Powerful*, edited by Robin Morgan. New York: Random House, 1970.

Nilsen, Aileen P. "Sexism in English: A Feminist View." In *Female Studies* 6. Available from Feminist Press, Old Westbury, New York.

_____ *et al*, eds. *Sexism and Language*. Urbana, Ill.: National Council of Teachers of English, 1977.

Pierce, Christine. "Natural Law Language and Women." In *Woman in Sexist Society: Studies in Power and Powerlessness*, edited by Vivian Gornick and Barbara Moran. New York: Basic Books, 1971.

Reik, Theodore. "Men and Women Speak Different Languages." *Psychoanalysis* 1-2 (1954): 3-15.

Sayers, Dorothy. "The Human Not-Quite Human." In *Masculine/Feminine*, edited by Betty Roszak and Theodore Roszak, New York: Harper and Row, 1969.

Sissmann, L.E. "Innocent Bystander: Plastic English." *Atlantic Monthly* (October, 1972): 32-37.

Stanley, Julia P. "Paradigmatic Woman: The Prostitute." In *Papers in Language Variation*, edited by David L. Shores and Carole P. Hines (Birmingham, Ala.: University of Alabama Press, 1977), pp. 303-321.

_____. "Gender-Marking in American English." In *Sexism and Language*, edited by Aileen Pace Nilsen *et al*. Urbana, Ill.: National Council of Teachers of English, 1977, pp. 43-74.

_____. "Sexist Grammar." *College English*, 39:7 (March, 1978).

Stanley, Julia P. and Susan W. Robbins. "Going Throught the Changes: The Pronoun *She* in Middle English." *Papers in Linguistics* 9: 3-4 (Fall, 1977).

Stannard, U. *Mrs. Man*. San Francisco: Germain Books, 1977.

Stanton, Elizabeth Cady, ed. *The Woman's Bible*. New York: European Publishing Co., 1895.

Steadman, J.M., Jr. "Affected and Effeminate Words." *American Speech* 13:1 (February 1938): 13-18.

Strainchamps, Ethel. "Our Sexist Language." In *Woman In Sexist Society: Studies in Power and Powerlessness*, edited by Vivian Gornick and Barbara Moran. New York: Basic Books, 1971.

Svartengram, T. Hilding. "The Use of Feminine Gender for Inanimate Things in American Colloquial Speech." *Moderna Sprak* 48 (1954): 261-92.

Thorne, Barrie and Nancy Henley, eds. *Language and Sex: Difference and Dominance*. Rowley, Mass.: Newbury House, 1975.

Tiedt, Iris M. "Sexism in Language: An Editor's Plague." *Elementary English* 50 (October 1973): 1073-4.

Trebilcot, Joyce. "Conceiving Women: Notes On the Logic of Feminism." *Sinister Wisdom* XI, forthcoming.

Troth, Emily. "How Can A Woman MAN the Barricades? Or Linguistic Sexism Up Against the Wall." *Women: A Journal of Liberation* 2:1 (Fall, 1970): 57.

Vetterling-Braggin, Mary; Frederick A. Elliston; Jane English, eds. *Feminism and Philosophy*. Totowa, N.J.: Littlefield, Adams and Co. 1977.

Warren, Mary Anne. "Language and Woman" and "Lakoff." In *The Nature of Woman*, edited by Mary Anne Warren. Box 69, Point Reyes, California: Edgepress, 1980.

Warshay, Diana. "Sex Differences in Language Style." In *Toward a Sociology of Woman*, edited by Constantina Safilios-Rothschild. Lexington, Mass.: Xerox College Publishing, 1972.

Wasserstrom, Richard. "Racism and Sexism." In *Philosophy and Women*, edited by Sharon Bishop and Marjorie Weinzweig. Belmont California: Wadsworth Press, 1979.

Weinreich, U.; W. Labov; M. Herzog. "Empirical Foundations for a Theory of Language Change." In *Directions for Historical Linguistics*, edited by W.P. Lehmann and Y. Malkiel. Austin, Texas: University of Texas Press, 1968.

Withington, Robert. " 'Lady,' 'Woman' and 'Person.' " *American Speech* 12:2 (April 1937): 117-21.

Notes On Contributors

ROBERT BAKER has taught philosophy at the University of Iowa and Wayne State University. He is now at Union College in Schenectady, N.Y. In addition to coediting *A Workbook in Logic* and *Philosophy and Sex*, he has published papers in epistemology and social philosophy.

ELIZABETH L. BEARDSLEY has taught philosophy at the University of Delaware and at Lincoln University. She is currently Professor Emeritus in Philosophy at Temple University, doing work on ethical theory, moral psychology, and the philosophy of law. She has published a number of essays on ethics and the philosophy of language and is a past vice-president of the American Society for Political and Legal Philosophy. Her work-in-progress includes a book on moral development as well as a collection of her papers to be called *Moral Criticism*.

JANE DURAN is a teaching assistant and graduate student in philosophy at Rutgers. She received her A.B. from the University of California at Berkeley and her interests include epistemology, philosophy of mind, and 20th century analytic philosophy in general. She is currently working on a course in contemporary moral issues at Douglass College, Rutgers.

JACQUELINE FORTUNATA received her doctorate in philosophy from the University of Minnesota. She is presently developing courses (for women managers and others) on computer-based education at the Control Data Corporation in Minneapolis, Minnesota.

MARILYN FRYE is, in patriarchal terms, a feminist philosopher and associate professor at Michigan State University. By her own naming, she is "a Spinster, a writer of essays, composer of speeches, and inventor of another way." Her most recent publication was "Some Reflections on Separatism and Power," in *Sinister Wisdom*, volume 6.

PATRICK GRIM is an assistant professor of philosophy and director of the master's program in philosophical perspectives at the State University of New York at Stony Brook. He is co-editor of *The Philosopher's Annual* (Rowman and Littlefield, 1978 and 1979) and has published articles on a variety of topics in a number of philosophical journals. His current work is in theoretical ethics.

SARA ANN KETCHUM teaches ethics, political philosophy, philosophy of Marxism, and philosophy and feminism at Dartmouth College at Hanover, New Hamshire. She has published articles in these fields in philosophy journals and anthologies, and has read papers at conferences, institutes, and colleges. Her current research project is on theoretical problems related to the inclusion of reproduction in social/political philosophy and, in particular, in Marxian political theory.

CAROLYN KORSMEYER is an associate professor in the Department of Philosophy at the State University of New York at Buffalo. In addition to feminism, her major philosophical work is in aesthetics. She is currently at work with colleagues in four other fields on a book which examines the impact of feminism on academic scholarship.

ELEANOR KUYKENDALL received her doctorate in philosophy from Columbia University and recently completed two years of research on linguistics in Cambridge, Mass. She is currently Director of the Paris Philosophy Program of the State University of New York at New Paltz in affliation with the Sorbonne. She has published several articles on linguistics and feminism and edited *Philosophy in the Age of Crisis*.

ROBIN LAKOFF teaches linguistics at the University of California at Berkeley. Her *Language and Woman's Place* and *Why Women Are Ladies* are considered by many to be the pioneering foundations for much of current thought on the issue of sexist language.

MICHAEL LEVIN is the author of *Metaphysics and the Mind-Body Problem* as well as many articles on the philosophy of science and foundations of mathematics. He teaches philosophy at the City College of the City University of New York in Brooklyn.

JANICE MOULTON teaches at the University of Kentucky. She has served as executive secretary for the Society for Women in Philosophy. She is the author of *Guidebook for Publishing Philosophy*, coauthor (with G.M. Robinson) of *The Organization of Language* and has contributed to *Signs, Journal of Philosophy, Teaching Philosophy*, and (despite the name) to *International Journal of Man-Machine Studies*.

B.C. POSTOW teaches philosophy at the University of Tennessee in Knoxville. Her special interests include social and political philosophy, ethics, and the philosophy of feminism, and she has contributed to several journals on all of these subjects.

LAURA PURDY is currently an assistant professor of philosophy at Wells College in Aurora, N.Y. She has published several articles on the subjects of abortion and euthanasia and is currently working on a book on biomedical ethics. She is now in the process of preparing papers on the right to be killed and on problems of affirmative action for women in academe.

STEPHANIE ROSS is an assistant professor at the University of Missouri in St. Louis. She teaches a philosophy and feminism course there in connection with the Women's Studies Certificate Program. Her research interests include aesthetics, perception, and moral psychology.

SARA SHUTE received her Ph.D. in philosophy in 1977 from Washington University in St. Louis, and she is now an assistant professor of philosophy at Marietta College in Marietta, Ohio. In addition to feminist philosophy, she is currently interested in problems of perception.

ALAN SOBLE received his Ph.D. in philosophy from SUNY/Buffalo. He is the editor of *The Philosophy of Sex: Contemporary Readings* (Littlefield, Adams and Co., 1980) and has taught at the University of Texas at Austin, Southern Methodist University, the University of New Orleans, and is now at Wheaton College in Norton, Massachusetts.

A.J. STENNER received a doctorate in philosophy from Michigan State University and currently teaches at Washington University in St. Louis, Missouri. His research interests include logic, philosophy of science, and philosophy of language.

KRISTE TAYLOR teaches philosophy at the University of New York at Stony Brook where she is currently completing her dissertation on referential semantics and ontological commitments. Her areas of interest include contemporary metaphysics, philosophy of language, and modal logic.

LAURENCE THOMAS, who is primarily interested in the relevance of psychology to moral theory, teaches at the University of North Carolina. His trilogy of papers on self-respect include, "Capitalism versus Marx's Communism," *Studies in Soviet Thought* (1979).

VIRGINIA VALIAN does research on language acquisition and on the cognitive structure of writing at Columbia University. She has published articles on various problems in psycholinguistics and cognitive psychology. She is also writing a book on the emotions of creative intellectual work.

MARY VETTERLING-BRAGGIN received a doctorate in philosophy from Boston University and is currently an Associate Scholar in the Department of Philosophy at Lehigh University. She coedited *Feminism and Philosophy* (Littlefield, Adams and Co., 1977) and has published papers on the philosophies of natural science, social science, and children's rights.